Collins

Revised Edition 6

# EXPEDITIONS

## An Integrated Course in Social Studies

Urmi Chakraborty • Sayee Lakshmi • Swati Shukla

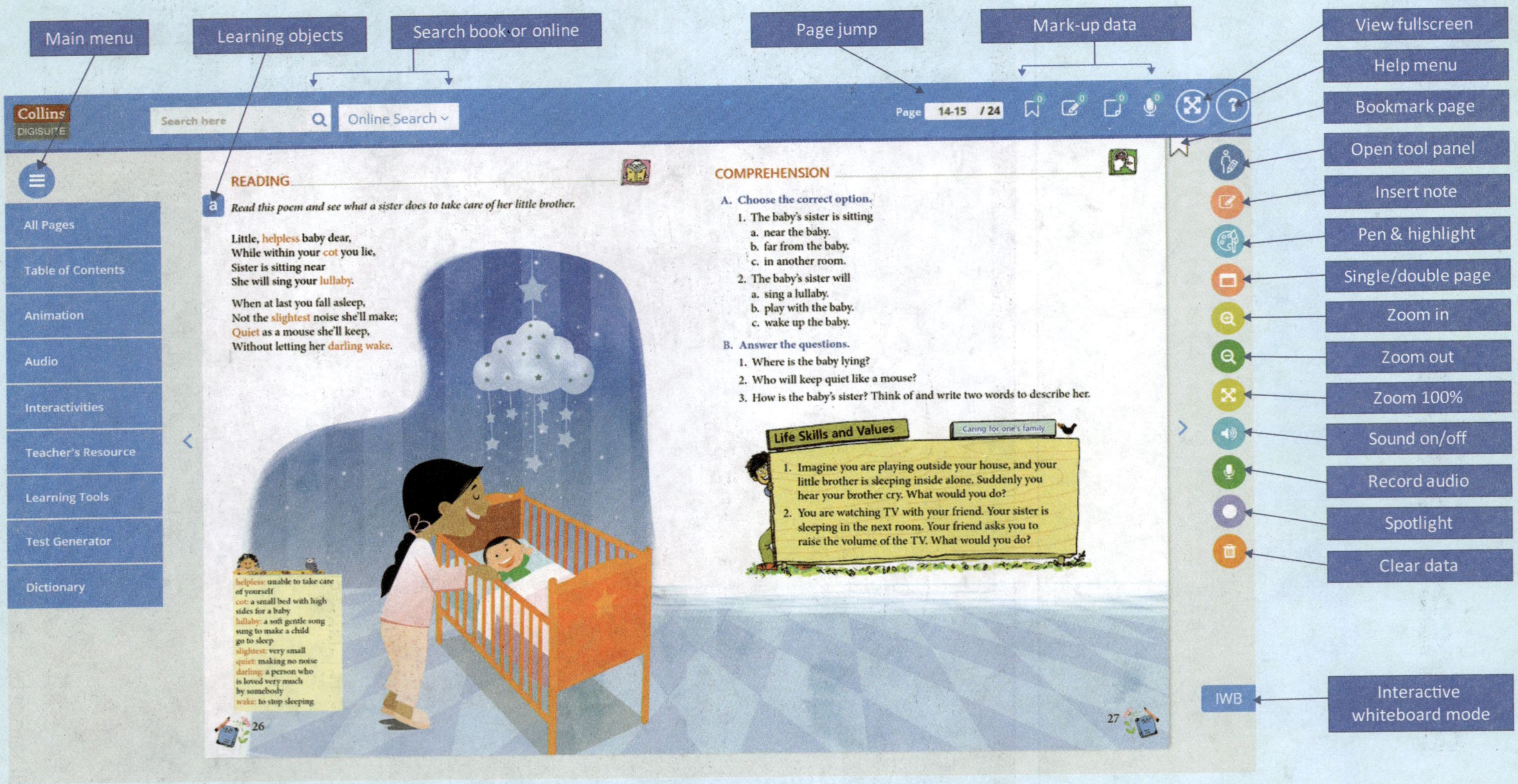


## Student + Teacher

- **a** animations
- **ilt** instructor-led tutorials
- **ia** activities
- **w** worksheets
- audio
- **g** games
- **v** videos

## Teacher-only

- **lp** lesson plans
- **w** worksheets
- **tn** teacher's notes
- **ak** answer keys

# Preface

*If I cannot learn the way you teach, teach the way I can learn.*

***Expeditions*** (Revised Edition) is a comprehensive course in Environmental Studies and Social Studies for the primary and middle school. This series for classes 1 to 8 has been designed taking into account the multidisciplinary nature of Environmental Studies and Social Studies. Following an interactive approach, the series caters to the young learners through inferential and experiential tasks, and stimulating content. The need for sustainable development holds the key to the future of mankind and young learners need to be sensitized to it through a gradual study to build environmental and social awareness.

***Expeditions*** (Revised Edition) is based on the underlying principle of the National Curriculum Framework that every learner can learn. This series maximizes opportunities to learn through its wide variety of tasks and facilitates easy learning and comprehension of the concepts at the primary level. Multiple intelligence-based tasks cater to the needs of all learners. With a learner-centric approach for effective teaching and learning in the classroom, the series promotes experiential learning. Course materials are drawn from the curriculum and provide examples from real-life situations to foster knowledge building and understanding. The series provides ample scope for the learners to observe, reflect, hone their thinking skills and develop effective communication skills. Learners are guided to look at the environment in a holistic manner and see the underlying unity in the physical and social environment.

**Key Features**

- **Take off** assesses the prior knowledge of the learners.
- **Warm up** has pre-reading tasks for discovery-based learning where learners can infer and relate to the topic.
- **Fact quest** provides interesting titbits of information and **Find out** tasks encourage referencing skills.
- **Explore/Investigate/Consider** are analytical tasks set to test a student's comprehension skills and foster their interest in further exploration of the key idea(s).
- **Case Study** re-counts in-depth investigations of a single person, group, event or community.
- **World Connect** highlights stories and events from around the world related to the chapter.
- **Eco feat** sensitizes learners towards conservation of the environment.
- **Recall** provides mind maps and flowcharts to reinforce learning.
- **Work out** at the end of the units facilitate understanding, recall and reinforcement, and assessment.
- **Think** focuses on Higher Order Thinking Skills.
- **Life skills and values** equips learners with the basic skills they need to excel in life and helps to build the right attitudes and values in learners.
- **Enjoy** has varied creative tasks.
- **Info Time** provides interesting information on topics related to the chapters studied.
- **Outline maps** are given for map practice.

The comprehensive teacher's resource materials are aimed at facilitating teaching and assessment. Feedback and suggestions to improve the course further are welcome.

# Key Features

**Take off**

- Studying the past helps us to understand the present and do better for the ............................ .
- ............................ were creatures that lived in the past.
- Looking at old ............................ helps us learn about our past.

Assesses the prior knowledge of the learners

**Warm up**

Dinosaurs lived on Earth a long time ago. What subject teaches us about them?

Has warm-up tasks that initiates the learners into the topic and help them relate to it

**Fact quest**

*Nirvana* means liberation from the cycle of birth and rebirth, through right deeds and actions.

Provides interesting titbits of information

**Recall**

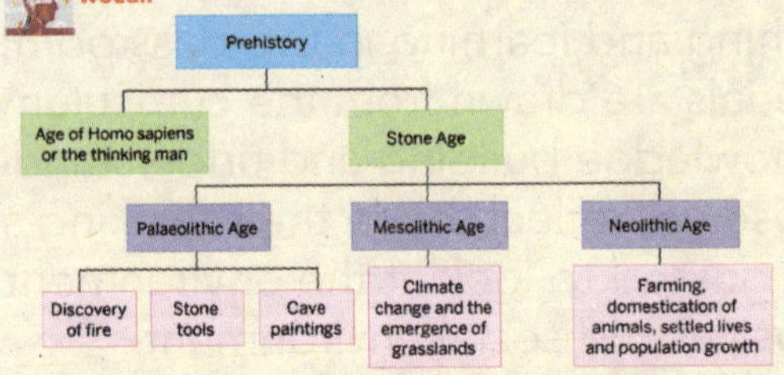


Is a ready reckoner of the chapter

**Case Study**

**The Gandhara School of Art**

During the rule of Kanishka in the first century CE, there was a lot of influence of the Greeks and the Romans on Indian art. This Graeco-Roman style of art flourished in the north-western region in Gandhara

In-depth investigations of a single person, place, event or community

**World Connect**

In Wiltshire, England, stands the Stonehenge, a prehistoric monument belonging to the Neolithic Period. It consists of a ring of standing stones. Archaeologists believed that it was built between 3000 and 2000 BCE.

Highlights stories and events from around the world related to the chapter

**Find out**

Name an ancient Indian civilization which we came to know of through archaeological sources.

Tasks to encourage referencing skills

**Eco feat**

The global temperature has risen by 5 to 7 degrees in the past 5000 years. The predicted rate of global warming is at least 20 times more in the next century.

Sensitizes learners towards conservation of environment

**Explore**

In 1609, Galileo Galilei heard of an invention from Holland known as the telescope. This object could make distant objects appear much closer. He decided to build his own telescope. He made great improvements to the telescope and began to use it to view the planets. Soon, Galileo's version of the telescope was being used throughout Europe. Galileo made many discoveries using his telescope including the four large

**Consider**

Soon after independence from the British, Sardar Vallabhbhai Patel single-handedly undertook the most difficult task of bringing together over 565 princely states of India under the umbrella of a single Indian Union, which became the foundation of the Indian Republic. The diverse nature

**Investigate**

In one of his inscriptions, Ashoka had written...

*'King Piyadasi made provision for two types of medical treatment: medical treatment for humans and medical treatment for animals. Wherever medical herbs suitable for humans or animals are not available, I have had them imported and grown. Wherever medical roots or fruits are not available,*

Analytical tasks set to test a student's comprehension skills and foster their interest in further exploration of the key idea(s)

## Work out

A. Fill in the blanks.

1. History is the study of the ..................................
2. The arrangement of events or dates in the order of their occurrence is known as .................................. .
3. The *Ramayana* is a .................................. source of history.

**Reinforces learning and facilitates assessment**

## Think

Crack the puzzle.

1. I belong to that period when writing was not invented. ..................................
2. I am a river civilization that developed around the River Indus. ..................................

**Focuses on Higher Order Thinking Skills**

## Life skills and values

Apart from the exchange of goods belonging to different countries of the world, merchants and traders had another interesting role. They helped spread the religious and cultural ideologies of the places they visited. For example, Islam was introduced in India by the traders from the Arabic world. Today, cross-cultural programmes are frequent among people belonging to all walks of

**Equips learners with the basic skills they need to excel in life**

## Enjoy

Did you know that every artefact has a story to tell? List the names of five or more objects found in the past, in your notebook. Speak in class about any one of these objects regarding where it might have come from, whom it might have belonged to and what period it is from.

**Has varied creative tasks**

### Suggested Assessment 1

SUGGESTED ASSESSMEN

**Max Marks: 80** **Max.Time: 3 hrs.**

**History** **Marks: 30**

A. Fill in the blanks. (½ × 6 = 3)

1. .................................. is the period in human history when humans did not leave behind written records.
2. Humans had mastered the art of farming by the .................................. Stone Age.
3. Apart from transportation, the wheel was also used to make .................................. .
4. .................................. was the first city to be discovered in the Indus Valley.
5. In the Vedic Period, society was divided into .................................. varnas.
6. Mahajanapadas could be a monarchy or a

**Worksheets facilitate evaluation**

## Web link

For more information, log on to:

https://www.dkfindout.com/us/history/stone-age/

Last accessed on 30 September, 2019

**For extended learning**

**Info Time**

### Major Milestones in History

- 5,00,000 BCE to 10,000 BCE — Palaeolithic Age
- 10,000 BCE–8000 BCE — The Mesolithic Age
- 5000–7000 BCE — The Neolithic Age
- 4,000 BCE–2,000 BCE — Chalcolithic Age
- 3300 BCE — The Bronze Age
- 1500 BCE — The Aryans migrated to the Indian subcontinent
- 600 BCE — The formation of *janapadas* and *mahajanapadas*
- 540 BCE — Vadhamana Mahavira was born

**Provides interesting information on topics related to the chapters studied**

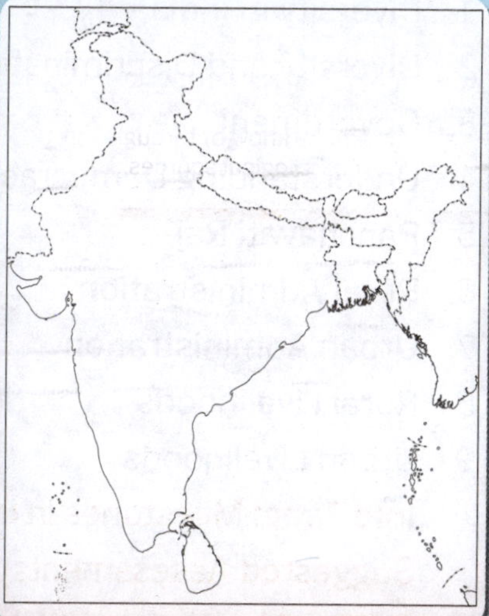

**Outline maps are given for map practice**

# Contents

## History


1. Discovering the Past 7
2. The Hunter Gatherers 15
3. The Agriculturist: The Neolithic Period 23
4. The Advent of Urbanization and Civilization in India 30
5. The Vedic Period 40
6. Janapadas and New Kingdoms 48
7. New Ideas and New Religions 56
8. The Mauryan Empire 65
9. Reappearance of Urbanization 74
10. Contact With Other Parts of the World 82
11. The Gupta Period 91
12. Our Cultural and Scientific Wealth 101

Info Time: Major Milestones in History 109


## Geography


1. The Solar System 110
2. Globes: Latitudes and Longitudes 118
3. Motions of the Earth 129
4. Maps 135
5. Major Domains of the Earth 142
6. Major Landforms of the Earth 152
7. Our Country—India 160
8. India—Climate, Natural Vegetation and Wildlife 170

Info Time: Earth's Biggest Milestones 179


## Social and Political Life


1. Diversity in India 180
2. Diversity and Discrimination 188
3. Government 195
4. Understanding Democracy 201
5. Panchayati Raj 209
6. Rural Administration 217
7. Urban Administration 223
8. Rural Livelihoods 231
9. Urban Livelihoods 239

Info Time: Milestones in India's Polity 246

Suggested Assessments 247

Outline Maps 263

# 1 Discovering the Past

## Take off

- Studying the past helps us to understand the present and do better for the .......................................... .
- .......................................... were creatures that lived in the past.
- Looking at old .......................................... helps us learn about our past.

## Warm up

Dinosaurs lived on Earth a long time ago. What subject teaches us about them?

We have already learnt in the previous class that history is the study of the past. It includes everything that took place since life began on Earth billions of years ago. It tells us about important events of the past and of changing human cultures, beliefs, politics and lifestyles.

## Fact quest

Science, astronomy, mathematics and medicine, are all a part of history. Aryabhatta calculated the length of the solar year and the value of *pi*, Varahamihira wrote books on astronomy and Sushruta wrote on medicine and surgery. We learn about all of these in history!

## The Importance of Studying History

- History helps us to connect the past to the present, and the future. By understanding our past we appreciate the developments of the present and look forward to building our future.
- History is the study of life, culture and traditions of different groups of people that lived at different times. It sensitizes us towards appreciating the rich cultural traditions left behind by our **predecessors**.
- History also proves useful for people involved in different professions and skills, like architects, engineers, sculptors, weavers and artists because they can include traditional styles and ideas in their work.

**predecessors:** ancestors

- History helps environmentalists understand the reasons for the depletion of natural resources over a period of time and to think about remedial measures to sustain our environment.
- The study of this subject helps us to develop a questioning mind and a broad vision as it is not limited to a particular aspect but includes a variety of topics like economy, education, politics, society and many more.

## Ways of Writing Dates in History

To denote time periods, we use BCE which stands for Before Common Era and CE which stands for Common Era.

### Counting years

**Decade:** A period of 10 years

**Century:** A period of 100 years

**Millennium:** A period of 1000 years

One century has a hundred years. The first century CE started on 1 January, 1 CE and ended on 31 December, 100 CE while the fifteenth century comprises the period between the years 1401 CE and 1500 CE. Which century are we living in right now?

A **timeline** helps us to understand history. It helps us to understand what happened when, how much time passed between different events and most importantly, it helps us to put events and instances in the order of their occurrence. This can be also termed as **chronology**.

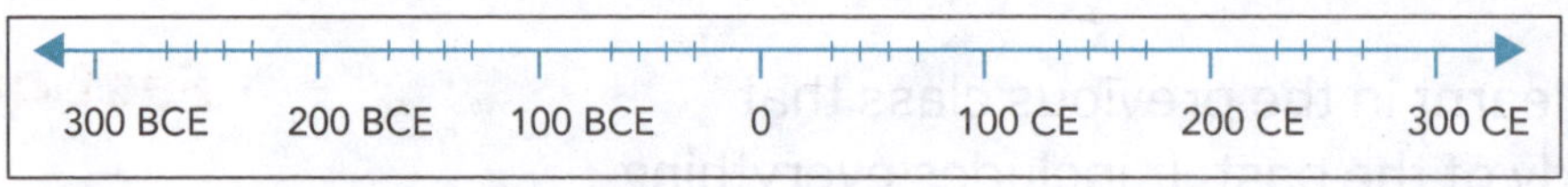


▲ Timeline

## Ways of Studying the Past

The period before history, where events were not recorded and humans did not know how to write, is called **prehistory**. History is the period that comes after humans learnt how to read and write. In order to learn about history and prehistory, **archaeologists** study different kinds of sources of history. Broadly, these sources can be classified into two types—**literary sources**, which are related to books or written records, and **archaeological sources**, which are related to **excavated** remains. Now let us examine these sources one by one.

▲ Archaeologists at work

**chronology:** the arrangement of events or dates in the order of their occurrence; **excavated:** remove earth carefully from (an area) in order to find buried remains

## Archaeological Sources

Archaeologists study material remains from the past like fossils, vessels, burial sites, artefacts, relics and weapons, through the process of excavation. These are called archaeological finds. By examining them, archaeologists can reconstruct the past by finding out how old they are, what they were used for and what type of material was used to make these objects. **Historians** also help us learn about our past. They study inscriptions, manuscripts and archaeological finds to reconstuct the past.

> **Find out**
>
> Name an ancient Indian civilization which we came to know of through archaeological sources.

**Monuments** are important structures, built to honor the memory of a person, to convey historical or political information of significant events or simply to improve the appearance of the location.

▲ Gateway to India, Mumbai

▲ An inscription on the Qutub Minar

**Inscriptions** are important messages, records or accounts of the orders of various kings, engraved on hard surfaces like pillars, temple walls and caves.

**Coins** belonging to different dynasties, have been discovered in different parts of the world. Gold, silver and copper were the three major metals used to forge these coins. Most of what we know about dynasties of the past rests chiefly upon what information has been derived from these coins.

▲ Coins in ancient India

**Burial Sites** have been discovered in different parts of the world which serve as rich sources of information to historians and archaeologists alike. In some sites, food and tools have been found along with the skeletal remains of early humans. This shows that the people believed in life after death. Important sites include the Shanidar Cave in Iraq.

**Paintings and sculptures** shed valuable light on the progress of human civilization. The cave paintings of Bhimbetka depict the life of early humans. These paintings exhibit scenes from the early humans' daily lives, such as hunting scenes and many other scenes. From these paintings, archaeologists get to know about life in prehistoric times.

## Literary Sources or Written Records

Many years ago when paper had not been invented, humans wrote on palm leaf or the bark of birch trees. These were known as **manuscripts**. Manuscripts are important sources of information that tell us about our past. There are experts who decode and **decipher** these ancient texts.

Literary sources may be religious or non-religious. They detail the lives of the kings and the common people, along with their religious beliefs and practices.

▲ An ancient manuscript

Some of the religious works are epics like the *Ramayana* and the *Mahabharata*, Indian scriptures like the *Vedas* and Buddhist literature like the *Jataka Tales*. These texts were written in ancient languages like Sanskrit. Some non-religious works include Kautilya's *Arthashastra*, Kalidasa's *Abhijnanashakuntalam*, folk tales like the *Panchtantra* and Banabhatta's *Harshacharita*.

| Sources | |
|---|---|
| **Archaeological** | **Literary** |
| Artefacts | Religious literature |
| Monuments | Secular literature |
| Coins | Biographies |
| Inscriptions | Traveller's accounts |
| Burial sites | Chronicles |

## Fact quest

Archaeologists use tools like picks and shovels to excavate fossils. In areas where digging is difficult, they use bulldozers too. Sometimes, they use simple things like spoons and brushes to extract the fossil.

## Investigate

In one of his inscriptions, Ashoka had written...

*'King Piyadasi made provision for two types of medical treatment: medical treatment for humans and medical treatment for animals. Wherever medical herbs suitable for humans or animals are not available, I have had them imported and grown. Wherever medical roots or fruits are not available, I have had them imported and grown... Along roads I have had wells dug and trees planted for the benefit of humans and animals ...'*

Based on what you have read, what impression do you have of King Ashoka?

## Co-relation between History and Geography

The geography of a place directly impacts its history. While history includes human experiences, geography focuses on how humans relate to the physical environment. Some of the earliest civilizations developed around river valleys as water and food were easily

**decipher:** convert (a text written in code, or a coded signal) into normal language available to them and the soil around these river valleys was fertile. The Harappan Civilization, one of the earliest civilisations, developed on the banks of river Indus.

Apart from river valleys, mountain passes too have been instrumental in shaping the history of a place. The Khyber Pass connecting Afghanistan and Pakistan was as an important trade route and paved the way for foreign invasions like those of Alexander the Great and Genghis Khan. People from different regions also interacted and shared ideas along this route, paving the way for the **integration** of different cultures and customs.

## Eco feat

Acid rain, caused by local foundries and an oil refinery, have brought about the degradation of the Taj Mahal. In an effort to control the effects of pollution, tourist traffic is not allowed near the site. However, despite the efforts, the Taj Mahal continues to lose its luster.

▲ **Alexander the Great**

▲ **Genghis Khan**

## World Connect

The Rosetta stone, which was discovered in France in 1799, is famous for holding the clue which led to the deciphering of the Hieroglyphic script—a script which baffled historians and scholars for centuries. This stone provided the key to understanding Egyptian hieroglyphs, without which a large part of the history of ancient Egypt would have remained unknown to us. This stone was found at el-Rashid in Egypt and is currently stored in the British Museum where it has been since 1802.

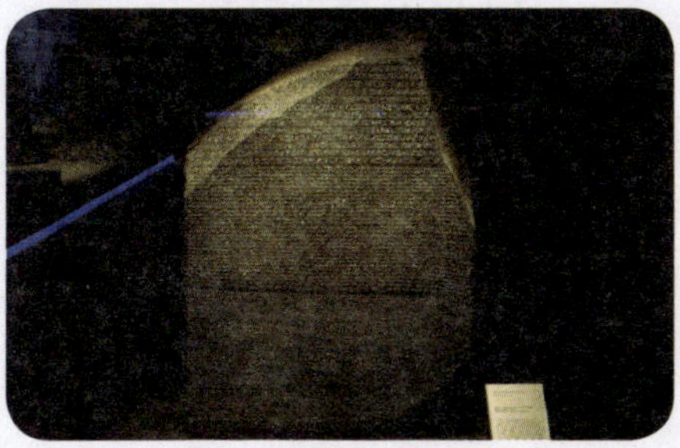

## Recall

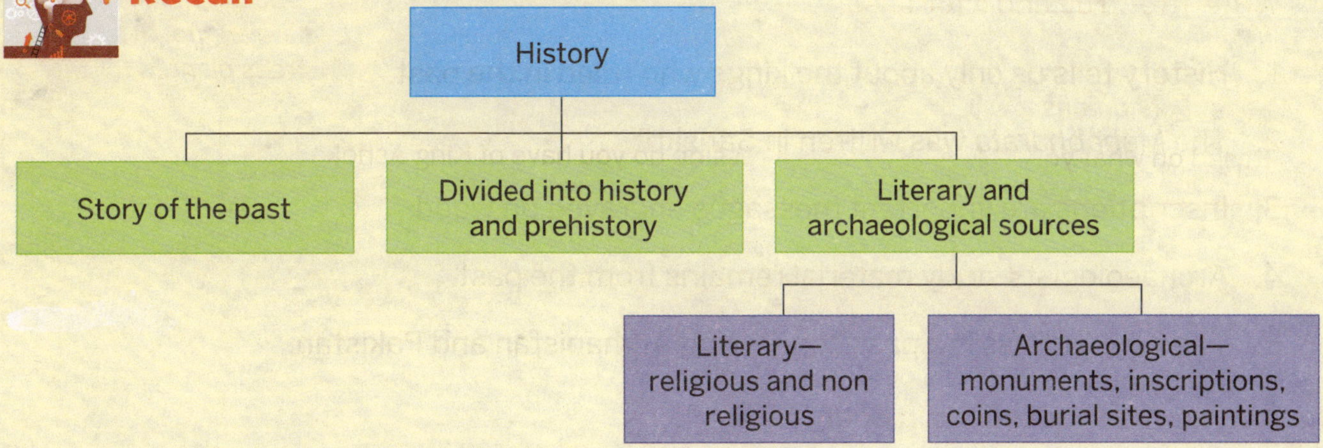


**integration:** the intermixing of people who were previously apart

## Work out

**A. Fill in the blanks.**

1. History is the study of the ..................................... .
2. The arrangement of events or dates in the order of their occurrence is known as ..................................... .
3. The *Ramayana* is a ..................................... source of history.
4. People who study the material remains of ancient civilizations are known as ..................................... .
5. An old building of historical value is termed as a ..................................... .

**B. Fill in the blanks with the correct answers.**

1. A person who examines ancient sites and objects is called an ..................................... .
   a. historian  b. scholar  c. scientist  d. archaeologist
2. A ..................................... helps us to put events and instances in the order of their occurrence.
   a. calendar  b. manuscript  c. timeline  d. non-religious text
3. A decade consists of a period of ..................................... .
   a. 10 years  b. 20 years  c. 100 years  d. 200 years
4. Literary sources include ..................................... .
   a. books  b. biographies  c. manuscripts  d. All of the above
5. ..................................... are archaeological sources.
   a. Coins  b. Cave paintings  c. Monuments  d. All of the above.

**C. Write T for true and F for false.**

1. History tells us only about the kings who ruled in the past. ☐
2. The *Mahabharata* was written in Sanskrit. ☐
3. Inscriptions are important messages engraved on wood. ☐
4. Archaeologists study material remains from the past. ☐
5. The Khyber Pass is a pass connecting Afghanistan and Pakistan. ☐

**D. Answer these questions in brief.**

1. Why is it important to study history? Give any two reasons.

2. Why are foreign travellers' accounts important in the study of our past?
3. Identify the difference between prehistory and history.
4. What is a manuscript?
5. Name two literary sources.

E. Answer these questions in detail.

1. List some objects excavated by archaeologists to study the pas
2. Why do we study history?
3. Explain CE and BCE in your own words.
4. What are inscriptions and what information do they provide?
5. With the help of examples, explain in detail how geography and history are interconnected.

## Think

Crack the puzzle.

1. I belong to that period when writing was not invented. ..........................
2. I am a river civilization that developed around the River Indus. ..........................
3. I am the key to understanding Egyptian hieroglyphs. ..........................
5. I am an engraved on hard surfaces like pillars, temple walls and caves.

..........................

## Life skills and values

We find walls of many historical monuments spoilt by scribbles as shown in the picture.

1. Do you think it is correct to scribble on historical remains?
2. How would you react if you see someone scribbling on the walls of a monument in front of you?

## Enjoy

Did you know that every artefact has a story to tell? List the names of five or more objects found in the past, in your notebook. Speak in class about any one of these objects regarding where it might have come from, whom it might have belonged to and what period it is from.

## Web link

For more information, log on to:

https://owlcation.com/humanities/What-is-History-Introducing-History-For-Kids

Last accessed on 30 September, 2019

# 2 The Hunter Gatherers

## Take off

- The study of material remains like fossils, vessels and burial sites is called ............................................ .
- Ancient civilizations flourished near ............................................ .
- Cave paintings tell us about the lives of ............................................ humans.

## Warm up

What do you think it was like for early humans to live out in the open? How different is it from camping?

In the beginning, the Earth was almost lifeless. There were only traces of simple plants which grew in the sea while the rest of the land remained rocky and bare. As time progressed, breathable air built up around the Earth making it possible for life to survive. The first human beings which appeared on the Earth had ape-like features. About 300,000 years ago, these humans evolved into what we call ***Homo sapiens*** or the 'thinking man'. The study of this period is based entirely on the material remains left by these humans.

## The Stone Age

During the prehistoric period, life was **primitive**. Prehistoric people lived in caves and were hunter-gatherers. They ate the meat of animals which they hunted, gathered fruits and vegetables and caught fish. However, plants and animals were not always available to them in one place. Some plants only grow in some seasons and would not be available all through the year. Animals had to move from place to place in search of food. Usually, they would move to places where there is easy access to water. If humans stayed in one place for too long, they would end up eating all the food available to them. Sometimes, the change of seasons meant they had to go out in search of a better place to live in. Therefore, they had to move from one place to another in search of food.

**primitive:** belonging to an early stage in the development of humans or animals

Early humans wore animal **hides** for clothes and used stone tools for hunting. This period is called the **Stone Age** and is marked by the use of stone tools and weapons. Archaeologists have uncovered some of these stone tools, although it is likely that early humans used animal bones and wood too. They used these tools for cutting meat and hides and for chopping fruits and roots. Based on the types of tools used, the Stone Age can be divided into three periods—the **Paleolithic Age**, the **Mesolithic Age** and the **Neolithic Age**.

**Find out**

Why do you think prehistoric man preferred to use tools made from stone?

## The Palaeolithic Age

The Palaeolithic period is the longest in the prehistoric era and dates from approximately 5,00,000 BCE to 10,000 BCE. During this period, humans were **nomadic** and wandered from place to place in groups that included men, women and children. They collected fruits, roots and honey and hunted animals for food.

### The Discovery of Fire

Fire was the most spectacular discovery of the Palaeolithic period. How was fire discovered? There are several assumptions or theories, regarding this. Early humans might have discovered fire when lightning struck dry grass, or they might have noticed sparks while striking two stones together. They found fire useful in scaring away wild animals and in keeping themselves warm during the winter months. They also discovered that it was a source of light for them in darkness. Soon after, they found that plants and meat tasted better after being roasted on fire, thereby discovering the art of cooking. Eventually, early humans learnt to use fire to make better tools and weapons.

Fire was very important during the Ice Age. Without fire, early humans would not have survived.

**Eco feat**

The global temperature has risen by 5 to 7 degrees in the past 5000 years. The predicted rate of global warming is at least 20 times more in the next century.

▲ Early humans sitting around a fire

### Stone Tools

Archaeologists have divided prehistoric tools into three categories. They are core tools, flake tools and blade tools.

- **Core tools** were the largest and most primitive. One of them was a fist-sized piece of rock and was generally used for pounding and smashing. Large stones were chipped

**hide:** animal skin; **nomadic:** wandering from place to place like nomads with no permanent home to get the required shape. These stones had sharp edges. Examples of core tools are hammers and hand axes.

- **Flake tools** were created by striking flakes from a stone core. Early humans found it easy to use these tools because they could be made and repaired easily and could be sharpened.
- **Blade tools** tools were created by striking a long narrow flake from a stone core. In this process, the stone was reduced till it formed the shape of a sharp blade. The blade had sharp sides and were at least twice as long as they were wide. These blades were used mostly during the Upper Palaeolithic Period. At times, they were mounted on top of bamboo sticks to use as spears.

▲ Stone tools

▲ A microlith used as a spearhead

## The Palaeolithic Artist

Observe the picture of the cave painting. Can you ever imagine early humans as artists?

▲ A cave painting

Cave paintings are etchings or drawing made on the walls or ceilings of rocky caves by dwellers usually with a sharp tool or blade or even a branch of a tree. Early humans painted on caves and cliff faces. Historians are not clear why these paintings were made but the assumption is that these paintings may have been associated with some kind of ritual or a way of communicating with each other. The paintings show hunting scenes, animals, human figures and everyday things that the artist would see around him. These paintings also reveal that prehistoric humans moved in small nomadic groups, hunting and gathering food. Natural colours like yellow ochre, hematite, manganese oxide and charcoal were used.

▲ A prehistoric man painting on a cave

Prehistoric rock paintings are present all over the world. In India, there are about 150 painting sites that have been discovered. The most famous one is located in Bhimbetka in Madhya Pradesh.

The cave paintings at Bhimbetka are good sources of information on prehistoric life. These paintings attest to the fact that prehistoric humans lived in the area, which was perfectly suited to their needs.

▲ Rock shelters in Bhimbetka

**Fact quest**

Prehistoric art has been found in Africa, Asia, Europe and Australia. Over 200 cave art sites have been found in France and Spain. These paintings include bulls, stallions and bisons.

## Location of Palaeolithic Sites

Palaeolithic sites have been found in places where good quality stones were found as stone tools were significant to the early humans. These sites were the earliest workshops and were known as **factory sites**. When the early humans stayed in these factory sites for a long time, they became **habitation** sites.

Archaeologists have discovered most of these Palaeolithic sites near river banks. They had easy access to water and food. Fishing became an important activity. Also, people did not know how to store water and so, had to live near water sources.

The banks of the rivers Tapi, Godavari and Krishna have yielded a large number of Palaeolithic sites. In Tamil Nadu, Palaeolithic sites have been discovered near rivers such as Palar, Penniyar and Kaveri.

## Mesolithic Age

The Mesolithic Age was a period where many transformations took place. It was, however, very brief and lasted from 10,000 BCE to 8,000 BCE. While man continued to hunt and gather, domestication too became an important feature of this period. The wild dog was the first animal to be domesticated, which was followed by domestication of sheep, goats and cattle. People started making tools which were sharper and more effective during this age. These tools came to be known as microliths.

**habitation:** the act of living in a particular place

This was also the time when climatic changes took place all over the world. The weather became warmer, which led to the **emergence** of grasslands and eventually, herbivorous animals. The early humans started observing animal behaviour and habits and the idea of rearing and taming them came to their minds. They also observed the natural growth of grasses like wheat and barley.

## Neolithic Age

The Neolithic Age is also known as the New Stone Age and it took place approximately 10,000 years ago. It is the last stage of the cultural evolution of the early humans. The emergence of grasslands led to the beginning of farming. By observing the environment and nature, early humans learnt to cultivate food and began living settled lives. The population also increased during this period.

### Find out

Why did early humans domesticate sheep and goat?

The stone tools belonging to this period were more refined and polished. The early human's dependence on domesticated animals increased in this period as advancements in agriculture were made. Humans learnt to grow crops. As a result, dependence on hunting, gathering of wild plants and fishing reduced. New crafts such as pottery and the art of weaving, developed around this time period.

### Investigate

Look at the picture and answer the questions.

- What do you think this tool was used for?
- Do we use a similar tool in our kitchen? What do we use it for?
- Why did the early humans need different types of tools?

### Case Study

**Hunasagi**

A number of tools belonging to the early Palaeolithic period have been discovered in Hunasagi in Karnataka. Limestone, a raw material available locally, was mostly used to make these tools. Some tools comprised of stone tools and weapons made from a reddish brown **chert.** The number of tools discovered from these sites suggests that the area was a habitation as well as a factory site of the Palaeolithic period. At some smaller sites, waste flakes and chips of stone have been found, which suggests that tools were made in these sites. Tools with long blade-like structures have also been discovered from these sites.

Q. What kind of tools were discovered from this region?

**emergence:** the process of becoming visible after being concealed; chert: a hard, dark, opaque rock that is rich in silica

## World Connect

In another part of the world, some 40,000 years ago, early humans painted inside a cave at Maros in Sulawesi, an island in Indonesia. These cave paintings show human hands outlined against a background of red paint and two detailed drawings of an animal described as a 'pig-deer'. These paintings have been considered to be one of the oldest cave paintings in the world.

▲ A cave painting in Indonesia

## Recall

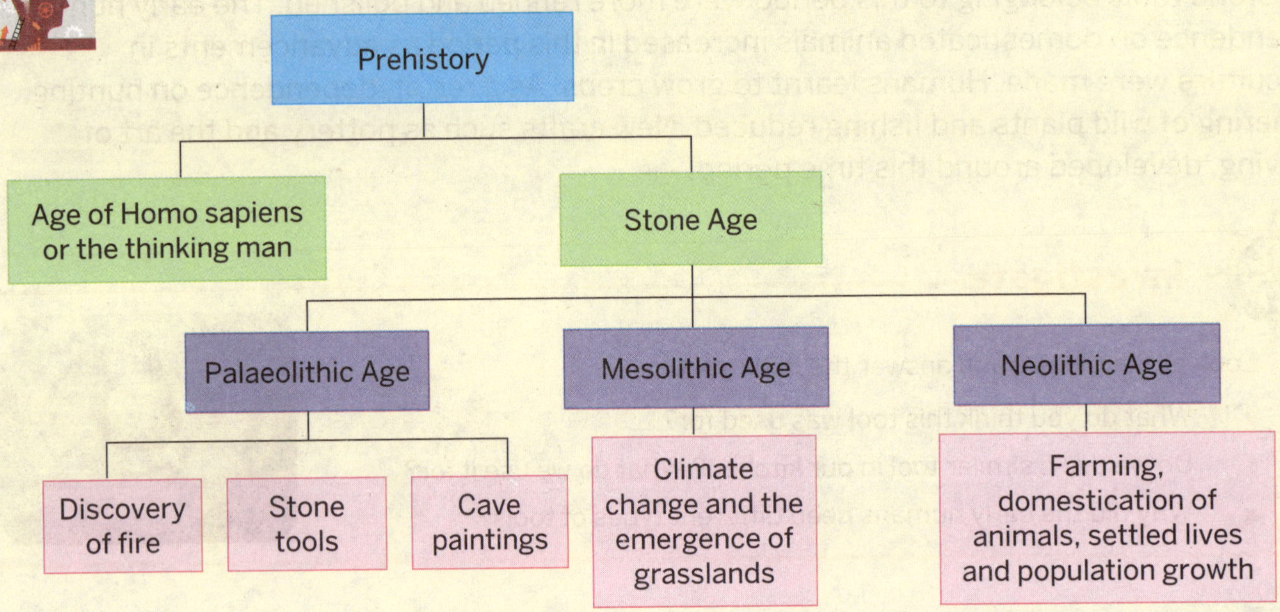


## Work out

A. Fill in the blanks.

1. The first human who appeared on the Earth had .................................. features.
2. Early humans wore animal .................................. for clothes.
3. Prehistoric humans were called .................................. as they moved from place to place in search of greener pastures.

4. Natural colours such as .................................. and .................................. were used in cave paintings, by the primitive humans.
5. Stone tools were of three types, namely, .................................., .................................., and .................................. tools.

B. Fill in the blanks with the correct answers.

1. The Neolithic Age is the .................................. .
   a. Old Stone Age
   b. Middle Stone Age
   c. New Stone Age
   d. Chalcolithic Age
2. Fire was discovered in the .................................. .
   a. Neolithic Period
   b. Palaeolithic Period
   c. Mesolithic Period
   d. Chalcolithic Age
3. In the Palaeolithic period, people were .................................. .
   a. hunter-gatherers
   b. farmers
   c. potters
   d. fishermen
4. Microliths were tools which were .................................. .
   a. small and sharp
   b. blunt
   c. large
   d. wood
5. Early humans used .................................. tools for hunting.
   a. metal
   b. stone
   c. wooden
   d. brick

C. Write T for true and F for false.

1. The early prehistoric humans lived in caves. ☐
2. Tools belonging to the Palaeolithic period were made of metals. ☐
3. Blade tools were used mostly during the Palaeolithic period. ☐
4. Domestication of animals began in the Palaeolithic Age. ☐
5. Cave paintings have also been discovered in other parts of the world, such as Indonesia. ☐

D. Answer these questions in brief.

1. How did early humans obtain food?
2. What were the key features of the Neolithic period?
3. Name the Palaeolithic sites of India.
4. List the sources through which we come to know about early humans.
5. Why did early humans live near water sources?

E. Answer these questions in detail.

1. How was fire a useful discovery for early humans?
2. Why were the hunter-gatherers always on the move?
3. What are the features of the Mesolithic Period?.
4. Why do you think prehistoric humans painted on the walls of the caves?
5. Draw a comparison between a core tool and a microlith. Which one do you think was better and why?

## Think

What do you think life was like during the Ice Age? Would it have been possible for humans to survive without fire?

## Life skills and values

Prehistoric humans communicated in sign language or with paintings. Imagine you have a new student in your school, from a foreign country, whose language you are not familiar with. How will you tell the new student about your school?

## Enjoy

Write a short story based on the title, 'Travel in Time: Meeting the Stone Age People'. Present the story in the classroom.

## Web link

For more information, log on to:

https://www.dkfindout.com/us/history/stone-age/

Last accessed on 30 September, 2019

# 3 The Agriculturist: The Neolithic Period

## Take off

- Early humans used .................................... tools to hunt.
- Early humans were .................................... as they moved from one place to another.
- .................................... tell us about the lives of early humans.

## Warm up

Early humans were hunter-gatherers. Do you think people today are still doing similar activities for food?

The Neolithic Age was the period of **transition** from hunter-gatherers to farmers. This marked a tremendous change in their lifestyle. They settled down in one place and also learnt to domesticate animals. It was during this period that early humans discovered the use of the wheel. Their tools too, improved significantly and they learnt the art of pottery. Some important sites of this period in the Indian subcontinent are Chirand, Hallur, Daojali Hading, Mehrgarh, Burzahom, Paiyampalli and Koldihwa.

## Eco feat

Many farmers today, like early humans, practise organic farming, which involves growing crops without chemicals. The use of chemical fertilizers affects the quality of the soil, water bodies and also harms the people who consume the produce.

### The Beginning of Farming

The formation of grasslands led to the growth of several grain-bearing grasses. Early humans noticed that plants grew over a period of time and that they usually grew in areas where seeds were dispersed. Thus, they learnt to sow seeds and to harvest them at the right time.

## Find out

What are the different ways in which the Neolithic people used the food grains?

**transition:** the process or a period of changing from one state or condition to another

They also understood that plants needed water to grow. They cultivated wheat, oats, barley and pulses. Farming meant a better supply of food grains. So, their dependence on hunting and gathering of food reduced. There was an increase in human population, leading to an increase in demand for food. Thus, early humans began to settle in one place for long periods of time to farm and cultivate crops. They built strong, permanent houses and lived together as a community.

▲ Early humans farming

## Case Study

**Chirand**

Chirand, a small village in the Saran district of Bihar, is situated on the northern banks of the river Ganga. The excavations in Chirand have revealed artefacts belonging to the Neolithic, Chalcolithic and Iron Age periods. Archaeologists have been able to mark the transitions in human habitation patterns and lifestyle, dating from 2500 BCE to 30 CE. Evidence of houses belonging to the Neolithic period have been excavated from this site. About 25,000 **potsherds** were excavated. These pottery remains were mostly black and red ware. A large prehistoric mound, which has been used by archaeologists to record the periods between the Neolithic Age and the pre-medieval period, was excavated here. Pendants, earrings, bangles, discs and combs from the Neolithic period were also found.

Q. Describe the type of pottery found in Chirand.

## Domestication of Animals

Once early humans became food producers, the need to care and tend to their plants became a priority in their lives. They also domesticated different animals such as sheep, goats, and cows. This provided them with a regular supply of meat and milk. Perhaps they also learnt that these animals could help them in their agricultural work. Archaeologists have uncovered remains of animal bones at Burzahom, present-day Kashmir, and Hallur in present-day Andhra Pradesh suggesting that animals were domesticated.

## The Beginning of Settlements

Early humans began building houses. These houses were mainly round, oval or rectangular **pit houses**. There were steps leading to these pit houses. Archaeologists have discovered **hearths**, both inside and outside the house. One example of the pit house was found at Burzahom in Kashmir. Pots too were found, perhaps, for storing surplus grains.

The Neolithic people soon began to live in groups. These groups led to the formation of tribes. Tribal people are those who live close to nature.

**potsherds:** broken pieces of ceramic, especially those found at an archaeological site; **hearth:** the floor of a fireplace

## Improved Tools

Tools became more advanced and **sophisticated** and had **multipurpose** uses. These tools were polished, more durable and could be shaped easily. They were made of different types of rocks like amphibolites, jadeite and basalt. With these new and strong tools, like axes, Neolithic people could clear forests for agriculture. Wood from the felled trees was used for the construction of houses, furniture and other household things. People also made use of mortars and pestles for grinding grain.

▲ Stone tools

▲ Black earthenware from Burzahom, Kashmir. Neolithic period, 2700 BCE.

## Pottery

As people started producing surplus food, there was a need to store these grains. Initially people started weaving baskets out of grass. Then they started making pots out of clay and sun-baked them. Later, **kilns** were also used to bake the pots and designs were made on them.

### Investigate

The Fertile Crescent has often been called 'the cradle of civilization' as it was home to many ancient civilizations. Agriculture, urbanization, writing, trade, science, history and organized religion all began in this region. Located in the Middle East, this region curves from the Persian Gulf and around modern-day southern Iraq, Syria, Lebanon, Jordan, Israel and northern Egypt.

On a map, find this region and name three things that began there.

## The Invention of the Wheel

The invention of the wheel was one of the most important achievements of the Neolithic people. It brought about the development of the earliest forms of vehicles—a wagon, four wheels and an axle. They could now travel faster and comfortably. The wheel also helped them to transport heavy objects from one place to another. Potter's wheels soon came to be used for making pottery and is also used to draw water from water wells.

▲ Evolution of the wheel

**sophisticated:** having, revealing, or involving a great deal of worldly experience and knowledge of fashion and culture; **multipurpose:** having several purposes or functions; **kiln:** a furnace or oven for burning, baking, or drying

## Additional Crafts

Although there has been no archaeological evidence which indicates that the early humans indulged in weaving and basketry, clay fragments bearing impressions of textiles or basketry have been uncovered in many sites. Weaving of cloth, textiles and straw mats was a common practice amongst the Neolithic people. They used materials like flax and wool. Baskets were used to store goods, woven straw mats were used for resting and fine nets were used for fishing.

**Fact quest**

There is evidence of the use of naturally available materials like stone, sea shells, animal bones and, very rarely, clay as jewellery. During the final Neolithic period, silver and gold were used.

## Burials

During the Neolithic period, the dead were buried inside their houses, beneath the floor or in simple pits. They were buried along with items such as stone tools, pottery, jewellery, animal offerings, amongst other things. These practices suggest that people believed in life after death. Some burial sites have been found at Mehrgarh.

▲ An excavated burial

## Case Study

**Mehrgarh (North-west region)**

Mehrgarh is located in present-day Pakistan. It is situated near the Bolan Pass. Mehrgarh is a Neolithic site dating back to about 7000 to 3200 BCE. It is one of the earliest sites with evidence of farming and herding in South Asia.

▲ A terracotta figure

This area was very fertile. The fertility of this area made it possible for people to grow wheat and barley. This is evident from the remains of charred grains that have been found. Animals such as sheep, goat and cattle were domesticated by the people of Mehrgarh. Apart from this, they also tamed animals such as deer. Archaeologists have divided the study of the Mehrgarh site into seven periods. It is observed that the site gradually progressed from hunting-gathering to the cultivation of plants. During the early period, they lived in mud houses and made tools from stone and bone. In the later period, agriculture became the main occupation. Houses made of wood and tools made from metals now appeared. Hand-made pottery also appeared in the later periods. Human figures made of terracotta and pottery, with exotic designs, have been discovered from this site. Numerous burials have been found at this site, many with elaborate burial goods such as pots, beads, stone and bone tools. Ornaments of sea shell, limestone and sandstone have been found, which suggest that the people were fond of wearing jewellery.

Q. What kind of crafts have been excavated from Mehrgarh?

## Chalcolithic Age (4,000 BCE - 2,000 BCE)

The Chalcolithic Age was the period that followed the Neolithic Age. It was also called the Copper Age as it was the period where humans came to use metals, particulary, copper. Copper was first the metal to be used. Later, it was mixed with tin and this came to be known as **bronze.** The transition of tools from stone to metal was a slow and a long-drawn process. The earliest metal tools resembled the stone tools in shape and size. The earliest settlements belonging to the Chalcolithic Age in India extended from the Chota Nagpur Plateau to the Gangetic Plains.

### World Connect

In Wiltshire, England, stands the Stonehenge, a prehistoric monument belonging to the Neolithic Period. It consists of a ring of standing stones. Archaeologists believed that it was built between 3000 and 2000 BCE. Some archaeologists and historians suspect the Stonehenge to be an ancient burial ground. Deposits containing human bones date as early as 3000 BCE. It is also believed to be a temple made for the worship of the Earth deities. It has also been called an astronomical observatory marking important events in the prehistoric calendar. The construction of the Stonehenge is a remarkable engineering feat. It consists of a bank and ditch arrangement called a henge. The site and its surroundings have been added to the UNESCO's list of World Heritage Sites and it is a legally protected monument.

▲ Stonehenge

### Recall

- Neolothic Period
  - Beginning of farming
  - Domestication of Animals
  - Beginning of settlements
  - Improved tools
  - Additional crafts – weaving and basketry
  - Pottery
  - Invention of the wheel

## Work out

**A. Fill in the blanks.**

1. The Age where early humans used both metals and stone was known as the ................................................ .
2. The beginning of farming and domestication of animals led to early humans living ................................................ lives.
3. Ornaments in the Neolithic period were made of sea shells and ................................................ .
4. The ................................................ wheel was used to make pots.
5. Burial sites show that people believed in life after ................................................ .

**B. Fill in the blanks with the correct answers.**

1. During the Neolithic period, the dead were buried ................................................, beneath the floor or in simple pits.
   a. in graveyards  b. in stone graves
   c. inside their houses  d. outside their houses
2. The stone that was used in making tools during the Neolithic period was called ................................................ .
   a. jadeite  a. basalt  c. amphibolites  d. all three
3. Neolithic sites are found in ................................................ .
   a. Mehrgarh  b. Mathura  c. Ujjain  d. none of these.
4. A new skill associated with the Neolithic period is ................................................ .
   a. weaving  b. pottery
   c. both pottery and weaving  d. none of these

**C. Write T for true and F for false.**

1. The Mesolithic Period came before the Palaeolithic Period. ☐
2. The Neolithic people buried their dead. ☐
3. The discovery of fire is associated with the Chalcolithic Age. ☐
4. Wheat and barley were two important crops of the Neolithic Period. ☐
5. People began to use copper during the Chalcolithic Age. ☐

**D. Answer the these questions in brief.**

1. What are pit dwellings?

2. How did the wheel help early humans?
3. How did the domestication of animals benefit early humans?
4. Give examples of the crops grown by the Neolithic people.

E. Answer these questions in detail.

1. Draw a comparison between the Palaeolithic and Neolithic periods.
2. The wheel was a revolutionary invention in the Neolithic period. Explain this.
3. What were the materials used for making ornaments during the Neolithic period?
4. Explain the burial customs of the Neolithic period.
5. What are the reasons that led early humans to begin living together as a community?

## Think

When archaeologists excavated a site at Daojali Hading, in Assam, they discovered jadeite stone, which, they suspect, must have been brought from China. What does the finding of jadeite suggest?

## Life skills and values

From what you have learnt about the Stone Age, list the jobs that would have been available during that period.

## Enjoy

A. Collect some straw and try to weave a basket out of the straw.

B. Divide the class into five groups. Each group can choose one site from amongst Chirand, Hallur, Daojali Hading, Mehrgarh and Burzahom. Find out about the location, farming, tools, domestication of animals, use of wheels, houses, pottery and other artefacts in these sites. Make a power point presentation for each site and share it with the class.

## Web link

For more information, log on to:

https://www.history.com/topics/pre-history/neolithic-revolution

Last accessed on 30 September, 2019

# 4 The Advent of Urbanization and Civilization in India

## Take off

- ................................................ was the first metal to be used by man.
- The ................................................ age marked the transition from the Stone Age to the age of metals.
- The first metal that came to be used is ................................................ .

## Warm up

Why do people move from villages to big cities and towns?

**Civilization** is that aspect of human life wherein, the human society reaches an advanced stage of social development and organization. A civilized society is one where highly developed forms of government, culture, industry, and common social norms exist. By this time, people had begun to live in cities and had found the time to develop different interests, like music, religion and painting. The earliest civilizations developed during the Bronze Age. They developed around the river valleys. Basic needs such as water and food were easily available near the rivers. Also, the land near the river banks was fertile and suitable for agriculture. Minerals like copper were also found near the rivers. Rivers were also used for transportation which led to trading.

▲ The ancient city of Mohenjo-Daro

## The Indus Valley Civilization

The Indus Valley was home to one of the world's largest civilizations. It began nearly 5,000 years ago in an area corresponding to modern-day Pakistan and northern India on the banks of the river Indus. It belonged to the Chalcolithic or the Bronze Age. **Artefacts** made of copper and stone have been found in various sites belonging to this civilization. This civilization was named after a place called Harappa in Pakistan. It was the first Indus Valley site to be excavated in the 1920s.

There were many towns and cities in the Indus Valley Civilization. The largest of them were Harappa and Mohenjo-Daro. It is believed that the cities of Harappa and Mohenjo-Daro had a population of about 80,000 people.

**Fact quest**

In 1856, the British railroad engineers discovered ancient bricks that were exactly alike. Those bricks were the first clues to the ancient civilization that once thrived in the Indus Valley.

The Indus Valley Civilization extended across present-day Baluchistan, Sindh, Punjab, Haryana and Rajasthan. The most important sites that were excavated were Harappa and Mohenjo-Daro in present-day Pakistan, Kalibangan in Rajasthan, Ropar in Punjab, Lothal in Gujarat, Banawali and Rakhigarhi in Haryana and Dholavira in Kachchh.

## Cities of the Indus Valley Civilization

**Harappa:** This archaeological site at Punjab in Pakistan consists of the ruins of a fortified city.

**Mohenjo-Daro:** Built around 2500 BCE, Mohenjo-Daro literally means 'mound of the dead'. This archaeological site is situated in the Sind province of Pakistan and has been declared a World Heritage Site by UNESCO in 1980.

**Kalibangan:** This town of the Indus Valley Civilization had developed at the confluence of the Drishadvati and the Saraswati rivers in Rajasthan. The unique fire altars found in Kalibangan are one of its most significant features.

▲ **Indus Valley Civilization**

**artefacts:** objects made by people typically one of cultural or historical interest

**Lothal:** Lothal was the most prominent trading centres of the Indus Valley Civilization. It is located in Gujarat. Valuable gems, beads and valuable ornaments were traded with West Asia and Africa via the Arabian Sea from Lothal.

### Find out

Pictures representing words or phrases were used to record the important events of people's lives. Today, pictographs are still used. Look at these signs, and write down what they stand for.

## Sources

The main sources for studying the history of the Indus Valley Civilization are the terracotta seals, which were mostly square in shape. These seals have animal and human figures engraved on them. The script is yet to be deciphered and will unveil much more than what we know today.

## The Skilled Engineers of the Indus Valley

Engineers of this ancient civilization were very skilled and their towns were well planned. There is clear evidence of the use of burnt bricks in making drains and roads. These bricks were baked in ovens outside the limits of the town.

### Find out

What are the names of the two Indian archaeologists who discovered the remains of Harappa and Mohenjo-Daro in the 1920s?

**The Planned Towns:** The Harappan towns were well-planned. They were divided into two parts .The upper part, described as the citadel by archaeologists, was built on a raised platform. All important buildings like the Great Bath, the granaries and the town hall are found here. The second part was the lower town, which included residential buildings or houses, all laid out in a grid.

**Store houses:** Elaborate store houses have been found in Mohenjo-Daro, Harappa and Lothal. All the surplus grain was stored in these store houses which were situated near the river bank. Harappa had more than six of them.

**The Great Bath:** Another prominent structure of the Indus Valley Civilization found at Mohenjo-Daro was a very special tank, which archaeologists called the Great Bath. It was like a large swimming pool. This was a magnificent and outstanding structure. It was watertight and layered with bricks and mortar. There were changing rooms along the sides. The Great Bath may have been used for ritual bathing purposes.

▲ The Great Bath of Mohenjo-Daro

**Town Hall:** There is evidence of a structure which may have been an assembly hall or a town hall.

**Houses and streets:** The houses were two-storeyed and built on either side of the streets. The number of rooms varied from two to twenty and each house had a central courtyard and a bathing area. Evidence of a circular oven and a mortar and pestle have been found. Houses were separated by a network of roads cutting each other at right angles, forming a grid-like pattern. The entrances to the houses never faced the main road, but opened towards secondary roads and smaller alleyways.

The primary or main streets pointed in a north to south direction, whereas, secondary streets stretched from east to west. Corners were rounded, which suggests that the planners kept the difficulty of turning carts in mind.

**Drainage system:** The drainage system in these cities was very impressive. The drains were water tight which prevented the leakage of dirty water. Wooden screens filtered solid waste and prevented it from getting washed away by water. As a result, clogging and over-flowing of dirty water was avoided. There were inspection holes and detachable covers, which made the process of cleaning easier. The house drains were connected to the main drains.

## Life and Occupation of the People

Farming was an important occupation of the Harappan civilization. The people grew rice, wheat, barley, pulses, peas, sesame, linseed and mustard. Ploughs and sickles were used and different methods of irrigation were adopted. Apart from this, they also reared animals for milk. Fishing was another occupation they engaged in. Their seals reflect their awareness of animals like goats, sheep, bison and humped bulls.

We have already learnt that the cities were well-planned. This tells us that there were people who planned the construction of buildings and streets in the city. Most probably, this work was done by the rulers. Scribes were people who could write on the seals.

▲ **Dancing Girl, a bronze statue found at Mohenjo-Daro**

Many people were engaged in different kinds of crafts. Pottery-making was an important occupation. Most of the pots were red ware and were used as storage pots and burial containers. Evidence shows us that the people also knew how to spin cotton. Archaeologists have found spindles which were used to spin thread. The evidence of ornaments proves that they liked to adorn themselves with jewellery which were made of gold, silver and bronze beads. Stones like lapis lazuli, agate and carnelian were used for making these beads. There were also special workshops where the people made different things like bronze sculptures and artefacts.

Copper and bronze were also used to make weapons and tools like knives and razors. Some vessels made of thin metal sheets have also been found. While the grown ups were engaged in different crafts and skilled jobs, the children amused themselves with games such as marbles, rattles, mobile toy carts and whistles.

## Investigate

*'Amongst the objects excavated at both Mohenjo-daro and Harappa, are a large number of small rectangular blocks, mostly of a tawny or light grey banded chert, but also of other hard rocks, such as gneiss. In one or two cases their form is cylindrical, but for the most part, they are cubical. The blocks are well finished and polished, and are generally in a good state of preservation. None bear any inscription or mark indicating a value. The results obtained from weighing these blocks show conclusively that they are weights belonging to a definite system.'*

This is an extract from a book by Sir John Marshall, who was the Director General of the Archaeological Survey of India in the 1900s, when excavations led to the discovery of the cities of Harappa and Mohenjo-Daro.

- For what purpose did the Indus Valley Civilization people use the system of weights and measures?
- What can we infer about trade with other places, from these weights and measures?
- Write down at least three modern uses of weights and measures.

## Trade

Evidence of seals, weights and measures suggest that active trade relations was carried out as Mesopotamian seals were found in Harappa. The dockyard in Lothal suggests brisk trade. The cities were connected with rural, agricultural communities, through a strong trade system. Trade is reflected in the widespread distribution of beads, ornaments, pots, metal tools and seals. While the people were self-sufficient, there were some items which had to be brought in from distant places. Archaeologists suspect that copper may have been brought in from Rajasthan and tin from Afghanistan. This suggests that trade had carried out between these places.

▲ Terracotta figurines

## Seals

Most of the seals have a knob at the back through which runs a hole. It is believed that the seals were used by merchants for stamping purposes. Most seals have a pictorial inscription on them. Some important seals excavated are the pashupati seal, the unicorn seal and the bull seal. These seals were mostly used for trading purposes. Archaeologists believe that these seals were used for stamping purposes. Once packets or bags are closed, traders would dip the seals on wet clay and press it on the closing. This way, people could see that when the seal was intact, it means that the bag has not been opened.

▲ An Indus Valley seal

## The Decline of the Indus Valley Civilization

The Indus Valley Civilization is said to have come to an abrupt end due to a combination of several factors. Natural calamities such as floods and earthquakes are believed to have destroyed the area leading to the migration of people to different regions. It is possible that climatic changes led to drought conditions. Perhaps the rivers changed their courses or dried up, thus affecting the agriculture of the place. Conditions of cities like Lothal, and Dholavira might have deteriorated and hence impacted trade and led to the decline of the civilization.

## Case Study

### Comparative Study of Two Different Cities of Gujarat

**Dholavira** is one of the largest settlements of the Indus Valley Civilization. It is located at Khadir Beyt in the Rann of Kutch. Unlike the other Indus Valley cities, which were divided into two parts, Dholavira was divided into three parts. The city was constructed as per a pre-existing geometrical plan. It was designed in the shape of a **parallelogram**. It had a citadel, a middle town and a lower town. The city was well-fortified, with entrances and a gateway.

Dholavira stands as one of the most distinctive and impressive sites of the Indus Valley cities. It was known as the lake city of the Indus Valley Civilization and because of its strategic location, it was called a paradise in the desert. The people were adept in technology and knew about the technique of water harvesting. They were artistic people who made ornaments with Lapiz Lazuli, agate, silver, gold, etc.

A large signboard (35 cm to 37 cm tall, 25 cm to 27 cm broad) has been discovered here. This was probably placed at the northern gate of the citadel so that it could be seen from a distance. It is made of gypsum. It could also have been placed in a public area where people could read it.

Another important discovery was that of an open space, which archaeologists believe, resembled a stadium. It has been named Rangbhoomi.

One unique feature of Dholavira was its sophisticated water conservation system. The city had massive stone reservoirs which were used to store freshwater brought by the rains. The stored water was useful in the desert-like climate of the region.

Dholavira is estimated to be older than the port city of Lothal.

**Lothal** is one of the most prominent cities of the Indus Valley Civilization, located in the Bhal region of modern-day Gujarat. It is believed to be a prominent trading centre of this civilization. This is because evidence of a dockyard has been discovered there. This site is considered to be the earliest dock, which connected the city to the ancient course of the Sabarmati river, placing it on the trade route between many cities. The people of Lothal traded in precious stones such as gems, beads, ornaments, and even had overseas trade. It is said that Lothal had the most prosperous trade relationships with Mesopotamia (Modern Iraq), Egypt, Persia and probably even African countries. A mound, a township and a marketplace have been unearthed at the site. Today, the excavated sites of the city of Lothal, stand adjacent to the Archaeological Museum, where the most prominent antiques from the Indus Valley Civilization are displayed.

The city of Lothal had elaborate storehouses too. Constant threats of tropical storms and floods, eventually, led to the destruction of the port town of Lothal.

Q. Write two similarities and two dissimilarities between the cities of Dholavira and Lothal.

## World Connect

### Mesopotamian Civilization

The Mesopotamian Civilization was the earliest of all civilizations. *Mesopotamia* is a Greek word which means 'between the rivers', in this case specifically, the area between the Tigris river and the Euphrates river. The civilization lasted for over 3000 years. Its people were the first to devise a system of writing, develop mathematics and learn to work with metal.

**parallelogram:** a four-sided plane rectilinear figure with opposite sides parallel

The Mesopotamian cities were divided into three parts, one area was set aside for religious purposes, the other was fortified and the third was the outer town. The central portion comprised a temple, built on a ruined area, called the Ziggurat. The people worshiped several gods and goddesses at the Ziggurat. The Ziggurats were constructed with layer upon layer of mud bricks in the shape of a pyramid. The temple on top served as the Gods' home and was beautifully decorated.

Mesopotamia's political structure represented an early form of democracy. Frequent wars led to the emergence of warriors as leaders and eventually gave rise to the monarchical system.

## Recall

- **Indus Valley Civilisation**
  - **Cities**
    - Harappa
    - Mohenjo-Daro
    - Kalibangan
    - Lothal
  - **Features**
    - Planned towns
    - The Great Bath
    - Town Hall
    - Store houses
    - Streets: grid-like pattern
    - Drainage System
  - **Life and occupation**
    - Farming
    - Reared animals and fishes
    - Crafts like pottery making, cotton weaving, jewellery and ornaments making, weaponry and metallurgy
    - Rulers probably planned the cities and scribes wrote on seals
    - Trade and seals

## Work out

A. Write T for true and F for false.

1. The Mesopotamian Civilization developed along the banks of the Nile River. ☐
2. Toys of the Indus Valley Civilization were made of terracotta. ☐
3. The Lothal dock was located in present-day Pakistan. ☐
4. The Great Bath was believed to be used for religious purposes and rituals. ☐
5. A large signboard was discovered in Lothal. ☐

B. Fill in the blanks with the correct answers.

1. .................................... was the first Indus Valley Civilization city to be excavated.
   a. Rangpur  b. Lothal  c. Harappa  d. Dholavira
2. .................................... were people who could write on the seals.
   a. Scribes  b. Craftsmen  c. Farmers  d. Rulers
3. The civilization that came up on the banks of the river Tigris was called the .................................... Civilization.
   a. Chinese  b. Egyptian  c. Indus Valley  d. Mesopotamian
4. The Indus Valley Civilization seals were made of .................................... .
   a. burnt brick  b. copper
   c. terracotta  d. both options a and b
5. .................................... was a city of the Indus Valley Civilization.
   a. Mysore  b. Bhimbetka  c. Kurnool  d. Kalibangan

C. Fill in the blanks.

1. The raised upper part of the Harappan city was termed as the .................................... .
2. The Indus Valley people believed in life after.................................... .
3. Seals were used as .................................... .
4. Stones ...................................., agate and carnelian were used for making beads.
5. The Great Bath was situated in .................................... .

D. Answer these questions in brief.

1. What do you understand by civilization?
2. What were store houses used for?
3. Name three occupations of the Indus Valley people.
4. What has the upper part of the city been called by archaeologists?
5. What were seals made of?

E. Answer these questions in detail.

1. How were the houses and streets designed?
2. The drainage system and the Great Bath reflected excellent planning. Explain this.
3. Describe the seals found in Harappa. What were they used for?
4. How can we say that the Indus Valley people traded with other countries?
5. Write down the main differences between Dholavira and Lothal.

## Think

Look at the picture and answer the questions.

1. Why did the Indus Valley people decide to live in the Indus Valley?
2. How do we know that the people were peace loving?

## Life skills and values

*'The uniform organisation of the town and its institutions give evidence that the Harappans were very disciplined people.'*

Do you agree with this statement? Do you think discipline is important? Why?

## Enjoy

Make mud pots

You will need mud and water

1. Take a cup of mud and mix it with some water.
2. Shape the mud into miniature pots. They can have handles on them too.
3. Leave it in the sun to dry.
4. Once dried, you can paint them.

## Web link

For more information, log on to:

https://www.harappa.com/slideshows

Last accessed on 30 September, 2019

# 5 The Vedic Period

## Take off

- The Harappan Civilization developed along the banks of the river .................................................
- The Great Bath was located in .................................................
- Indus Valley people built ................................................. cities.

## Warm up

What can we learn from reading books?

In the last chapter, we saw the emergence of developed cities and the beginning of urbanization. However, the Indus Valley civilization did see a decline, and it was during this time that a new group of people came to the Indian subcontinent.

By 1500 BCE, nomadic cattle herders from Central Asia migrated into the Indian subcontinent. They crossed the Hindu Kush mountains and came into contact with the Harappan Civilization. We learn about them from the ***Vedas***. The *Vedas* were sacred and religious texts of a group of people who called themselves the Aryans. These texts however, only came to be written down 200 years ago. Before that, they were recited and memorized and were passed down through the ages, orally. Students memorized the *Vedas* and when they grew up, they became teachers and taught other students. This tradition was called *shruti*.

Based on the information derived from the *Vedas*, the Aryans settled in the region around river Indus and its tributaries. They called this land the Sapta-Sindhu. They later **migrated** to the Indo-Gangetic

## Fact quest

The Iron Age is the period occurring after the Bronze Age (Chalcolithic Period). It is at this time that iron production began. In history, the Iron Age is the last principal period in the three-age system (Stone Age, Bronze Age and Iron Age), for classifying prehistoric societies.

**migrated:** (of a person) move to a new area or country in order to find work or better living conditions

Plain and the Deccan Plateau. The Aryans were known to be simple people. Their arrival marks the beginning of the Iron Age in India. They brought the horse and the horse-drawn chariot to the Indian subcontinent.

## Sources of History

The sources of studying the culture of the people who lived during this time can be broadly divided into the literary and the archaeological sources.

### Literary Sources

The *Vedas* are rich sources that help us understand the period. They were written by sages or priests, and tell us about important practices and rituals and also lists the rules the people needed to follow in society. There are four *Vedas*. They are the *Rig Veda*, the *Sama Veda*, the *Yajur Veda* and the *Atharva Veda*.

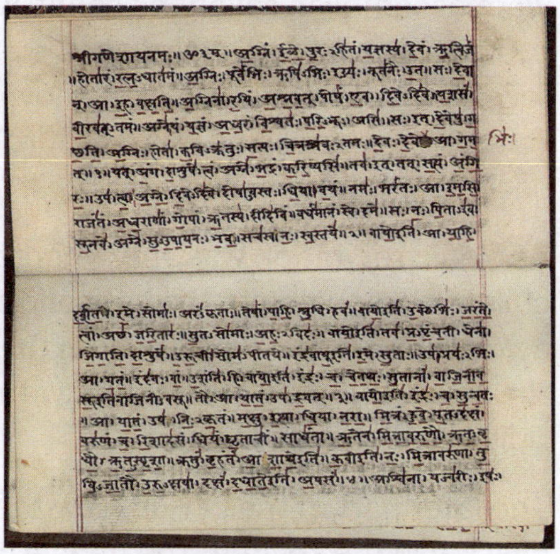

▲ An Indian Hindu scripture

The *Rig Veda* is the oldest of these books and is believed to have been composed approximately 3,500 years ago. It contains 1,028 hymns called *suktas*. These hymns were in praise of Agni, the god of fire, Indra, the warrior god and Soma, a plant from which a special drink is prepared.

The *Sama Veda* comprises hymns sung by priests during important ceremonies and sacrifices.

The *Yajur Veda* contains a set of rules that must be followed while performing different religious ceremonies and sacrifices.

The *Atharva Veda* contains songs, charms and magical spells to keep evil away.

**Find out**

In which language were the *Vedas* written?

### Archaeological Sources

The Vedic people used four types of pottery—black and red ware, black-slipped ware, painted grey ware and red ware. The most popular type was the red ware. However, the most distinctive pottery of the period is the painted grey ware. The Aryans introduced painted grey ware pottery to the Indian subcontinent. This pottery comprised bowls and dishes, painted with geometric patterns in black. This kind of pottery was used either for rituals, or for eating by the people from the upper classes.

▲ A historian sorting through fragments of red ware pottery

## Early Vedic Period

The information that we get from the *Rig Veda* draws upon the life and culture of the people living in the **Early Vedic period**.

### Social and Political Life

Early Vedic society lived in tribal settlements or tribes called *jana*. These janas were governed by a ruler called *rajan* who was elected on the basis of his physical strength and bravery. In order to advise the ruler, there were assemblies called the *samiti* which were attended by the entire village, whereas, the assembly attended by few, very special people, was known as the *sabha*. Priests also played an important role in the social society and were called *purohitas*.

▲ Inside a gurukula

As Vedic recitation was very important to these people, the children belonging to the household of the priests studied in a *gurukula*, under a guru, whom they served. The children of the rulers oriented themselves with skills like archery, horse riding and chariot racing.

**Eco feat**

Why were gods and goddesses associated with nature worship?

The later part of the period, saw the emergence of social division in the society. The people who did not belong to the same group, spoke different languages and did not perform sacrifices came to be called *Dasas*. Later, this term came to refer to slaves or servants. Mostly, these comprised of the people captured in war.

## Occupation

The Aryans lived semi-nomadic lives at the beginning. They were hunter-gatherers and lived off the land, moving from one place to another. By the 12th century BCE, the Vedic society had **transitioned** from this semi-nomadic life to settled agriculture. The people reared cattle and engaged in agricultural practices for their food. Cattle was the main source of wealth for the Aryans and the amount of cattle a family owned signified the family's social status. Fruits like berries, dates, *ber*, *amla* and *jamun* were collected.

**Investigate**

The *Rig Veda* mentions the names of learned women such as Viswara, Apala and Ghosa who composed hymns like men. What does this tell you about the society of the period?

**transition:** the process or a period of changing from one state or condition to another

## Later Vedic Period

Later Vedic society came to be divided into four groups, according to their birth. The highest in the hierarchy were the *Brahmins*, who were mainly teachers, advisors and priests. The second group of people were the *Kshatriyas*, who were rulers and warriors. The third group were the *Vaishyas*, who worked as cattle herders, potters, weavers and other craftsmen. The last group were the *Shudras*, who had to serve the other three groups. Initially, this was simply a division of labour but later, the division became rigid and members of the same family had to follow the same occupation.

Inter-caste marriages were not allowed and the position of women deteriorated. The ruler's position became hereditary and his position became unquestionable.

Towards the later Vedic period, the significance of cattle came to be replaced by land. Archaeologists have found seeds of barley, wheat, rice and pulses that suggest that people were agriculturists and lived in villages. Iron came to be used during the later half of the Vedic period. Iron smiths had an important position in the economy. There were potters, craftsmen, weavers, carpenters, jewellers, chariot-makers and tanners.

## Burials

Many **burials** have been excavated in many sites in the Deccan, south India, north-east and Kashmir. The dead were buried with their heads facing the north along with pots containing their belongings. From the burials, we come to know the position of a person in the society. When a person is buried with many ornaments and household items, it indicated that he or she was a prominent member of a tribe. Some burials have only a few objects. This suggests some difference in status amongst the people who were buried. Sometimes, iron tools and weapons, skeletal remains of horses and horse equipment have been found in these burials.

When some burials have more than one skeleton, it may be estimated that they may have belonged to the same family. The people who were buried later were brought through a round or rectangular entrance, known as **porthole.** Stone boulders were placed near these burials so that it was easy to locate them. Perhaps, the people would return to these burial sites to pay their respect to the deceased.

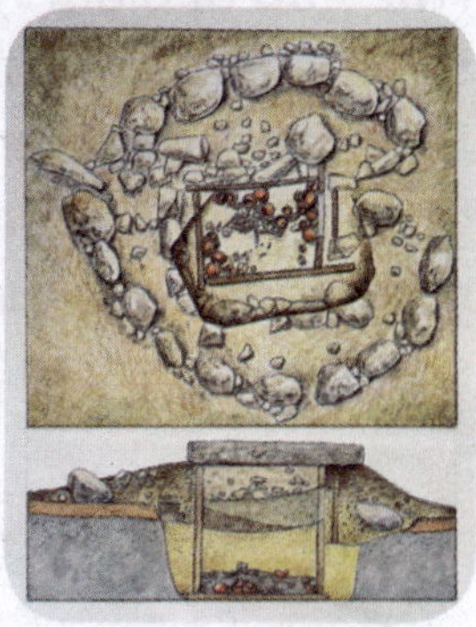

▲ A porthole

### The Megaliths

The term 'megaliths' refers to large stones used to construct a monument. Megaliths have been found in the Deccan Plateau in south India. These are huge stone **boulders** that are circular in shape. These were **earmarked** as burial sites.

Many megaliths have been found with agricultural tools, black and red ware pottery and ornaments. The agricultural tools suggest that the people were agriculturists. Traces of grains

**boulders:** large rocks, typically ones that have been worn smooth by erosio; **earmarked:** designated for a particular purpose too have been found near the megaliths. Some of the well-known megalithic sites are Brahmagiri and Inamgaon.

## Case Study

**Inamgaon**

Inamgaon is a site excavated near Pune in Maharashtra on the banks of river Ghod, a tributary of river Bhima. This settlement existed between 1700 BCE and 600 BCE. The people used copper and stone to make tools. Agriculture was the main occupation, as seeds of barley, wheat, rice, pulses and millets have been discovered at this site. The other occupation of the people of Inamgaon must have been domestication of animals such as cattle and sheep, because bones of these animals have been found. Apart from this, traces of kiln-baked red ware pottery with geometric designs have been unearthed at Inamgaon. People appear to have been religious as figures of gods and goddesses have been excavated. Several megaliths, having more than one skeleton, along with vessels, suggests that people of the same family were buried at the same spot. The vessels were meant to keep food and water for the dead. In many instances, burials were found within the houses. A special burial was found here, where the skeletal remains of a man were unearthed in a large, four-legged clay jar in the courtyard of a very big house. Archaeologists believe that this could have been the body of a ruler or a chief.

Q. Write a note on the burial practices of the Vedic period in Inamgaon.

# Contributions of the Vedic Age

The Vedic Age was an important period in the history of India. It was during this period that India presented to the world, its rich cultural heritage, through Vedic literature. Through the *Vedas*, we learn about several gods, like Indra, (the god of rains), Agni (the god of fire), Soma (the god of plants), Surya (the sun god), Varuna (the sky god) and several hymns composed to pay respect to them. During the later Vedic period, people began worshipping gods like Brahma, Vishnu and Shiva. Rituals became elaborate and complex, and the priest community became very important. The Sanskrit language which is considered to be the mother of most Indian languages originated during the Vedic period. Therefore, Vedic culture played a significant part in the history of India.

## World Connect

**Yellow River Valley Civilization**

Around 4000 BCE, the Yellow (Hwang-Ho) River Valley Civilization began in China. This civilization marked the beginning of many Chinese empires. Early Chinese tribes followed the patriarchal system of society. Men held roles as leaders of the society, while women had no role to play. Ritual sites were also significant to the early Chinese civilization. Those who had access to ritual sites had political power. Shrines were dedicated to the ancestors, and worshipers paid tribute to their ancestors in the hopes that they would have successful harvest and prosperity. Gifts included objects such as jade carvings and pieces of pottery. Archaeological evidence suggests that violence was a common occurrence in the Yellow River Valley Civilization. Although violence led to changes in political leadership, no significant cultural changes occurred.

## Recall

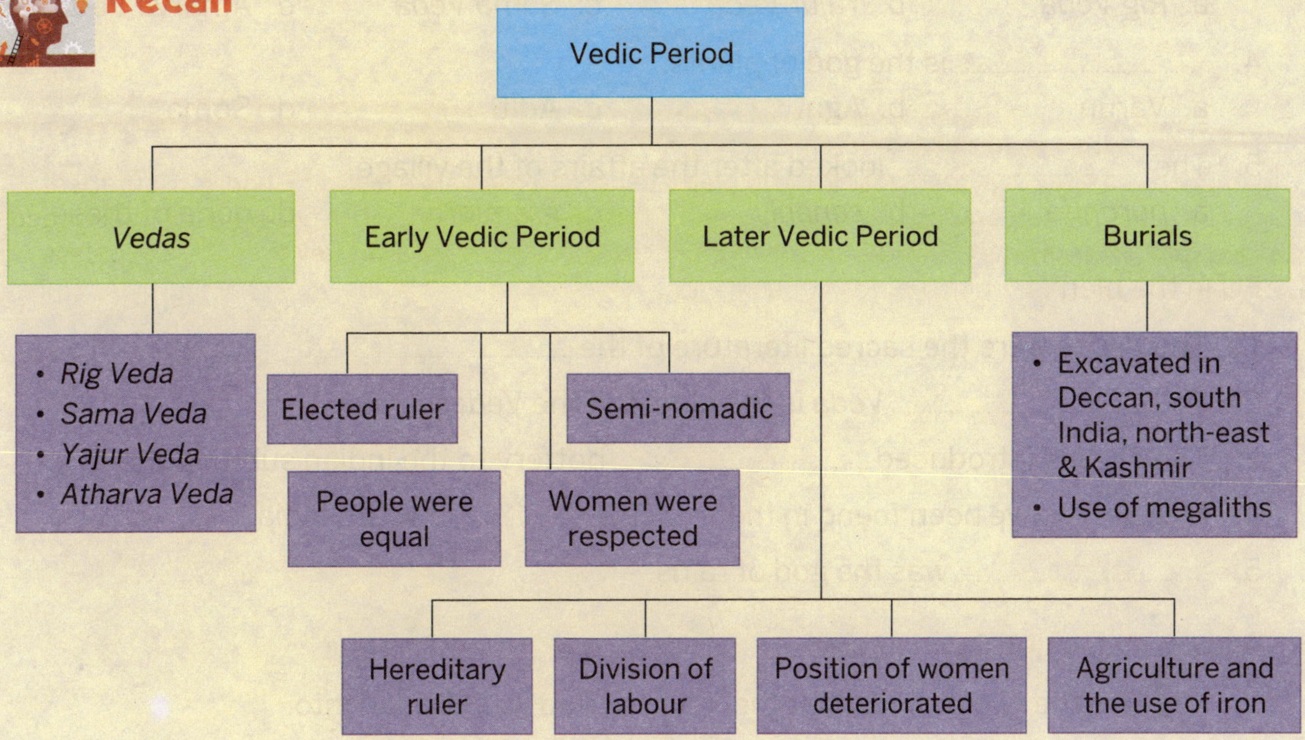


## Work out

**A. Answer in one word.**

1. I am the oldest *Veda* and contain 1028 hymns. .................................... .
2. Children, in the Vedic age, came here to learn the *Vedas* and other skills. .................................... .
3. I am the god of fire, honoured in the Vedic period. .................................... .
4. I am the mother of many Indian languages, and originated during the Vedic age. .................................... .

**B. Fill in the blanks with the correct answers.**

1. The *Rig Veda* has hymns composed to honour .................................... .
   - a. various gods
   - b. the ruler
   - c. the head of the family
   - d. None of these
2. Some historians believe that the Aryans migrated from .................................... .
   - a. Europe
   - b. India
   - c. Both options a and b
   - d. Central Asia

3. The ................................ is the Veda that has rules.
   a. *Rig Veda* b. *Yajur Veda* c. *Sama Veda* d. *Atharva Veda*
4. ................................ is the god of plants.
   a. Varun b. Agni c. Aditi d. Soma
5. The ................................ looked after the affairs of the village.
   a. *purohita* b. *senani* c. *gramini* d. none of these

## B. Fill in the blanks.

1. The *Vedas* were the sacred literature of the ................................ .
2. The ................................ *Veda* is the oldest of the *Vedas*.
3. The Aryans introduced ................................ pottery to the Indian sub-continent.
4. Megaliths have been found in the ................................ in south India.
5. ................................ was the god of rains.

## C. Answer these questions in brief.

1. Mention the two periods that the Vedic period was divided into.
2. What was the role of the *sabha* and the *samiti* in the Vedic age?
3. What did the children do in the *gurukula*?
4. Name the different occupations followed by the people of the Vedic Age.
5. Where is Inamgaon located?

## D. Answer these questions in detail.

1. What did the burials contain?
2. Explain the main contribution of Vedic literature in shaping the culture of India.
3. Write short notes on:
   a. Megaliths b. the Ashrama System
4. Name the different gods and goddesses that the Aryans worshipped.
5. Write a note on the contribution of the Vedic period in the history of India.

## Think

Look at the picture and answer the questions.

1. What is this girl doing?
2. Do girls enjoy an equal status with boys today?

## Life skills and values

The *Kshatriyas* were the warrior class whose role was to fight wars and protect their people. What are the good qualities of a soldier? Make a list of all the virtues that the *Kshatriya* would have possessed during the Vedic period.

## Enjoy

The Vedic period is the basis of the society in India. In pairs, talk to your elders and find out,

1. whether the *varna* system still exists in the Indian society today.
2. whether the Panchayati Raj is based on the *sabha* and *samiti* of the Vedic period.
3. whether the position of women has changed in Indian society today.

Write an report on your findings and share it with the class.

## Web link

For more information, log on to:

https://www.culturalindia.net/indian-history/ancient-india/vedic-civilization.html

Last accessed on 30 September, 2019

# 6 Janapadas and New Kingdoms

## Take off

- The Aryans were a group of people who migrated from .................................. to India.
- The .................................... is the oldest of the *Vedas*.

## Warm up

Both boys have to share the room. How do you think it should be divided?

## Janapadas

In the last chapter, we had learnt about how tribes began to form. People started living together in tribes called *janas*. Each tribe had a leader or a ruler called a *rajan*. As the population increased, tribes became larger. A group of tribes constituted a village called a *grama*. Soon, these *gramas* became large territories, thereby giving the *rajan* more and more power. These large territories came to be called ***janapadas***. In the early Vedic period, the *rajan* was chosen by the *janas*. However, in the later Vedic period, powerful men established their own supremacy, declaring themselves to be the rajans of the *janapadas*.

Some sites from this period, excavated by archaeologists, include the Purana Qila in Delhi and Hastinapur near Meerut (UP). Archaeologists have excavated these sites and have found that people lived in huts and took up farming and domestication of animals as occupations. A number of earthen pots have been uncovered in these sites.

▲ **An earthen pot from the Vedic Period**

### Ashwamedha Yagna

At times, a rajan would perform the *Ashwamedha Yagna* or horse sacrifice to prove his supremacy over other rulers. In this ritual, a horse belonging to the ruler would be let loose to wander into the neighbouring kingdoms. If the neighbouring rulers stopped the horse, they had to fight the king who owned the horse. However, if the horse was allowed to roam freely, it signified that the ruler accepted the **supremacy** of the king who was performing the *Ashwamedha Yagna*. The *yagna* was performed by specially-trained priests in front of a large gathering. This included all the rulers who had accepted the King's supremacy, as well as the people of his kingdom. The horse would then be guided back to the kingdom from whence it came and sacrificed. After the sacrifice, the king would be declared supreme and all the rulers who attended the yagna would give gifts to the king.

▲ A painting of the Ashwamedha Yajna

## Varnas

By this time, the *varna* system had become extremely rigid. While the two upper classes, the *Brahmins* and the *Kshatriyas*, enjoyed power and status, the two lower classes, the *Vaishyas* and the *Shudras*, were exploited by the upper classes. The *Shudras* formed the lowest rung in the social hierarchy. They, along with landless peasants, had no rights and were treated as slaves. They were expected to serve the upper castes and because the *varna* system was **hereditary**, people from these castes were typically born into oppression. This fostered feelings of contempt and disdain among the lower castes towards the system as a whole as well as to people from the upper caste. This period ushered in swift advances in ideas and thoughts. By this time, a large number of people were opposed to the rigid turn that religion had taken.

## Mahajanapadas

Soon *janapadas* became bigger and more powerful. These evolved into *mahajanapadas* which were powerful kingdoms. Most of these *mahajanapadas* were located in the Gangetic Plains. The *mahajanapadas* had capital cities, and were **fortified**. Forts were probably built to safeguard the kingdom from attacks. Building such walls required thousands and thousands of bricks as well as workers. This means that the kingdoms were not only large but also wealthy.

▲ Mahajanapadas (600–300 BCE)

**supremacy:** the state or condition of being superior to all others in authority, power, or status; **fortified:** (of a place) defensible, due to walls, trenches, etc

Across the Indo-Gangetic Plains, there arose sixteen kingdoms during the Vedic period. These sixteen *mahajanapadas* are described in the *Vedas* and other ancient literature. They were Anga (in present-day Bihar), Assaka (in present-day Maharashtra), Avanti (in present-day Madhya Pradesh), Chedi, also known as Cheti, Gandhara, Kamboja, Kasi (in present-day Varanasi), Kosala (in present-day Uttar Pradesh), Kuru, Machcha or Matsya (in present-day Jaipur in Rajasthan), Magadha (in present-day Bihar), Malla, Panchala, Surasena, Vajji or Vriji and Vamsa or Vatsa (in present-day Uttar Pradesh).

Other cities like Tamralipti, Shravasti and Bhrigukachchha, gained importance because of their presence on the trade routes. These *mahajanapadas* were ruled by monarchs, who were considered to be divine representatives by the people. They maintained armies and employed many people to do different kinds of work as officials.

## Urbanization

This period was marked by major developments which included the use of iron, paddy transplantation, the imposition of taxes, the growth of trade and urban settlements, the growth of new skills and crafts and the emergence of new religions and ideas. The developments in agriculture and crafts led to the emergence of many trade towns which were mainly located near rivers. Several important trade routes developed at this time and some cities became important market centres.

### Agriculture

The new rulers started realizing the importance of agriculture. The discovery and use of iron led to the clearing of forests for agricultural purposes. Farmers could now cultivate food crops better, as the iron plough was more effective than the wooden one. Also, they no longer scattered seeds on the ground and waited for the seeds to sprout. They could directly plant saplings, ensuring that more plants survived. This was eventually followed by trade of the **surplus** production.

**Eco feat**

Agriculture has a lot of effect on the environment. Trees have to be cut to obtain space for planting of crops. This leads to soil erosion, as roots of trees hold the soil together. Also, planting a single crop repeatedly leeches the soil of its nutrients. Fertilizers used for agriculture, also have an adverse effect on the soil. A large amount of freshwater is used up for irrigation. Agriculture will, however, continue to increase with an increase in the world's population.

### Taxes

The rulers needed to pay salaries to the soldiers and officials. This means, they needed a large sum of money to come in at regular intervals. Thus, the system of taxation was introduced. Resources collected through taxes were used to pay salaries to soldiers, to build forts and carry out public welfare jobs. The rulers realized the importance of a strong and powerful army, to build a large empire. Money from the taxes was used for the development of a strong army.

**Find out**

What taxes do we pay now?

**surplus:** excess, extra

The main tax was on agricultural produce as agriculture was the main occupation of the people. Taxes were also imposed on craftsmen. These could have been collected in the form of labour. Herders were also expected to pay taxes. They were, perhaps, paid in kind, usually in the form of animals and animal produce.

### Crafts

More and more people started practising various crafts like pottery, carpentry, blacksmithing and weaving. Many different types of pots have been excavated from the ruins of these ancient kingdoms. They stand as evidence to the skill that prevailed at that time.

## Monarchies and Republics

Most of the *mahajanapadas* that existed during the period were **monarchies**, that is, they were ruled by kings or *rajans* and the throne was hereditary. The *rajans* were revered by all, including the Brahmins. Alongside these monarchies, there also existed the **republics**, known as the *gana-sanghas*. The term *gana-sangha,* is made up of two words, *gana*, which means equal, and *sangha*, which means governance. This was a political system, in which, the ruler or chief was elected. Hence, his position was not hereditary. These *gana-sanghas* were generally spread out on the foothills of the Himalayas. They generally consisted of a single clan, such as the Shakyas, the Koliyas and the Mallas. A famous *gana-sangha,* was the Lichchavi clan, with its capital at Vaishali. Mahavira, the founder of Jainism, belonged to this clan. Gautama Buddha, the founder of Buddhism, belonged to the Shakya clan of Kapilavastu. Sometimes, the republics consisted of a **confederacy** of clans, such as the Vajjis or Vrijjis and Vrishnis.

We learn about these *mahajanapadas* from various Buddhist and Jain texts. The *Jataka Tales*, the *Bhrahmanas*, the *Upanishads*, and the epics—the *Mahabharata* and the *Ramayana* are all sources of information on the *mahajanapadas*.

### Investigate

*A villager and his wife had a hen that laid a golden egg every day. The greedy couple decided to kill the hen to collect all the golden eggs that they supposed, were stored inside the hen. Having done so, they found, to their surprise, that the hen differed in no respect, from their other hens. The foolish pair, thus hoping to become rich all at once, deprived themselves of the gain of which they were assured day-by-day.*

—An adaptation of 'The Goose That Laid the Golden Eggs', the *Jataka Tales*

1. This story teaches its readers a moral. What moral do you think it is?
2. What does this story tell us about the age in which it was composed?

**confederacy:** a league or alliance, especially of states joined by an agreement or treaty

## Fact quest

The people began to question the *Brahmins*' authority in making laws. At times, the *Kshatriyas* forced the *Vaishyas* or the traders into giving them **tributes**. Internal differences also emerged within the ranks of the nobility.

## Case Study

**Magadha**

Magadha had become the strongest *mahajanapada* at that time. It had powerful rulers like Bimbisara and Ajatashatru who focused extensively on conquering other *janapadas*. They were brave rulers and fought many wars to expand their kingdom. They also indulged in matrimonial alliances to extend their kingdom. Bimbisara was successful in conquering and controlling the kingdom of Anga with its important port at Champa. He was an excellent administrator and carried out many public utility services like building roads and improving public infrastructure. He encouraged trade and improved the means of transport in the kingdom. His son Ajatshatru also worked towards building the empire.

Magadha had rich iron deposits, because of which better tools and implements could be made. The land was fertile as both rivers Ganga and Son flowed through the region. The rivers acted as natural barriers against enemies. They also helped in the transportation of goods from one place to another. The dense forests of Magadha provided wood for building houses. Elephants that were captured from these forests were trained for war purposes. These all contributed in making Magadha the strongest *mahajanapada* of the time.

Rajagriha was the first capital of Magadha. Later, Pataliputra became the capital. Some of the greatest empires of India originated from Magadha. The Gupta dynasty and the Mauryan dynasty ruled over Magadha. Religions such as Buddhism and Jainism also flourished here.

**Vajji**

The Republic of Vajji, with its capital at Vaishali, was a confederacy of eight clans, of which, the Licchavis, the Vajjis and the Videhas were famous. The kingdom of Vajji extended from the north of the river Ganga till the Maḍhesh region of Nepal. It was the first kingdom to practise the republican form of government called the *gana-sangha*. There were several *rajans* in Vajji, who took care of the administration. These rulers would meet at assemblies to discuss major issues. The decision would be taken with the **consensus** of all present in the assembly.

Around 600 BCE, the Licchavi rulers of Vajji became disciples of Buddha and Mahavira. It is believed that Buddha organized the administration of the Buddhist Sangh on the lines of the government at Vajji.

Q. What was the primary difference between the two kingdoms?

**tributes:** gifts that are intended to show gratitude, respect, or admiration; **consensus:** a general agreement

## World Connect

▲ Confucius

Confucius was a Chinese thinker, philosopher, educator and a political figure, who lived between 500–400 BCE. His teachings, preserved in the *Lunyu* or *Analects*, deal with the life of an ideal man. He explains how a person should live his life and interact with others and which forms of government and society should an individual accept and participate in. The philosophy of Confucius laid stress on personal morality as well as the morality of the governing authority. He believed in strong family loyalty, respect towards elders by children in a family, worshipping of ancestors and sincerity in relationships. His famous golden rule was 'Do not do to others what you do not want done to yourself.'

## Recall

**Janapadas and New Kingdoms**

- *Janapadas*
  - Tribes called *jana*
  - The *rajan* was the ruler
  - Important sites are—Purana Qila in Delhi and Hastinapur
  - Ashwamedha Yajna
  - Varnas
- *Mahajanapadas*
  - Fortified cities
  - Sixteen *mahajanapadas*
  - Improved agricultural practices
  - Taxation
  - Crafts
- Monarchies and Republics
  - Monarchies were ruled by kings or monarchs
  - In republics, the ruler was elected
  - Magadha became the strongest empire

## Work out

A. Fill in the blanks.

1. .................................... was the earlier capital of Magadha.
2. .................................... was an important city for trade.
3. The *Ashwamedha Yagna* was performed by specially-trained .................................... in front of a large gathering.
4. The main tax was on .................................... .
5. Mahavir belonged to the .................................... clan.

B. Give one word answers.

1. I am a sacrifice done to show the king's power. .................................... .
2. I am the ruler who conquered the kingdom of Anga. .................................... .
3. I was the founder of Jainism. .................................... .
4. I paid my taxes in the form of animals and animal produce. .................................... .

C. Fill in the blanks with the correct answers.

1. .................................... was the term used for republic.
   a. *Janapada* b. *Mahajanapada* c. *Sabha* d. *Gana-sanghas*
2. The .................................... formed the lowest rung in society.
   a. Brahmins b. Kshatriyas c. Vaishyas d. Shudras
3. The port of Champa was associated with .................................... .
   a. Vaishali b. Taxila c. Anga d. Bodhgaya
4. .................................... was not a *mahajanapada*.
   a. Avanti b. Kosala c. Vatsa d. Gupta
5. .................................... was well known for its important trade routes.
   a. Champa b. Shravasti c. Tamralipti d. Vajji

D. Answer these questions in brief.

1. What is the difference between *janapada* and *mahajanapada*?
2. Name the book from which we learn about the *mahajanapadas*.
3. Why were people unhappy with the varna system?
4. Who is a *rajan*?
5. Name two monarchies and two republics.

E. Answer these questions in detail.

1. Explain the *varna* system. Identify the upper classes and the lower classes in this social hierarchy.
2. Explain the developments that took place, leading to urbanisation in this period.
3. Why were taxes introduced by the rulers?
4. Explain the difference between monarchies and republics citing examples.

## Think

Look at the picture and answer the questions.

1. Find out who built the Great Wall of China. What was the purpose of building it?
2. Find out if India has a fenced boundary with all its neighbours.

## Life skills and values

Imagine you are witnessing an *Ashwamedha Yagna* being conducted by the ruler of a *mahajanapada*. Describe the event to your friend.

## Enjoy

Form two groups in the class, each representing a clan. Imagine that there is a proposal to increase the land tax in a specific region. One group argues for the enhanced taxes while the other group argues against it.

## Web link

For more information, log on to:

https://www.newworldencyclopedia.org/entry/Mahajanapadas

Last accessed on 30 September, 2019

# 7 New Ideas and New Religions

## Take off

- Some *janapadas* evolved as more powerful kingdoms and were known as ................................................ .
- Along with monarchies there also existed republics called ................................................ .

## Warm up

Do you think it was fair for Rema to shout at Anya for making a mistake?

You have already learnt that during the later part of the Vedic Age, *janapadas* and *mahajanapadas* emerged and along with them came a period of religious unrest and discontent. By the sixth century BCE, vedic philosophy had lost its purity due to the *varna*-divided society. This was an age, that welcomed new ideas and thoughts.

## Investigate

*'Intelligence, sacrifice, disinterested service are the characteristics of the Brahmins. Valour, chivalry, forgiveness, ability to rule are the characteristics of the Kshatriyas. Trade, co-operation, agriculture and distribution of material wealth are the characteristics of the Vaisyas. Ungrudging manual labour and service are the characteristics of the Sudras.'*

—*Brahadaranyaka Upanishad*, Paraphrased-simplified-abridged by RR Diwarkar

What type of social system is being highlighted in these lines

## The Rise of New Religions

There were a number of causes that led to the rise of new religions. Firstly, vedic philosophy was primarily focused on expensive rituals and sacrifices performed by Brahmin priests. The practice of indiscriminately killing livestock in the name of sacrifices was becoming detrimental to the agricultural economy thereby, affecting the livelihood of the poor, who were mostly oppressed and suppressed.

Secondly, the *varna*-divided society was opposed by many people from the oppressed classes. The Brahmins dominated almost every aspect of social life and enjoyed special privileges. There was no equality amongst the people because the Brahmins enjoyed all the benefits.

Thirdly, most of the religious literature was in Sanskrit and could not be understood by the common people. That means most of the people could not partake in religious ceremonies.

Lastly, as societies and communities were getting urbanized, some people were opposed to idea of emphasis on material wealt and wanted to lead simple lives.

This was the period when more than 60 schools of thought emerged. Three out of these, caught the imagination of the people and were well received by them. They were Buddhism, Jainism and the teachings of the *Upanishads*.

## The *Upanishads*

The term 'upanishad' is derived from three words *upa* (near), *ni* (down) and *shad* (to sit). The *Upanishads* were created when groups of students sat near a sage, in the middle of a forest, and learnt age-old wisdom from the sage. They were presented in simple dialogues between a sage and his students. The *Upanishads* were composed in the Sanskrit language, during the later Vedic period. They contain the essence of the *Vedas*. There are over 200 *Upanishads*. Some important ones are the *Isha Upanishad,* the *Katha Upanishad,* the *Mandukya Upanishad* and *the Prashna Upanishad.* The *Upanishads* deal with the relationship of an individual with the universe. They contain detailed instructions concerning good conduct of the individual and explain how *moksha* or **salvation** can be attained from the cycles of births and rebirths. Men, particularly *Brahmins* and *Kshatryias* were the main participants. In some instances, women also participated. Poor people did not partake in these dialogues except in one instance, where the son of a slave woman was accepted as a student by a *Brahmin* and went on to become one of the greatest thinkers of the time. His name was Satyakama Jabala.

▲ An ancient manuscript

## Jainism

One of the oldest religions in the world, Jainism, derived its name through the Sanskrit verb root *ji,* meaning 'to conquer'. The person who has achieved enlightenment is known as *jina*, or the conqueror of self. According to the traditions of Jainism,

**Find out**

Why were the *Upanishads* created?

**salvation:** the state of being saved from the power of evil there were 24 *Jinas,* also known as *tirthankaras,* in history. The last of these *tirthankaras* was Mahavira, who is regarded as the real founder of Jainism. The followers of Jainism are known as Jains.

Vardhaman Mahavira was born in 540 BCE (or 599 BCE according to some followers) in Kundagrama near Vaishali (in present-day Bihar). He was a prince, the son of King Siddhartha and Queen Trishala. When Mahavira reached thirty years of age, both his parents died. He decided to **renounce** the world and left the comforts of the palace life for a life of hard penance. He finally attained salvation after more than 12 years of meditation and penance and began to be known as a *jina*.

**Eco feat**

Wildlife conservation is an attempt to preserve endangered animals and plant species, to protect them from extinction and allow the animals to roam around freely. Ahimsa too aims at respect for all living things and the avoidance of violence towards others including plans and animals.

▲ Statue of Lord Mahavira

## Teachings of Jainism

The main teachings of Jainism include:

1. *Ahimsa* means non-violence. Jainism believes in being non-violent towards all living beings. To avoid injuring any living creature, many Jains walk barefoot, and even cover their mouths with a cloth, so that they do not harm even the tiniest of insects. They even take care not to damage any plant or tree.
2. Jainism does not believe in performing *yajnas*, sacrifices and rituals. Mahavira made the religion simple and free of rituals.
3. Jainism forbids class distinctions and does not accept the caste system. It preaches equality for all human beings.
4. Jainism promotes simple living, a life free from material wealth. The followers have to give up everything that they own.

▲ Old Jain temples in Jaisalmer

5. Jainism focuses on speaking the truth and not stealing. They believe that the actions of a person in the past decide that person's afterlife.

**Find out**

Why did the traders support Jainism?

Jainism was difficult to follow as it had very strict rules. It was limited to a few sections of people. Farmers found it difficult because they had to kill insects during agricultural activities. However, this religion had the support of many traders.

**Fact quest**

*Nirvana* means liberation from the cycle of birth and rebirth, through right deeds and actions.

### Jainism Literature

The *Angas* and the *Purvas* are some literary sources to study Jainism. Apart from these, Tamil and Kannada literature also deal with the religious beliefs of the Jains and serve as literary sources of the period. Some of the archaeological sources inclued Ellora caves in Maharashtra and the Dilwara temples in Mount Abu, Rajasthan.

## Buddhism

Buddhism began in India, approximately 2500 years ago. The founder of Buddhism was Gautama Buddha, who was born around 566 BCE in Lumbini near Kapilavastu the border of present-day Nepal. Prince Siddhartha, as he was known before he became Buddha or the enlightened one, belonged to the Sakya clan. His father was King Suddhodana, the ruler of Kapilavastu, and his mother was Queen Maya. When Prince Siddhartha was young, he saw four sights that changed his life. The first sight was that of a sick man crying in pain. The second was of an old man and the third of a dead man. These three sights made him sad and he found that he could never enjoy the pleasures of the palace while the people of his kingdom suffered. The fourth sight was that of an **ascetic** who had renounced the world and was meditating under a tree. Seeing the ascetic, the prince decided to leave the palace and wander around like a monk, trying to find a solution for the sufferings of the world. Prince Siddhartha then wandered from place to place for six years in search of the truth. He finally achieved **enlightenment** while meditating under a peepal tree in Bodh Gaya in Bihar and came to be known as Buddha, the enlightened one.

▲ Buddha

**Find out**

What are the names of two Indian rulers who converted to Buddhism?

According to Buddha, the world is full of suffering, caused by human desires. **Renunciation** of desires is the path for attaining salvation. Salvation, according to Buddha, can be achieved by following the Eight Fold Path. This Eight Fold path, as preached by Buddha included:

**ascetic:** a person who lives in a simple and strict way, without physical pleasures, especially for religious reasons; **enlightenment:** to gain knowledge; **renunciation:** the formal rejection of something

- right action
- right determination
- right exercise
- right livelihood
- right meditation
- right memory
- right observation
- right speech

Like Mahavira, Buddha also propagated the theory of *Ahimsa* or non-violence.

A Buddhist manuscript

## The Spread and Growth of Buddhism

Buddhism was taught in Prakrit, which is the language of the ordinary people so that everyone could understand the message of the Buddha. The disciples of Buddha formed *Sanghas* or associations and travelled from place to place to propagate Buddhism. As a result, many tradesmen and craftsmen became followers of this religion.

Apart from India, Buddhism spread to many countries of Central Asia. In fact, Buddhism continues to be a popular religion in Japan, Korea, Thailand and China. Buddhism became an important aspect of the Chinese life. Many scholars went to China and Chinese monks came to India to learn Buddhism.

**Fact quest**

Menander I, a famous Bactrian king who ruled from Taxila, became a Buddhist. His discussions with Buddhist philosophers are recorded in the book *Milinda Panha*.

**Find out**

Who is the spiritual head of the Buddhists and where does he live?

## Sources of Buddhism

*Tripitaka*, a Sanskrit word which means 'three baskets' are the Buddhist scriptures. The three categories of the *Tripitakas* include the *Sutra Pitaka*, the *Vinaya Pitaka* and the *Abhidhamma Pitaka*. These *pitakas* contain the teachings of Buddha and tell us about his life.

The *Jataka Tales* contain stories regarding the previous births of Buddha in both human and animal form. The archaeological sources to study Buddhism include the Buddhist *viharas* or monasteries and the Mahabodhi Temple in Gaya. The early Buddhist monks lived in caves. Later, *viharas* or monasteries were built for them. These monks lived and preached from the monasteries.

**Fact quest**

The famous Sanchi Stupa was built by Emperor Ashoka. It has many relics of Buddha.

## Sanghas and Monastries

Both Buddhism and Jainism stressed on the importance of giving up material wealth and property to attain happiness. These people who left their homes in search of happiness are called the *sangha*. These people led simple lives. They meditated most of the time and begged for their food. They were encouraged to help each other and also to spread the message of Buddhism to the masses.

▲ Tawang monastery

During the period when they did not travel, for instance, during the rainy season, they retired in caves or temporary houses built by their supporters. Eventually, they felt the need for more permanent homes and so monasteries or *viharas* were built.

## Ashramas

During this period, when Buddhism and Jainism were becoming popular, the brahmins developed the system of *ashrama* which outlines special guidelines for *Brahmins*, *Kshatriyas* and *Vaishyas*. According to the system of *ashrama*, life is divided into four stages.

- *Brahmacharya*: the student life
- *Grihastha*: the family life
- *Vanaprastha*: when man contemplates or meditates in the forest
- *Sanyasa*: when man gives up on all worldly things and becomes a *sanyasi*

### World Connect

**Taoism**

Taoism is a philosophy or a way of life. It is believed to have been started by a man named Lao Tsu, who lived a little before Confucius in 600 BCE. The word '*tao*' means a 'way' or a 'path'. Lao Tsu believed that people needed to 'go with the flow' to remain happy in life. He believed that there were simple and natural ways for all actions in life. Instead of trying to find the hard way of doing things, people should take time to find simpler ways of accomplishing them. Lao Tsu also believed that every living being in the universe, be it humans, animals or plants, shared a universal life-force. There are two sides to this life-force called the yin (darker) and yang (lighter). A balance was required between the yin and the yang for a good life.

## Recall

**Conditions leading to the rise of new religions**

- Expensive rituals
- Varna divided society
- Ordinary people were not part of religious ceremonies
- People wanted to live simple lives

*Upanishads*
- Sage teaching students
- Composed in Sanskrit
- Presented in simple dialogues
- Deals with the relationship of an individual with the universe

Buddhism
- Gautama Buddha
- Four sights
- Eight fold path
- Ahimsa
- Sanghas
- Monasteries

Jainism
- Vardhaman Mahavira
- Ahimsa
- No caste and class distinctions
- Simple living
- Honesty and no stealing

## Work out

A. Fill in the blanks.

1. Most of the scriptures were written in the .......................... language.
2. The *Upanishads* deal with the relation of man with his ..........................
3. According to Jainism, there were 24 .......................... .
4. Buddha's father was the king of .......................... .
5. The Mahabodhi Temple is located in .......................... .

B. Fill in the blanks with the correct answers.

1. A .................................. is a place where Buddhist monks took shelter.
   a. *vihara* b. stupas c. pagoda d. none of these
2. The *Tripitakas* gives us information about .................................. .
   a. Hinduism b. Jainism
   c. Buddhism d. Both options b and c
3. Mahavira preached in the .................................. language
   a. Prakrit b. Pali c. Sanskrit d. Tamil
4. Buddha gained enlightenment in .................................. .
   a. Kushinagar b. Sarnath c. Bodh Gaya d. Kapilavastu
5. .................................. is when a man contemplates or meditates in the forest.
   a. Brahmacharya b. Grihastha c. Vanaprastha d. Sanyasa

C. Write T for true and F for false.

1. The *Upanishads* were written before the period of the *Rig Veda*. ☐
2. The *Jataka Tales* are stories about the previous births of Buddha. ☐
3. Mahavira was the first *tirthankara* of the Jains. ☐
4. Jainism believes in *Ahimsa* or non-violence. ☐
5. Taoism began in Japan in 600 BCE. ☐

D. Answer these questions in brief.

1. Who was the founder of Jainism and to which clan did he belong?
2. Why were farmers unable to follow Jainism?
3. What was the fourth sight of Buddha?
4. What does *upanishad* mean?
5. What was the cause of unhappiness according to Buddha?

E. Answer these questions in detail.

1. Explain the Eight fold path of Buddha.
2. How did Buddhism spread?
3. State the importance of monasteries.
4. What steps did Jains take to prevent injuring living creatures?
5. Explain the common features of Jainism and Buddhism.

## Think

Look at the picture and answer the questions.

1. What do you see in the picture?
2. How do people get these?
3. Name one religion that you have read about which prohibits the killing of animals.

## Life skills and values

Make a list of the principles of Buddhism that you can incorporate into your life. Write an essay on the relevance of Buddhism in today's times.

## Enjoy

Quiz fun

Test your knowledge and your classmates' to see if you've understood the chapter.

1. He belonged to the Sakya tribe. ..........................................
2. His mother's name was Queen Maya. ..........................................
3. This was the Buddhist monument built by Emperor Ashoka. ..........................................
4. This was the place where Buddha gained enlightenment. ..........................................

## Web link

For more information, log on to:

https://courses.lumenlearning.com/boundless-worldhistory/chapter/religion-in-the-indian-subcontinent/

Last accessed on 30 September, 2019

# 8 The Mauryan Empire

## Take off

- Vedic philosophy was too rigid, and focused on rituals and ............................................
- Both Buddha and Mahavira preached ............................................

## Warm up

Would you have woken up to help the cat? Do you think animals deserve to be loved and cared for?

Between the years 322 BCE and 185 BCE, India saw the growth of large and powerful **empires**. Empires are large kingdoms that grew because of ambitious rulers and the rich natural and economic resources that these regions had.

## Chandragupta Maurya

Chandragupta Maurya was the founder of the Mauryan Empire. His rise to power came with the help of his most trusted minister and chief advisor, Chanakya, also known as Kautilya in 321 BCE. His conquest of Pataliputra established a strong base for the Mauryan Empire. We know about the reign of Chandragupta in great detail from the Greek Ambassador, Megasthenese in his book, *Indika*.

### Fact quest

Chandragupta Maurya became a Jain monk during the last years of his life.

### Chanakya

Chanakya was previously a minister to the last of the Nanda rulers. He is regarded as a great political thinker and an economist. His political theories have been compiled in his book, the *Arthashastra*.

▲ Chanakya

▲ **Extent the Mauryan Empire**

## Bindusara

Bindusara, Chandragupta's son, succeeded him to the throne. He has been attributed with conquering almost the entire Indian peninsula. Like his father, Chandragupta Maurya, Bindusara

**Find out**

Identify at least two modern Indian states that were a part of the Mauryan Empire.

maintained friendly relations with the Greeks. He was tolerant to all religions and many saints visited his empire during this time.

## Ashoka

Regarded as one of India's greatest rulers, Emperor Ashoka ruled almost the entire Indian subcontinent. He has been called 'Ashoka the Great'. During his father's reign, Ashoka served as the governor of Taxila and Ujjain and went on to become the emperor in 268 BCE. Ashoka was a very ambitious ruler and used military strength in order to expand the empire. He launched brutal wars, which lasted for around eight years till the Kalinga War, which changed his life.

**Eco feat**

Some officials in the Mauryan Empire were specially appointed to take care of animals and forests. When Ashoka embraced Buddhism, he gave up hunting as a royal sport. He was the first Indian ruler to advocate conservation methods for wildlife in his edicts or public inscriptions.

### The Kalinga War

Kalinga was a kingdom in coastal Orissa (present-day Odisha). The war of Kalinga turned out to be an infamous battle. Over 1,00,000 people of Kalinga and more than 10,000 soldiers of Ashoka died in the war. This war was a turning point in Ashoka's life. He felt responsible for the loss of so many lives and decided to **renounce** war. He devoted the rest of his life to *ahimsa* (non-violence) and converted to Buddhism. Ashoka ruled for forty years after the Battle of Kalinga in peace, harmony and prosperity.

**Investigate**

(A) *'When king Devanampiya Piyadassi had been anointed eight years, (the country of) the Kalingas was conquered by (him).'*

(B) *'One hundred and fifty thousand in number were the men who were deported thence, one hundred thousand in number were those who were slain there, and many times as many those who died.'*

(C) *'After that, now that (the country of) the Kalingas has been taken, Devanampiya (is devoted) to a zealous study of morality, to the love of morality, and to the instruction (of people) in morality.'*

(D) *'This is the repentance of Devanampiya on account of his conquest of (the country of) the Kalingas.'*

—Extracts from the 13th rock edict

1. What does Ashoka talk about in these lines?
2. What impression do you have about emperor Ashoka after reading these lines?

**renounce:** to state publicly that you no longer have a particular belief or that you will no longer behave in a particular way

## Ashoka's Dhamma

*Dhamma* is the Prakrit form of the word *dharma* which means duty. The principles of *dhamma* were based on a code of conduct that would help people live virtuous lives. Ashoka's *dhamma* consisted of non-violence, tolerance towards all sects and religions, obedience towards parents, respect for Brahmins and all religious teachers, humane treatment of servants and generosity towards all.

Ashoka's *dhamma* was written in Prakrit, which was the language of the common people. He inscribed his *dhamma* on pillars, caves and rocks so that people could read and follow the messages on the inscriptions. He referred to the people as 'my children' in all his inscriptions. He believed that *dhamma* could resolve conflicts for the people. He appointed officials called *dhammamahamatta* who travelled to distant places and spread his message. These officials were even sent to Syria, Egypt, Greece and Sri Lanka to spread his *dhamma*.

▲ The Lion Capital of Ashoka, Sarnath

Ashoka sent his son and daughter to Sri Lanka and other countries of South-East Asia as **ambassadors** of Buddhism. He communicated directly to his subjects through his rock edicts. Usually, the top of the columns or pillars on which Ashoka's messages were inscribed was decorated with figures of lions and bulls. One such pillar in Sarnath, has four lions carved at the top. This pillar has come to be known as one of the most famous of Ashoka's pillars. This structure is now the national emblem of India.

## Ashoka's Administrative Measures

Ashoka was a very earnest king, who believed that a king's duty was not to enjoy and lead a relaxed life, but to serve the society.

- He introduced many reforms, some of which included an efficient civil service and land taxation reforms.
- During Ashoka's reign, cities and villages were protected by walls. Ashoka's messengers used specially built tunnels to move safely and quickly.
- Ashoka did a lot for the welfare of the people. He built roads, rest houses and universities for his people. He made hospitals for animals and people, offered loans to poor farmers.
- Ashoka promoted vegetarianism and himself quit meat to reduce unnecessary slaughter of animals.
- He encouraged and controlled international trade.
- He boosted agriculture with revolutionary ideas and improved the system of drainage and irrigation.

**Find out**

Why is Ashoka known as 'Ashoka the Great'?

**abmassadors:** representatives or promoters of a specified activity

## Mauryan Administration

We come to know about Mauryan administration from Chanakya's *Arthashastra*. It gives us information about the Mauryan Empire and their rules of governance. From it, we learn that the empire was divided into four provinces, each under a prince or a *kumara*. The provinces were divided into districts and these districts were further divided into villages. At the provincial level, the prince was assisted by ministers. Some of the functions undertaken at the district level were the review of the land, maintenance of law and order and collection of taxes. Here, the district head was assisted by junior officials. At the village level, the headmen looked after land records and assisted the district officials pertaining to matters of the village.

The Mauryan economy was driven by agriculture. The state-owned farms were large and rice, coarse grain, sesame, barley, wheat, mustard, grapes, sugarcane, pumpkin and medicinal roots were grown. Internal trade improved due to the new-found peace and stability in the empire. Chandragupta Maurya even introduced a single currency to be used throughout his empire. The Mauryans maintained a strong army which was well-equipped with infantry, cavalry, elephants, chariots and a navy. Spies were kept throughout the kingdom and they informed the rulers about what was going on inside as well as outside the kingdom. This enabled the rulers to remain updated on matters regarding the welfare of the people as well as in matters involving other kingdoms.

### Case Study

**Pataliputra**

Pataliputra (present-day Patna) was located at the **confluence** of the Ganga and the Son rivers. It flourished as the capital of the Mauryan empire (326-184 BCE), and again as the capital of the Gupta empire (320-550 CE). The Greek Ambassador Megasthenes, stayed in Pataliputra during the reign of Chandragupta Maurya. Megasthenes recorded his observations of the city in his diary, which is a useful source to study this period.

According to Megasthenes, Pataliputra was an elaborate city with amazing architectural buildings, such as towers, palaces, and gateways, that stood along with the houses of the ordinary people. The city was surrounded by a wooden wall, nine-miles-long and a mile-and-a-half wide, with over 400 towers and a deep **moat**. Megasthenes has also described the lavish palaces of Chandragupta Maurya, which were built of wood.

Agriculture was the main occupation of the people. Taxes were levied for the supply of water and the sale of goods. There was apparently no caste system. Women too were employed at the King's court. According to Megasthenes, six boards, with five members each looked after tax collection, trade and commerce, public works, foreigners, and industries in the city.

King Ashoka convened the Third Buddhist Council in this city. Pataliputra declined after the fall of the Mauryan Empire. The city was revived during the Gupta period, when it was made the capital of the Gupta Empire.

Q. What made Pataliputra such an important city?

**confluence:** the junction of two rivers

## Art and Architecture

▲ Sanchi Stupa, built by Ashoka

Some of the best contributions to art and architecture were made during this period, Some examples are the stupas, the pillar edicts of Ashoka, and the *viharas*. Stupas were a semi-spherical dome-like structure, built in various sizes. The upper portion was decorated by a wooden umbrella, signifying the importance of *dharma*. Polished monolithic pillars containing the Ashokan edicts were built all over the kingdom. The Ashokan pillar at Sarnath has the lion capital and the four lions positioned back to back, supporting the dharma known as the Ashoka Chakra. Many impressive viharas have also been found. Examples of such viharas are in Nagararjuna hills near Gaya in Bihar.

## Decline of the Mauryan Empire

The successors of Ashoka were very weak and the empire was too vast. It was not easy for the king to maintain control over the provinces that were located far-off from the centre. After the death of Ashoka, many distant provinces broke away and there were constant foreign invasions. The final blow came when an internal revolt led by the chief of the Mauryan army, Senapati Pushyamitra Sunga bringing an end to the Mauryan empire.

### World Connect

At another age and place, there lived another ruler who spread the beliefs and principles of another religion and **propagated** tolerance amongst the people. Constantine the Great was a Roman Emperor who ruled from 306 to 337 CE. He was the first Roman emperor to convert to Christianity. Constantine's support to Christianity was associated with his rise in power. At that time, Christians were persecuted by the Romans. Constantine was the first emperor to stop Christian persecutions and legalize Christianity along with all other religions in the Roman Empire. Constantine played an influential role in the proclamation of the Edict of Milan in 313 CE, which **decreed** tolerance for Christianity in the empire. The edict stated that Christians should be allowed to follow the faith without oppression. Earlier, people who practised Christianity were penalized and Church property confiscated. This edict removed penalties for professing Christianity. It protected not only Christians from religious **persecution**, but all religions allowing all the freedom to worship any deity of their choice.

▲ Constantine the Great

**propagated:** ideas or theories spread and promoted widely; **decreed:** to have ordered something officially and by law; **persecution:** ill-treatment towards a particular race or political or religious beliefs

## Recall

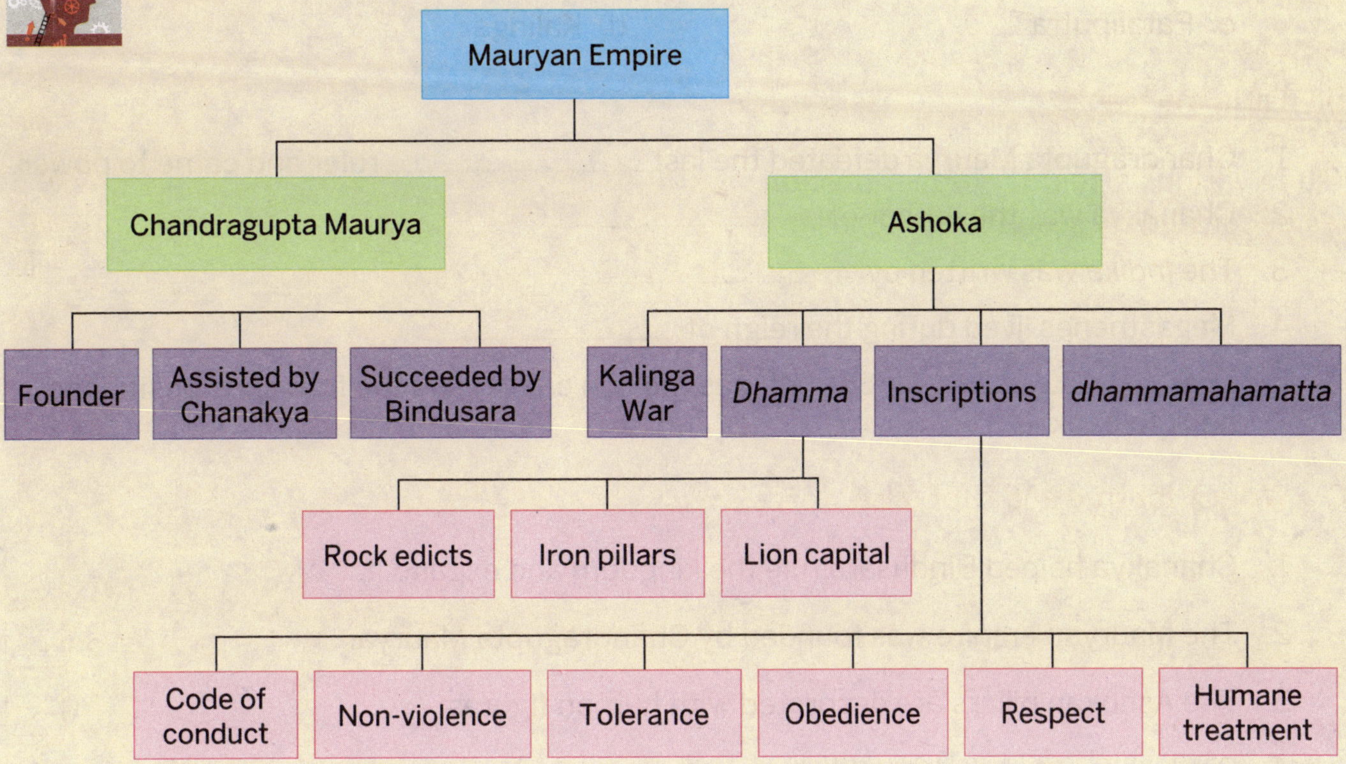


## Work out

**A. Fill in the blanks with the correct answers.**

1. The last battle where Ashoka fought his last war was in .......................................... .
   a. Pataliputra  b. Kalinga  c. Varanasi  d. Kosala
2. Chanakya was previously a minister to the last .......................................... rulers.
   a. Mauryan  b. Nanda  c. Gupta  d. None of these
3. .......................................... is an important Ashokan pillar near Varanasi.
   a. Sanchi stupa  b. Vihara
   c. Lion Capital of Ashoka, Sarnath  d. Ashoka chakra
4. Chandragupta Maurya even introduced a .......................................... to be used throughout his empire.
   a. chariot  b. single currency
   c. religion  d. none of these

5. .................................... was the Mauryan capital.
   a. Vajji
   b. Vaishali
   c. Pataliputra
   d. Kalinga

## B. Fill in the blanks.

1. Chandragupta Maurya defeated the last .................................... ruler and came to power.
2. Chanakya was the author of .................................... .
3. The *Indika* was written by .................................... .
4. Megasthenes lived during the reign of ....................................
5. The .................................... at Sarnath has the lion capital and the four lions positioned back to back.

## C. Write T for true and F for false.

1. Chanakya helped Bindusara rule the kingdom and expand it. ☐
2. The Mauryan empire was founded by Chandragupta Maurya. ☐
3. The Ashokan pillars are decorated with human figures. ☐
4. Bindusara was Ashoka's elder son. ☐
5. Ashoka converted to Buddhism after the Kalinga War. ☐

## D. Answer these questions in brief.

1. How was the Mauryan kingdom established?
2. Who was Chandragupta Maurya and who assisted him in becoming the king?
3. Who was Bindusara?
4. How did the battle of Kalinga change Ashoka?
5. What religion did Ashoka convert to?

## E. Answer these questions in detail.

1. The Mauryan Empire had an effective administrative system. Give reasons for this.
2. What do you understand by *dhamma*? Explain the main principles of *dhamma*.
3. What measures did Ashoka take to improve the lives of the people?
4. How did Ashoka spread his message of *dhamma*?
5. What were Ashoka's contributions to art?

## Think

Look at the picture and answer the questions.

This is an image of the Lion Capital of the Ashokan Pillar which is our national emblem.

1. Why do you think the four lions have been shown facing away from each other?
2. What does the Ashoka Chakra signify?
3. Does your passport carry the stamp of the Lion Capital of Ashoka? Where else do you find the image of the Lion Capital?
4. Why are the words 'Satyamev Jayate' written under our national emblem?

## Life skills and values

If you were Ashoka, what would be *dhamma* according to you and your classmates? List five to ten things which could be a part of your class *dhamma*.

## Enjoy

Imagine you are a reporter who has witnessed the Kalinga War. Prepare a report on it.

## Web link

For more information, log on to:

https://www.newworldencyclopedia.org/entry/Maurya_Empire

Last accessed on 30 September, 2019

# 9 Reappearance of Urbanization

## Take off

- The Mauryan Empire was founded by .................................................. .
- Emperor Ashoka was changed after the ..................................................... War.
- After the Kalinga war, King Ashoka adopted ............................................. as his religion.

## Warm up

How are the boys able to get what they want without using money? Before coins were invented, how did people buy and sell goods?

Why do you think that the urban settlements disappeared after the Indus Valley Civilization?

Archaeological excavations have revealed that **urban communities** flourished in India in the Indus Valley Civilization as early as 2500 BCE. In the Early Vedic period, the people were pastoralists and the concept of urbanization did not occur to them till the later part of the Vedic age when people started farming and settling down in one place. Gradually, the use of better iron implements led to surplus production in agriculture. It was this surplus production that led to the growth of trade and commerce and eventually, to the development of towns and cities. It was during the Mauryan period that many cities and towns emerged in different parts of India. Historians believe that the second phase of urbanization in India began around 300 BCE. This period of **second urbanization** saw large-scale expansion of town life in the Gangetic Plains.

**The features of the first urbanization and the second urbanization in the history of India**

| First Urbanization (2600–1700 BCE) | Second Urbanization (600–300 BCE) |
|---|---|
| Centre: North West India (Indus Valley) | Centre: Gangetic Plains |
| Main Towns: Harappa (Punjab), Mohenjodaro (Sind), Ropar (Punjab) | Main Towns: Hastinapur, Ujjain, Vaishali |
| Extensive mining of copper | Increase in use of iron |

**The features of the first urbanization and the second urbanization in the history of India**

| First Urbanization (2600–1700 BCE) | Second Urbanization (600–300 BCE) |
|---|---|
| Use of seals in trade | Use of punch-marked coins |
| Nature worship; worship of mother goddess | Rise of new religions |
| Agriculture as the main occupation | Growth of new crafts and industries |

## The Development of Agriculture

The beginning of the Iron Age resulted in the forging of better tools and weapons as iron was a better metal than copper in terms of sturdiness. The Aryans, who settled down in villages near the Indo-Gangetic plains, started clearing forests with the help of iron axes for agriculture. Earlier, the people used to burn the forests down to clear the ground for cultivation. Now, iron was effectively used in agriculture. The iron **ploughshare** was also introduced at this time. This helped in ploughing deeper into the hard soil and preparing the ground for cultivation. By this time, farmers had become better equipped in agricultural practices and methods. They learnt **transplanting**, which means that they grew paddy seedlings and then transported them to bigger fields. This increased agricultural produce twofold. Irrigation facilities had also improved by this period and contributed greatly towards farming. Canals, dams, wells, tanks and artificial lakes were built to help irrigate the farms. Irrigation not only increased farming productivity but also increased revenue. The more an agricultural produce, the more taxes are paid to the ruler and the more developed the kingdom gets. People learnt to grow three crops in a year. These innovations and developments in the field of agriculture ensured a surplus of food grains.

**Fact quest**

Indian silk and spices were traded along the Silk Route, which connected India, China and parts of western and central Asia. Indian pepper and pearls were famous in countries like Rome.

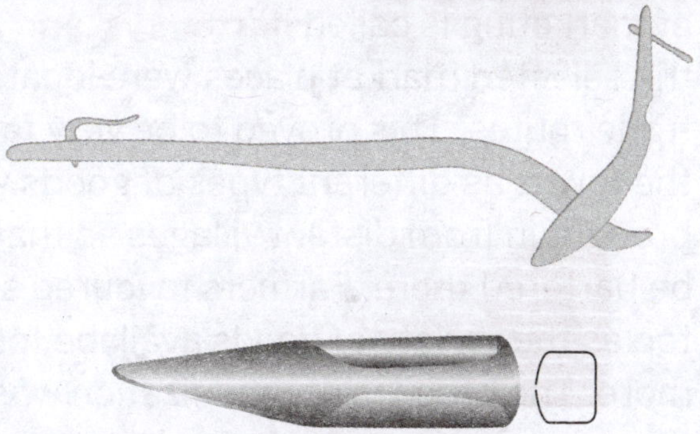

▲ Ploughshare–iron and wood

## Use of Labour

Before large-scale settlements had sprung up in the Gangetic Plains, the area was covered with thick forests and marshy land. Labourers were required to clear the land for cultivation. People now felt the need for an administrative system to control and direct such labour. Different agricultural communities came up in different regions. In south India, large landowners were known as *vellalar* and in north India, they were known as *grama bhojaka*. They employed ploughmen or had slaves to do the work. Independent farmers known as *grihapatis* were small landowners. Along with the growth of agriculture, there was a

**ploughshare:** the main cutting blade of a plough

growing need for skilled workers like craftsmen, metal workers, potters, chariot makers and many more.

## Formation of Guilds or *Shrenis*

The workers organized themselves into guilds or *shrenis*. The guilds formulated rules and regulations which catered to the needs of the workers. They ensured that the workers acquired a good supply of raw materials. They also imparted the training required for particular crafts. The guilds also introduced weights and measures, and provided a check on the quality of the goods produced. Matters pertaining to the price of the goods and the wages of labour were all decided by those who headed the guilds. The guild of merchants looked after matters relating to trade. Some even functioned as banks. This led to an increase in trade.

## Increase in Trade

Due to the increase in agricultural production and the development of new crafts and industries, towns became good market places and centres for trade. Villagers producing surplus grains would transport them to nearby towns and exchange their surplus grains for the goods produced in those towns. This system of marketing is called **barter system.** At times, the selected market places were located on the trade routes. This proved to be very favourable for the towns as different types of goods were brought in from distant villages so that they could be bartered there. Farmers favoured such towns too as the variety of goods availabe for barter was more. The process of urbanization was faster and more intense in such places. Ujjain was the most important urban centre to grow out of such a process.

▲ **Indian rugs**

Trade improved road connectivity and the transport system. A network of good roads connected important cities like Taxila, Ujjain, Mathura, Prayag, Kashi, Gaya, Pataliputra and Vaishali. Rivers were used for transportation and this led to the emergence of port cities, which, in turn, promoted inland trade. Trading networks not only emerged within India but also with other countries like Sri Lanka and Burma. A large number of Roman gold and silver coins have been discovered in Indian ports, primarily the ones located in the south of India. Besides this, India was famous

### Eco feat

Ivory goods made from the tusks of elephants and at times, rhinoceroses, were very popular in ancient times. Ivory was used to make piano keys in the olden days because of the white colour it produces when processed. However, today, endangerment of species has resulted in a ban on using ivory for goods.

for its ivory goods, carpets, medicines, essences and oils. Some important trading ports were Bhrigukachchha and Arikamedu. Trade also flourished after coins came into use.

## Use of Coins

Before the use of coins, people used the system of barter for goods and services. This means that they exchanged goods amongst themselves. In the Mauryan period, coins came to be issued—silver, punch-marked coins were the first to be used followed by copper coins. Since then, goods and services came to be exchanged for coins. Several punch-marked coins have been found at various sites.

**Find out**

What is the advantage of using brass and copper for coins?

▲ Punch-marked coins

## The Growth of Urban Centres

Urban centres had specific functions and were of different types. They were in contact with each other to fulfill their needs.

Powerful *mahajanapadas,* which had a capital became places where administrative and official matters were looked after. Towns like Madurai, Pataliputra and Ujjain, developed as capital cities. Some towns were used for the exchange of surplus production and came to be used as markets and centres of trade. These towns were called market towns. Trading was also done through sea and these developed into port towns.

**Investigate**

*'He shall receive only such gold coins as have been declared to be pure by the examiner of coins.'*

—Book II, The Duties of Government Superintendents, *Arthashastra* by Chanakya

This line was written during the same period. What do you think it suggests? Do you think there was any regulation in the creation of coins back then?

Places where major religions developed became important religious towns. Some cities served as centres for arts and crafts such as Vaishali and Varanasi. Kodumanal in Tamil Nadu was rich in mineral resources and became an industrial centre for semi-precious stones like sapphire and quartz. Towns like Mathura, Amravati and Kondapur were located on important trade routes and became important trading centres.

▲ Varanasi

## Case Study

**Mathura**

Mathura derived its importance as a center of trade due to its location where the trade routes of the north met with the routes to central India and the west coast. A fortified city, it has been important for more than 2500 years.

Mathura was the second capital of the Kushanas, a powerful empire (you will be reading about them in the next chapter), a religious centre and also a centre for arts and crafts. Archaeologists have discovered evidence of extremely fine sculptures in Mathura. Believed to be the homeland of Krishna, it became a holy city for Hinduism. There are many places of historic and religious importance in Mathura associated with Hinduism, Buddhism and Jainism.

Q. Write a note about the multiple significance of Mathura.

## Sources of History

We learn about the history of the period from various sources. Coins tell us about the period—how rich the kingdom was, which countries it traded with and how people lived. The *Jataka Tales* and Sangam literature are two works that tell us about the period. Accounts written by various travellers from around the world who visited during that time also highlight important features of the time. Archaeological findings also help archaeologists reconstruct history. These include extremely fine pottery, known as the Northern Black Polished Ware (NBPW) which was a form of pottery mostly found in the northern part of the subcontinent. It was polished and sophisticated and archaeologists believe that it was used by rich people of the period.

## World Connect

**Rome**

The city of Rome originated as a village in the 9th century. It was initially ruled by kings. When cities came up on the banks of the Ganga river in India, the Roman Republic was established. It was the capital of Italy. The most important ruler of Rome was Augustus who converted Rome from a city of bricks to a marble city.

▲ The Golden Colosseum at dusk, in Rome, Italy

There were **exemplary** architects in Rome who built public baths, water channels called aqueducts and many other things. Roman architecture is noted for its arches, domes, temples and amphitheatres. The Roman amphitheatre is a unique structure built from stone and is oval in shape. It appears like a modern football stadium. There were levels of seating around an open space where chariot-racing, public executions or other public activities were performed. The largest amphitheatre, the Colosseum, is located in Rome.

**exemplary:** serving as a desirable model; very good

## Recall

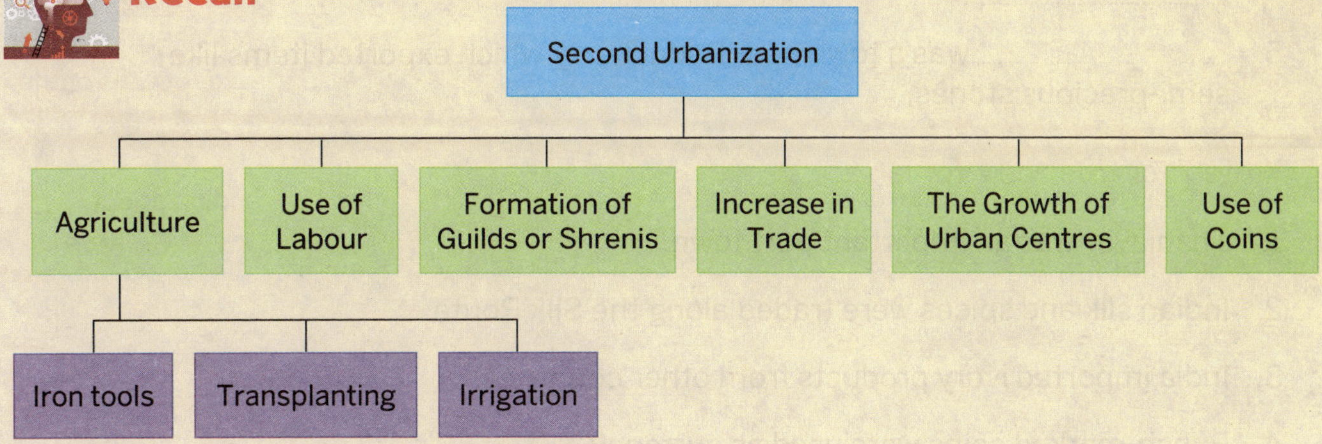


## Work out

**A. Fill in the blanks with the correct answers.**

1. The use of .................................. resulted in producing better implements for agriculture.
   a. aluminum  b. steel  c. bronze  d. iron
2. India traded with the .................................... Empire.
   a. Roman  b. Mughal  c. Gupta  d. Mauryan
3. The city of .................................... was a market town.
   a. Sopara  a. Arikamedu  a. Madurai  a. Tanjore
4. Sopara and Tamralipti were famous as .................................... .
   a. administrative centres  b. art centres
   c. religious centres  d. trading centres
5. Trade began because of .................................... .
   a. surplus production  b. export of goods to other places
   c. increase in product demands  d. All of the above

**B. Fill in the blanks.**

1. Before the use of coins, people used the system of .................................... for goods and services.
2. Trading was done through the .................................... routes.
3. Iron tools were used for clearing .................................... .

4. A large number of urban centres came up during this period bringing about .................................................. .

5. .................................................. was a town near Puducherry which exported items like semi-precious stones.

C. Write T for true and F for false.

1. Thanjavur was an important port town. ☐
2. Indian silk and spices were traded along the Silk Route. ☐
3. India imported ivory products from other countries. ☐
4. Punch-marked coins were used as currency. ☐
5. The guilds functioned as banks as well. ☐

D. Answer these questions in brief.

1. What is transplanting?
2. State the factor that led to surplus production.
3. What led to the emergence of specialized towns?
4. Name the literary sources that give us information on the urban towns or cities.
5. Name two port cities.

E. Answer these questions in detail.

1. Discuss the importance of guilds with reference to the traders.
2. Explain the specialties of Mathura.
3. State the function of an administrative town.
4. Write a note on the types of urban centres that existed during that period.

**Think**

Look at the picture and answer these questions.

1. What material has been used to make these coins?
2. What has been imprinted on them?
3. Are these coins still in use today?

## Map work

On an outline map of India, mark the important port, market and administrative towns of India.

## Life skills and values

Apart from the exchange of goods belonging to different countries of the world, merchants and traders had another interesting role. They helped spread the religious and cultural ideologies of the places they visited. For example, Islam was introduced in India by the traders from the Arabic world. Today, cross-cultural programmes are frequent among people belonging to all walks of life. Students, diplomats and businessmen often participate in these cross-cultural programmes.

Imagine you have been selected from your school to participate in a cross-cultural programme. Which country would you like to visit and why?

## Enjoy

A. Form groups of four and find out an interesting fact about a port town and a market town. Design a pamphlet to attract tourists from other countries to those spots.

B. Find out three ways in which the second urbanization is similar to the present-day India. Write an article on it.

## Web link

For more information, log on to:

http://glimpsesofhistory.com/second-urbanisation-6th-century-bce/

Last accessed on 30 September, 2019

# 10 Contact With Other Parts of the World

### Take off

- In the second phase of urbanization, workers and traders organized themselves into ..............................
- An example of a temple town was ..............................
- Surplus production led to growth in ..............................

### Warm up

Why do people travel to distant lands today?

Many years ago, maps did not exist and people were not aware of what existed beyond the territory which they occupied. Some even believed that the world was flat and if one travelled too far, he would fall off the edge of the Earth!

Few explorers who were curious about the world outside dared to go beyond their territory and discovered new lands and new cultures, charting new territories and paving new routes. It is because of these explorers that we know so much of the world now. Today, we can travel from one part of the world to the other without much trouble.

### Find out

Apart from adventure, was there any other reason for these explorers to travel to distant lands?

### Eco feat

Ancient explorers travelled on horses or camels. Today, we have faster means of travel such as cars, trains and aeroplanes. But these modern means of transport take a toll on the environment by adding to environmental pollution.

## Expansion of Trade

With the coming of the second phase of urbanization, trade took on an active form where people established contact with distant lands. Port cities developed along the Indian coastline. By 200 BCE, India had established trading relations with many countries like Greece, Rome, the Arab countries, China, South East Asia and Africa through both sea and land routes.

Indo-Roman trade flourished particularly during the reign of Emperor Augustus in Rome. India was famous for silk, muslin, ivory goods, pearls, precious stones, spices and medicines, among many other things.

▲ Ivory goods

▲ Silk

The rulers used the money from trade to develop the army and to **patronize** learned men who were generously rewarded with precious things. Evidence has proved that India always encouraged foreign trade. The Ashokan edicts talk about India's trade with foreign lands. Sangam literature mentions the generosity of these rulers. In exchange, traders from abroad brought wine, horses, silk, ceramic, glass, gold and perfumes amongst other things.

▲ Spices

## The Silk Route

The **Silk Route** is a historical term to denote a network of trade routes that existed between China and the Mediterranean.

Silk-making techniques were first invented in China around 7000 years ago. The Chinese are believed to have kept the methods of making silk as a closely-guarded secret. Gradually, as people began to travel to distant lands on foot or on camels and horseback, they carried the rich, glossy silk fabric with them. The paths they followed came to be known as the Silk Route.

This route linked the regions of the west and east through the Mediterranean. Many other things travelled along this long road—things not meant for import and export. These were ideas—ideas that changed the world.

## The Advent of Travellers and the Growth of Buddhism and Hinduism

### Buddhism

The Silk Route used by the traders led to the exchange of religious and cultural ideas. It helped many pilgrims come to India to study Buddhism and

**Fact quest**

Kanishka's greatest contribution to Buddhist architecture was the Kanishka Stupa discovered at Peshawar in Pakistan. Gold coins belonging to this period have the image of Kanishka on one side and that of Buddha on the other.

**patronize:** treat with an apparent kindness which betrays a feeling of superiority

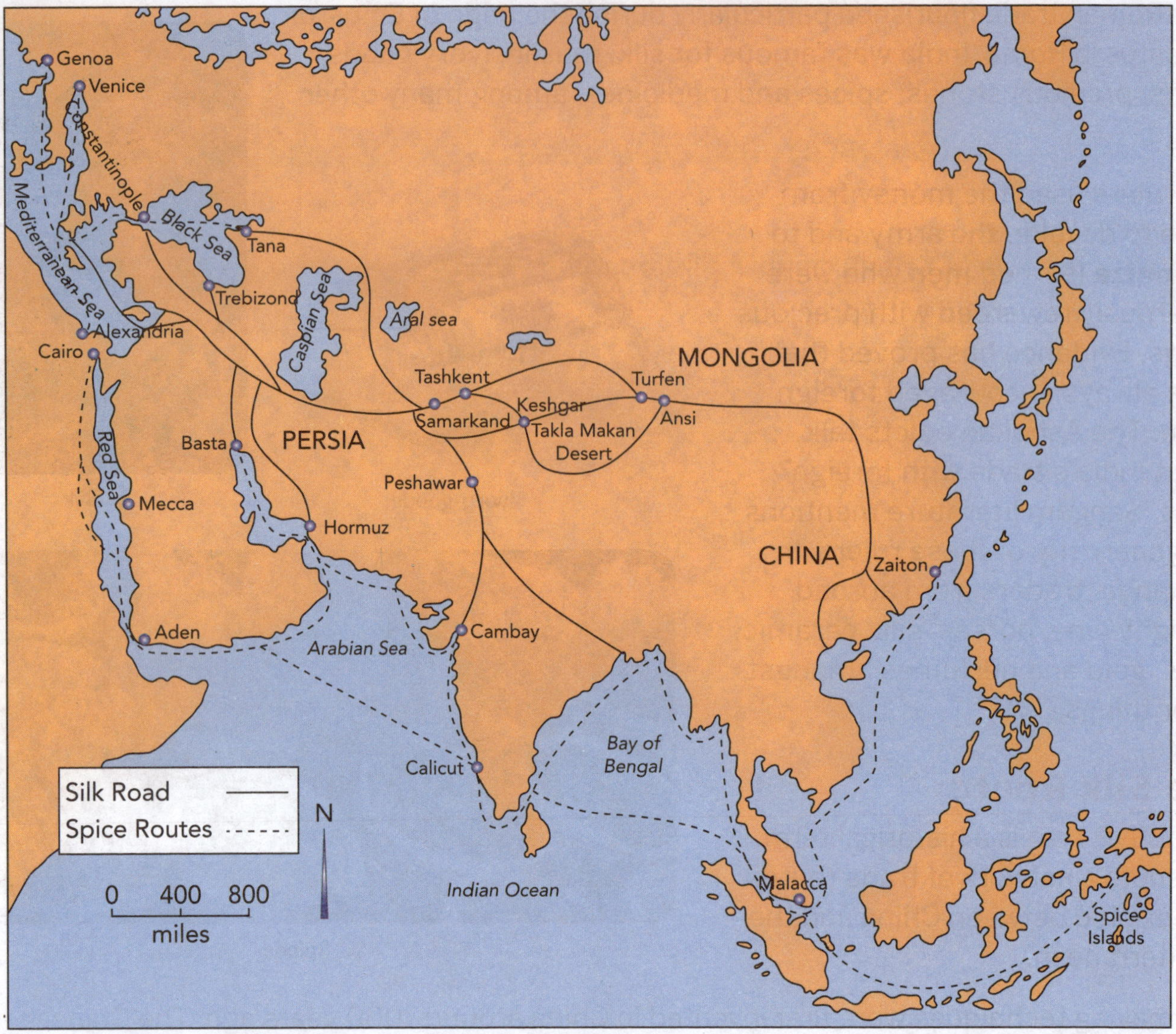


▲ **The Silk Route**

paved the way for future contacts. This route was used for the spread of Buddhism during Kanishka's rule. Kanishka also **convened** the fourth Buddhist Council in Kashmir where he invited more than 400 Buddhist monks to discuss the teachings of Buddha. It was during this time that a new form of Buddhism, Mahayana Buddhism, emerged. Here, statues of Buddha were made, while earlier, only symbols of him attaining enlightenment were shown, for instance, a sculpture of a peepal tree was shown to represent enlightenment. This new form of Buddhism also brought about a change in the practices of the followers. Earlier, the Bodhisattvas, after attaining enlightenment, lived in isolation and spent their days meditating. Now, they stayed on and helped the people.

Buddhism spread to many parts of India as well as the world. Emperor Ashoka was one of the first rulers to help spread Buddhism to many parts of the world. Kanishka, the emperor of the Kushana dynasty in the second century also patronized Buddhism. He

**convened:** assembled; **memoirs:** a historical account or biography written from personal knowledge sent missionaries to China and other countries to preach the teachings of Buddhism. Several Chinese monks and pilgrims visited India to see the birthplace of Buddha and the place where he attained enlightenment. Fa-Hien was one of the Chinese monks who visited India in the 5th century CE during the rule of Chandragupta Vikramaditya. Another Chinese pilgrim was Hiuen Tsang who visited India during the reign of King Harshvardhana in the 7th century CE. Both Fa-Hien and Hien Tsang left behind detailed and valuable accounts of the socio-political and religious life of the people in India.

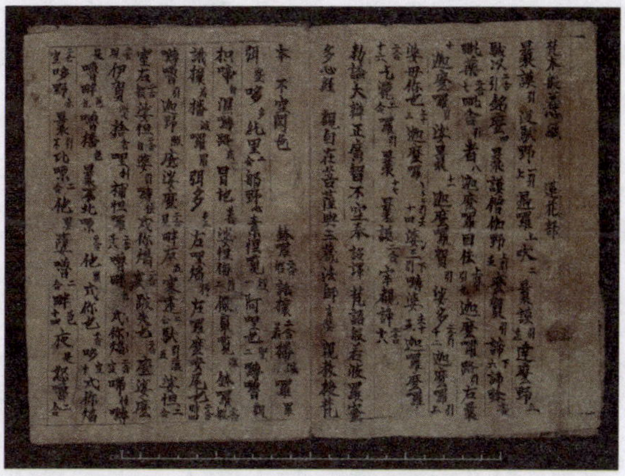

▲ Old Chinese manuscript believed to have been Hiuen Tsang's

### Investigate

*'In the night ride across the Wular lake a small storm made me worry for the safety of my manuscript (Rajatarangini). It seemed as if the goddess of wisdom—Sharada, represented by waters of Kashmir, was unwilling to let me abduct the manuscript.'*

—Hiuen-Tsang

Hiuen Tsang was unable to return with a copy of *Rajatarangini*, the history of Kashmir written by Kalhana. Why do you think Hiuen Tsang was so keen to take the manuscript with him?

### Hinduism

Around 300 BCE, gods such as Shiva and Vishnu emerged as the main Hindu gods. The rule of the Gupta Dynasty is known as the golden period in the history of Hinduism. In the Deccan region, the Satavahans promoted Hinduism. The Pallavas and the Cholas of south India, were also staunch followers of Hinduism and Hindu temple art flourished during their reign.

Gradually, Brahmanism underwent several changes. The concept of *bhakti* became more important than elaborate rituals and sacrifices. The idea of *bhakti* or intense devotion to God rather than on complicated rituals originated in south India (present-day Tamil Nadu and Kerala). Saints of this movement looked upon religion as a bond between the devotees and God. These saints were poets who composed hymns and *bhajans* in praise of God. People from all walks of life were encouraged to sing these hymns.

## New Kingdoms

### The Indo-Greeks

The **Indo-Greeks** comprised more than 30 Hellenistic kings who ruled in various parts of northwest and northern India between the 2nd century BCE to the 1st century CE. Demetrius was a famous king who invaded India in the 2nd century BCE. He crossed the Hindu Kush

Mountains and began the conquest of Northern Afghanistan and the area covered by the Indus river. Another great king of the Indo-Greeks was Menander I who converted to Buddhism. His famous conversation with the Buddhist monk Nagasena is mentioned in *Milinda Panha*, a Buddhist text. He is supposed to have to have issued bilingual coins using the Kharoṣṣhī script. The last of the Indo-Greek rulers was Strato II who ruled in the Punjab region.

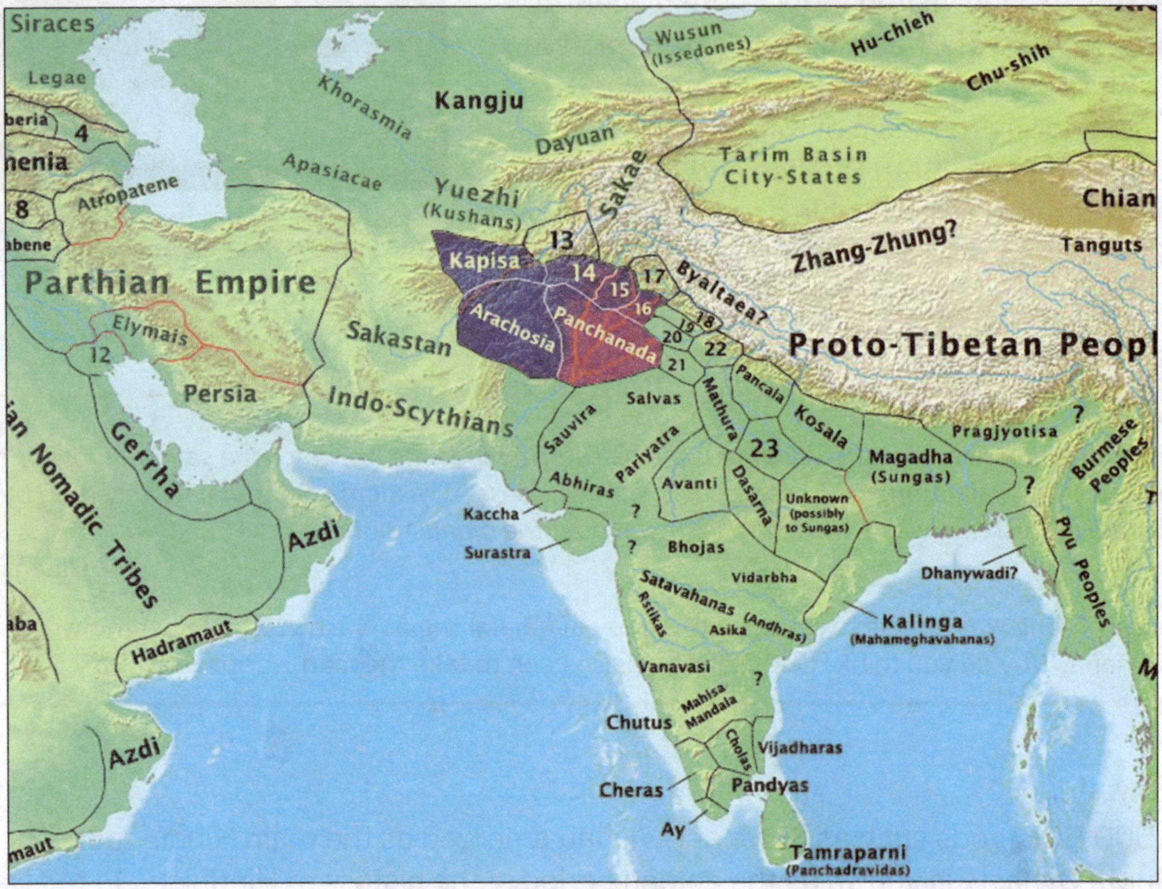


▲ The Indo-Greeks in 100 BCE

## The Sakas

▲ Rudradaman coin

The Sakas invaded India through the north-western part of the country and took control over Taxila and Mathura from the Indo-Greeks, only to face the hostility of the Satvahanas in the south and the Kushanas in the north. Important Saka kingdoms in the Indian region were in Taxila, Mathura, Nasik and Ujjain. The most famous Saka ruler was Rudradaman I. He was a great conqueror and his military expeditions are inscribed in the Junagadh rock inscription.

## Parthians

The Parthians had come to India from Iran. They ruled over a small part of the north-western territory of the Indian sub-continent. A famous Parthian ruler was Gondophernes, in the 1st century CE.

## Kushanas

The Kushanas were a powerful group of people who ruled north India and had their origin in China. The most well-known Kushana ruler was Kanishka. Kanishka ruled over a vast empire from Bactria to Pataliputra in the Gangetic Plains. The centre of his huge empire was Bactria. In India, the centres were Peshwar and Mathura. He was deeply inclined towards the Buddhist faith and **sponsored** the building of many Buddhist monasteries. It has been recorded that the important meetings of the Buddhist monks took place in Kashmir during his reign.

We have ample evidence of trade links existing with China, Central Asia, Egypt and Rome during the Kushana period which made their kingdom prosperous. A large number of gold and copper coins, bearing Greek, Hindu and Buddhist figures and deities, belonging to the Kushana period have been recovered. The Kushana kingdom reached its peak under Kanishka and his successors. The Kushanas were **instrumental** in spreading Buddhism, particularly Mahayana Buddhism in Central Asia and China. They also developed the Gandhara and Mathura schools of art. The Gandhara school of art was a perfect blend of Indian and foreign art styles. King Kanishka also encouraged Sanskrit literature. The famous Sanskrjt scholar Ashvaghosha lived during his reign.

## The Sangam Age

The word 'sangam' is a Tamil word which is derived from the word 'sangha' meaning an assembly or a *sabha*. The Tamil sangam consisted of different poets from different time periods who flourished under the patronage of the Tamil kings. Sangam literature speaks highly of three south Indian dynasties—the Cholas, the Pandyas and the Cheras—and refers to them together as *Tamilakha* or the Tamil realm.

### World Connect

Marco Polo was a 13th century Venetian merchant and adventurer who travelled from Europe to Asia in the years between 1271 and 1295. His account of what he saw during his twenty-four years of service in a high position in the court of Kublai Khan, the great Mongol Emperor, are detailed in the book *Livres des merveilles du monde* which means *The Travels of Marco Polo*. During the twenty-four years that he spent there, Marco Polo proved to be a valuable asset to the court of the Mongol Emperor and was sent on various important missions to China, Burma and even India. His account of the empire depicts his admiration towards the great Khan, the empire and the ceremonies, functions and culture of the Mongols. He became a favourite of the Khan and rose to a high position. He described the summer palace as the 'greatest palace that ever was.' He marvelled at the hall of the palace which he described in his

**sponsored:** provided funds for; **instrumental:** serving as a means of pursuing an aim accounts was covered with gold and silver and was so large that that over six thousand people could comfortably dine in it. The capital of Kublai Khan was called Cambulac meaning 'the city of the Khan' in present-day Beijing. From his travels, Marco Polo accumulated great knowledge about the Mongol Empire. He was greatly impressed by the empire's use of paper money, an idea that had failed to reach Europe, and its economy and scale of production. After many years of seeking permission to return home, Marco Polo was finally granted permission to escort a Mongol princess to Persia, where she was to marry a Persian prince. He headed home soon after. His stories and accounts give the reader the sense that he had clearly grown fond of this culture, despite his objective approach while writing the stories.

## Recall

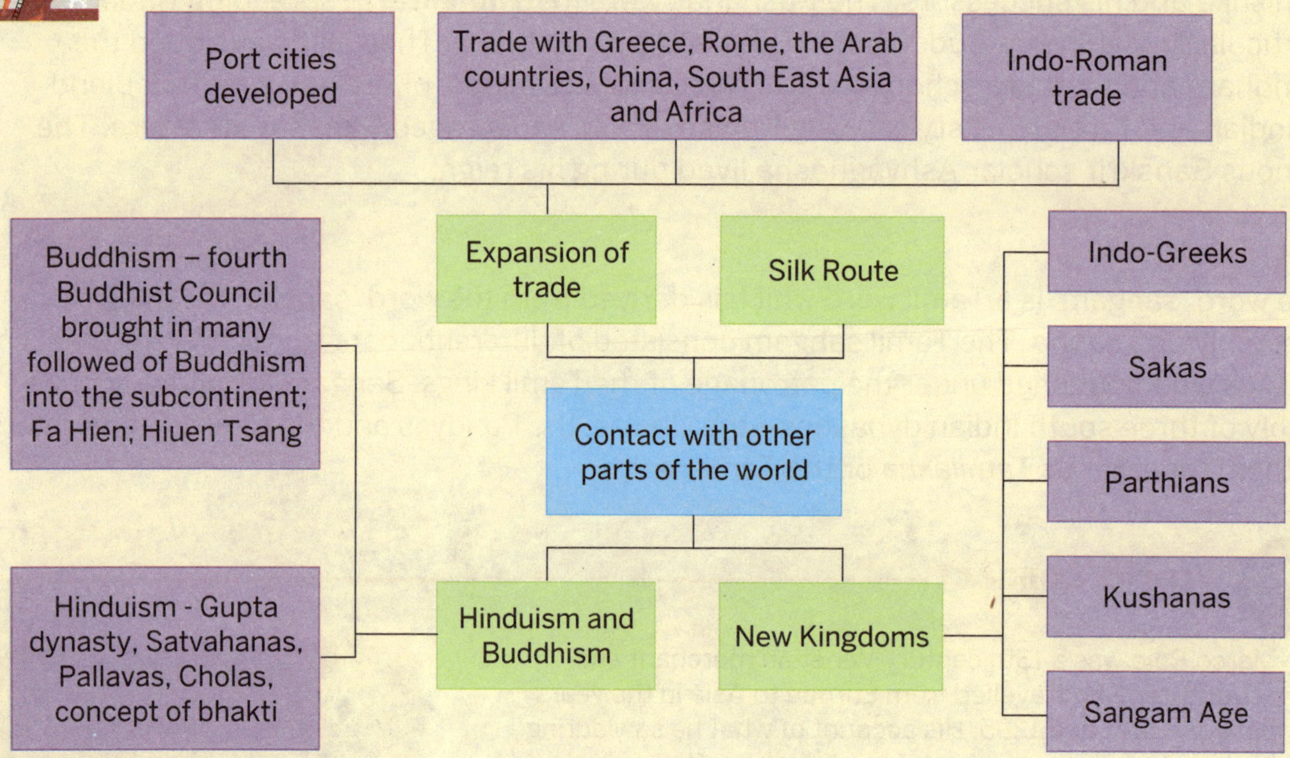


## Work out

A. Fill in the blanks with the correct answer.

1. The assemblies of poets held in South India is known as the .................................... .
   a. tamilkam   b. sangams   c. satraps   d. both a and c
2. The famous king Rudraraman I belonged to the .................................... .
   a. Pallavas   b. Cholas   c. Sakas   d. Parthians

3. The Parthians had come to India from .................................... .
   a. Central Asia   b. Iran   c. Iraq   d. Afghanistan
4. The Kushanas were instrumental in spreading .................................... in Central Asia and China.
   a. Mahayana Buddhism   b. Hinduism   c. Jainism
   d. none of these
5. The technique of silk-making first started in .................................... .
   a. Sri Lanka   b. China   c. France   d. India

B. Fill in the blanks.

1. Important .................................... kingdoms in the Indian region were in Taxila, Mathura, Nasik and Ujjain.
2. King .................................... was the greatest ruler of the Kushana dynasty.
3. Sangam literature was written in the .................................... language.
4. The idea of .................................... or intense devotion to one God emerged during this time.

C. Write T for true and F for false.

1. Hiuen Tsang visited India during the reign of Chandragupta Maurya. ☐
2. Fa-Hien visited India to learn Buddhism. ☐
3. Kanishka was a Chinese king. ☐
4. Kanishka convened the fourth Buddhist Council in Kashmir. ☐

D. Answer these questions in brief.

1. Who were the Sakas?.
2. What is Mahayana Buddhism?
3. Name the main gods and goddesses worshipped by the Hindus.
4. Who were the Parthians?
5. Which religion did the Pallavas and Cholas promote?

E. Answer these questions in detail.

1. Explain the significance of the Silk Route.
2. Discuss the main factors responsible for the popularity of Buddhism in ancient India.
3. How did Kanishka sponsor Buddhism?
4. Write about the expansion of trade during that period.

## Think

A. Look at the picture and answer the questions.

1. This picture is from an ancient silk scroll depicting 7th century Chinese Buddhist pilgrim & traveller Huien Tsang. Why did he come to India?
2. To what extent had he spread the message of Buddhism?

B. Many rulers wanted to control the Silk Route. Why do you think so?

## Life skills and values

*'Famous scholars like Fa Hien and Hiuen Tsang have taught many secrets of Chinese wisdom to Indians. In addition, they discovered many secrets within India itself. Hiuen Tsang had visited my own home town in Gujarat. From his works, we know today that there was a Buddhist monastery there.'*

–Prime Minister, Narendra Modi.

1. How do the accounts of foreign travellers help us reconstruct history?
2. Find out two quotes of Chinese wisdom from the Internet and discuss the meaning of these quotes in class.

## Enjoy

A. Imagine you have visited the beautiful city of Tanjore. If you have not visited the city, find out information about it from the Internet. Form groups of four and prepare a travelogue highlighting the main attraction of the Chola city, supplementing it with drawings.

B. Find out about the route of some famous explorers on the internet. Take a world physical map and trace the routes of Marco Polo, Megallan, Vasco da Gama and Christopher Columbus. Mark them with different coloured sketch pens.

## Web link

For more information, log on to:

https://en.unesco.org/silkroad/about-silk-road

Last accessed on 30 September, 2019

# 11 The Gupta Period

## Take off

- The network of trade routes from China to the Mediterranean was known as the ..................................................
- Fa Hien visited India during the reign of ..................................................

## Warm up

What can you buy with a ten paise coin today? Discuss.

After being in power for a period of well over a hundred years, the great Kushana Empire of the north, collapsed and broke away into many small kingdoms. In the midst of this, one dynasty, destined to rival the Kushanas in size and strength, was that of the Guptas. Magadha (modern Bihar) had lost its importance during the period of the Kushanas, but in the late 3rd century, under the leadership of Chandragupta I and his son Samudragupta, the Gupta Empire grew rapidly and came to include all of northern India from the Indus to the Brahmaputra and even extended south along the east coast of the peninsula. The Gupta period has been deemed the Golden Age of India as it came to dominate Indian history for the next two centuries.

▲ A modern statue depicting Chandragupta Maurya, Delhi

## Chandragupta I (320-335 CE)

The first important king of the Gupta dynasty, Chandragupta I, was married to the Lichchavi princess, Kumaradevi. He received Magadha as part of his wedding gift. He issued gold coins bearing his images along with those of his wife, Kumaradevi. Chandragupta I reigned for fifteen years and was followed by his son Samudragupta in 335 CE.

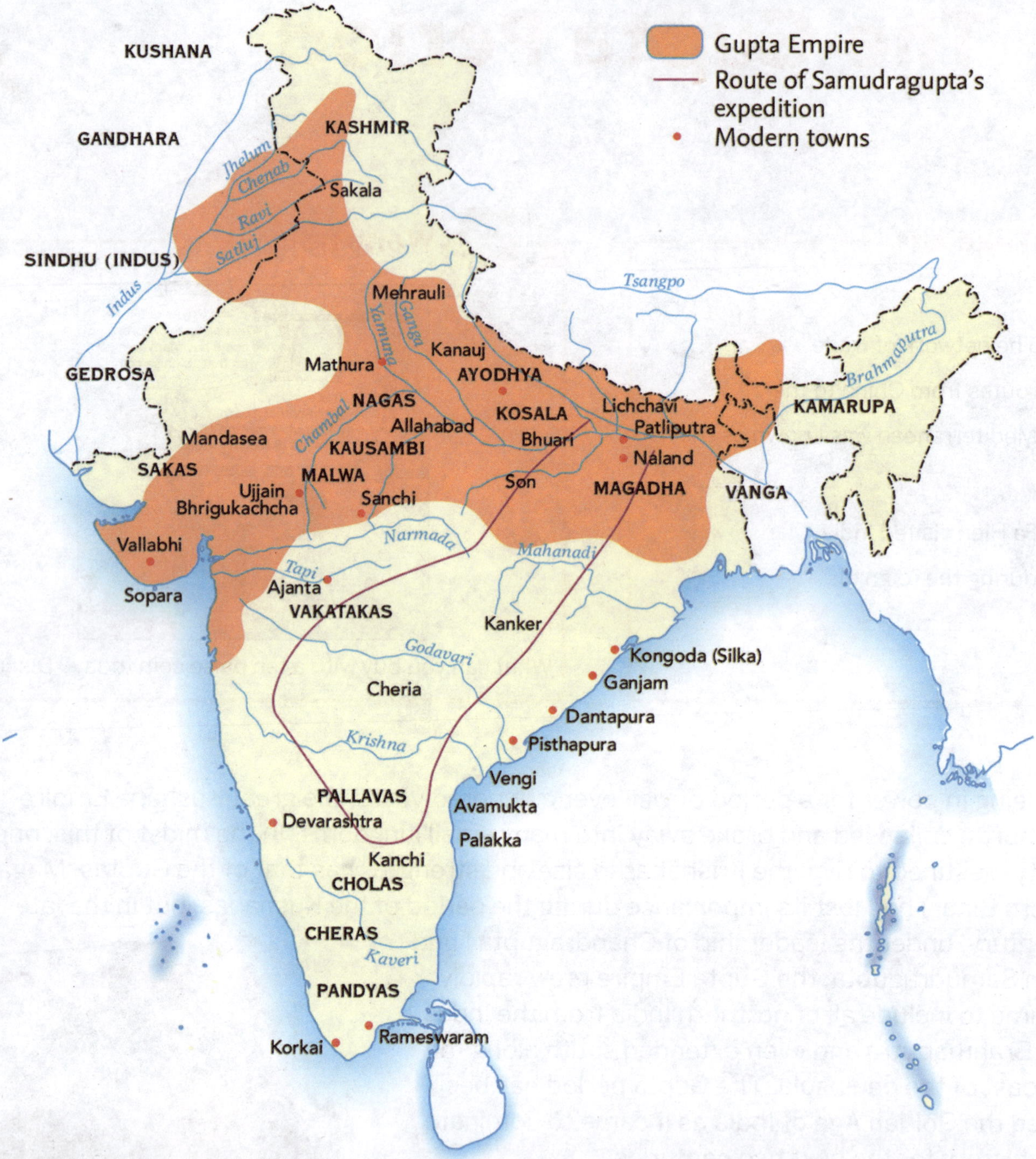


▲ Extent of the Gupta Empire

## Samudragupta (335-375 CE)

Samudragupta was one of the most well-known, respected and admired Gupta rulers known for his millitary victories and is said to have conquered many areas of the Indian subcontinent. Therefore, he has been called by many as the 'Indian Napoleon'.

**Find out**

What were the titles given to Samudragupta?

We know about Samudragupta mainly through an inscription on the Ashokan pillar in Allahabad. The inscription was written by Samudragupta's court poet, Harisena, in Sanskrit. This inscription tells us about his various conquests and that his principles towards these rulers varied. Some kingdoms which were annexed were made a part of his empire. Some rulers were allowed to rule again, while there were some who brought tributes. Certain rulers such as the ruler of Sri Lanka not only surrendered to him, but also offered his daughter's hand in marriage. We also learn about him from the coins issued by him. From them, we get to know that Samudragupta was attributed with many qualities. He was not only a warrior but also wrote poetry and played the *veena.*

## Chandragupta II (380-412 CE)

Chandragupta II can be regarded as one of the most prosperous rulers of the Gupta dynasty. We have already learnt that Fa-Hien visited India during the reign of Chandragupta II. He spent six years in India and was impressed by Chandragupta II, whom he described as a wise and **benevolent** ruler.

▲ Coins from the Gupta period

The famous Sanskrit poet, Kalidasa, was one of the nine gems in Chandragupta II's court. He has been widely regarded as the greatest poet and dramatist in the Sanskrit language. His plays and poetry are primarily based on the Hindu *Puranas.* They also give us glimpses into the life of the common people.

**Fact quest**

Chandragupta took on the title of Vikramaditya.

## Administration Under the Guptas

The Gupta rulers gave themselves high sounding titles like *Maharajadhiraja* and *Vikramaditya*, which suggested that they ruled over a large empire. Kingship was hereditary but the throne was not always occupied by the eldest son of the king. A council of ministers called the *mantri parishad* assisted the king in the administration of the state. These ministers were highly-paid and lived lavish lives.

The Empire was divided into provinces known as *bhuktis*. Each *bhukti* was placed under a prince. Bhuktis were divided into districts called *vishayas*, and each *vishaya* was placed under a *vishayapati*. The districts were made up of a number of villages. Each village had a council of elders headed by the village headman known as *gramika*.

A special feature of the Gupta Empire was the payment of **land grants** to the officials instead of salaries. The records were inscribed on copper plates. Only the army officials were paid in cash. Land grants were also made to the Brahmins and this land was generally tax-free. Land grants were also used as methods of payment to military leaders who who provided the

**benevolent:** well meaning and kindly

king with troops whenever required. They collected revenue from the land and used this to maintain the army and the equipment required.

Some posts were made hereditary. Harisena, the famous poet was made the *mahadandanayaka* or the chief judicial officer after his father, who was the previous chief judicial officer, died.

Besides these, the *nagara shresthi* (the chief merchant), the *sarthavaha* (the leader of the caravans), the *prathama kulika* (the chief artisan) and the *kayastha* (the most important scribe) all played important roles in the affairs of their state.

Eventually however, the local elites who had special privileges like land grants wielded more and more power. This led to the decentralization of the administration as the king himself came to be more and more dependent on them. They came to be called *samantas* as they were powerful people, independent of any kind of royal control. They maintained their own armies and helped the king by providing soldiers in times of need.

## Life of the People

The people lived a peaceful existence and were disciplined. The caste system was in existence, and the low caste people had to live outside the village. The Brahmins were given high positions in society. In large towns like Magadha, people were generally rich and prosperous. Rest houses were built on highways for travellers. Each town had numerous market places, banks, temples and many places of interest for the people. A number of charitable institutions and hospitals were built by them. While Hinduism was the main religion, Buddhism was also encouraged by them. By this period, the caste system had become even more rigid in the society. A number of sub-castes also came into existence. The plight of the lower castes was deplorable. The untouchables were ill-treated and made to live outside the city. The plight of the untouchables found mention in many accounts written by Fa-Hien. The position of women also saw no improvement. Formal education was denied to them, and they were considered to be inferior to men.

The Gupta Empire also saw the growth of education. The University of Nalanda, founded during the Gupta period, was world-renowned for imparting education. Nalanda was a famous university for **Hinayana Buddhism** in the kingdom of Magadha (present-day Bihar). Scholars like Zuan zang, Fa-Hien and Hiuen Tsang came to study Buddhism here. Nalanda flourished under the reign of the Gupta kings in the 5th and 6th centuries. Many foreign scholars from as far as Tibet, China and Central Asia visited the university. The accounts of these foreign travellers and students give us information about the university.

▲ The ruins of the university at Nalanda

The main occupation of the people was agriculture. The agriculturists paid one-sixth of their total produce as tax to the king. Apart from this there were specialist craftsmen involved in the designing of ivory work, and polishing stone. These craftsmen formed *shrenis* or guilds.

There was extensive and active trade in pepper, sandalwood, precious stones and perfumes.

### Religion

Hinduism was a popular religion during the Gupta period and it flourished under the **patronage** of the Gupta rulers. Hindu gods and goddess like Shiva, Shakti and Vishnu was worshipped. However, Hinduism underwent some changes during this period. There was an increase in the popularity of concepts such as *bhakti*. **Philosophical** debates would take place between both the Hindus and the Buddhists on the questions of the presence of God, attaining salvation, cycle of rebirths, etc. Both Buddhism and Jainism received support from the Gupta rulers. Jainism continued to be a popular religion amongst the traders.

### The Later Guptas

Kumara Gupta succeeded Chandragupta II and was powerful enough to maintain and protect the vast empire that he had inherited from Chandragupta II. He was succeeded by Skanda Gupta, who was **competent** but had to face the threat of the Huns from Central Asia.

Although the Huns were driven out of India, the Gupta Empire could not regain its former glory. The Gupta Empire was reduced to Magadha and a few adjoining areas thereby finally leading to its decline.

## Smaller Kingdoms

The end of the Gupta dynasty saw a rise in the number of smaller kingdoms in the north. Well-known among them was the king of a small place called Thanesar. He was Harshavardhan. Harsha came to the throne in 606 CE after the death of his elder brother. King Harshavardhan proved to be a great conqueror and administrator. He soon united the kingdoms of Thanesar and Kannauj and then succeeded in bringing Bihar, Odisha and Bengal under his command. He married his daughter to a king in Gujarat. After he came to the throne, Harsha moved his capital from Thanesar to Kannauj.

We come to know about Harshavardhana through the writings of his court poet, Banabhatta. Banabhatta's *Harshacharita* describes king Harshavarhdhan's early rise to power, his conquests and his administration.

We also get details of Harsha's rule from the accounts of the Chinese pilgrim Hieun Tsang. He is described as a modest, benevolent, energetic and active ruler. He established diplomatic relations with the Chinese Emperor and sent **envoys** to China. Upon his death, north India fell into complete chaos and confusion.

**patronage:** the support given by a patron; **philosophical:** relating or devoted to the study of the fundamental nature of knowledge, reality, and existence; **competent:** able to do something well enough to meet a standard; **envoy:** messenger or representative, especially one on a diplomatic mission

## Religion

Though in his initial years, Harshavardhan was an **ardent** follower of Shiva, he respected all religions. In his later years, he became a great follower of Buddhism and is said to have supported the Nalanda University.

**Fact quest**

Hieun Tsang studied in the University of Nalanda. He wrote a book called *Si-Yu-Ki*.

A great poet himself, King Harshavardhan composed three works in Sanskrit, namely, *Nagananda, Ratnavali and Priyadarsini.*

## Important Kingdoms of the South

Meanwhile, two kingdoms became very important in south India. They were the Chalukyas of Vatapi or Badami and the Pallavas of Kanchipuram.

▲ Aihole inscription

**Chalukyas:** In the sixth century CE, the Chalukyas set up their kingdom in the western side of the Deccan Plateau. Pulakeshin I established the Chalukya dynasty in 543 CE by taking control of Vatapi in Karnataka. The greatest Chalukya ruler who defeated Harsha was Pulakeshin II. We know about Pulakeshin II from the Aihole inscription composed by his court poet Ravikirti. Pulakeshin II's empire consisted of present-day Karnataka, Andhra Pradesh and Telangana. The rule of the Chalukyas mark an important period in the history of south India. For the first time in the history of India, a south Indian kingdom was to control the entire region between the Kaveri and Narmada rivers. The Chalukyas had an efficient administrative machinery, flourishing overseas trade and made significant contributions to art and architecture.

Pulakeshin II was successful in defeating Mahendravarman I, the Pallava ruler of Kanchipuram. However, in the Battle of Vatapi in 642 CE, Pulakeshin II lost to Mahendravaraman's son, Narasimhavarman. The battle resulted in his death and the establishment of the Pallavas in Vatapi.

**The Pallavas:** The Pallavas were a local tribe who controlled southern Andhra Pradesh and northern Tamil Nadu. The Pallavas had extensive trade in teak, sandalwood and textiles with the countries of Cambodia, Java and Sumatra. The Pallava kingdoms were very prosperous. Kaveripattanam was a busy port city of the Pallavas.

The Pallavas had a centralized system of administration. The state was divided into *kottams* and each *kottam* was placed under officials appointed by the king. There were a number of local assemblies. The *ur* and *nagaram*, were two such assemblies. The *ur* was a village assembly while the *nagaram* was an organisation of merchants. The Pallavas built tanks and wells for irrigation purposes. They also imposed taxes on the people. The main tax was on agricultural produce.

**ardent:** very enthusiastic or passionate

## Investigate

*Who was the exterminator of all kings; who had no* antagonist *(of equal power) in the world; whose fame was tasted by the waters of the four oceans; who was equal to (the gods) Dhanada and Varuna and Indra and Antaka; who was the very axe of (the god) Kritânta; who was the giver of many millions of lawfully acquired cows and gold; who was the restorer of the ashvamêdha-sacrifice, that had been long in abeyance;*

— This is an extract from an inscription about Chandragupta II, found in Mathura.

1. On the basis of the translation of the inscription given, write down at least four qualities of Chandragupta II.
2. Do you think the inscriptions are a good source of history? Why?

**Religion:** The period witnessed a lot of temples being built. Narasimhavarman built the famous Ratha temple at Mahabalipuram. These were rock cut temples. During this period, the role of the temple became very important. The Brahmins were made responsible for looking after the temple affairs. Brahmins were given a high status in the society. They were given land grants by the Pallava rulers. This period saw the rise of Shaivism and Vaishnavism and the decline of Buddhism and Jainism.

The Pallava rulers were patrons of the Sanskrit language and they encouraged the growth of the Tamil language too. It was during this time that the *Bhakti* movement gained momentum under the Alwars (the followers of Vishnu) and the Nayanars (the followers of Shiva).

The Pallavas were great patrons of art and literature. Their capital Kanchi, was a centre of learning and it attracted students from all parts of India and abroad. Dharampala, who later became the head of the Nalanda University, belonged to Kanchi. Great Sanskrit scholars like Dandin and Bharavi lived during the rule of the Pallavas. Tamil literature developed during this time. Music and dance also flourished during this period.

## World Connect

The Liu Song dynasty was founded by Liu Yu (363–422 CE) in China. Liu Yu who joined the army and soon rose to the position of a commander was responsible for defeating the rebel Huan Xuan. After Huan Xuan's fall, Liu Yu took the throne from the Jin dynasty and established the Liu Song dynasty. Liu Yu came to be known as Emperor Wu. Emperor Wu was one of the greatest rulers and it was under him that the southern Chinese Empire came closest to conquering the northern states. He was succeeded by Shaodi who proved incompetent and was removed from power. It was under the reign of the third emperor, Emperor Wen that there was political stability in the empire.

## Recall

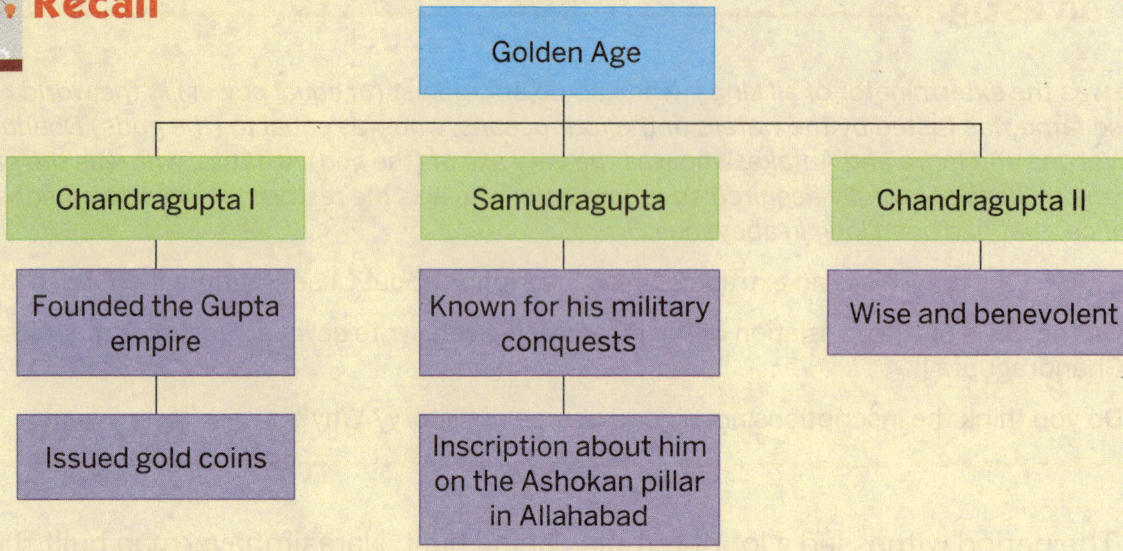


## Work out

### A. Fill in the blanks.

1. The ruler of Sri Lanka .............................. to Samudragupta.
2. The agriculturists paid .............................. of their total produce as tax to the king.
3. .............................. was the most powerful ruler of the Chalukya dynasty.
4. One of the nine gems who lived in the court of Chandragupta II and was a Sanskrit poet, was .............................. .
5. The Aihole inscription tells us about .............................. .

### B. Fill in the blanks with the correct word.

1. The capital of the Pallavas was called .............................. .
   a. Kannauj  b. Tanjore  c. Kanchipuram  d. Madurai
2. .............................. was known as the Indian Napoleon.
   a. Samudragupta  b. Chandragupta I
   c. Chandragupta II  d. None of these options
3. The term bhukti refers to a ..............................
   a. village  b. district  c. province  d. town
4. Harsha ruled in ..............................
   a. Thaneswar  b. Kannauj
   c. Pataliputra  d. Both Thaneswar and Kannauj

C. Solve the crossword.

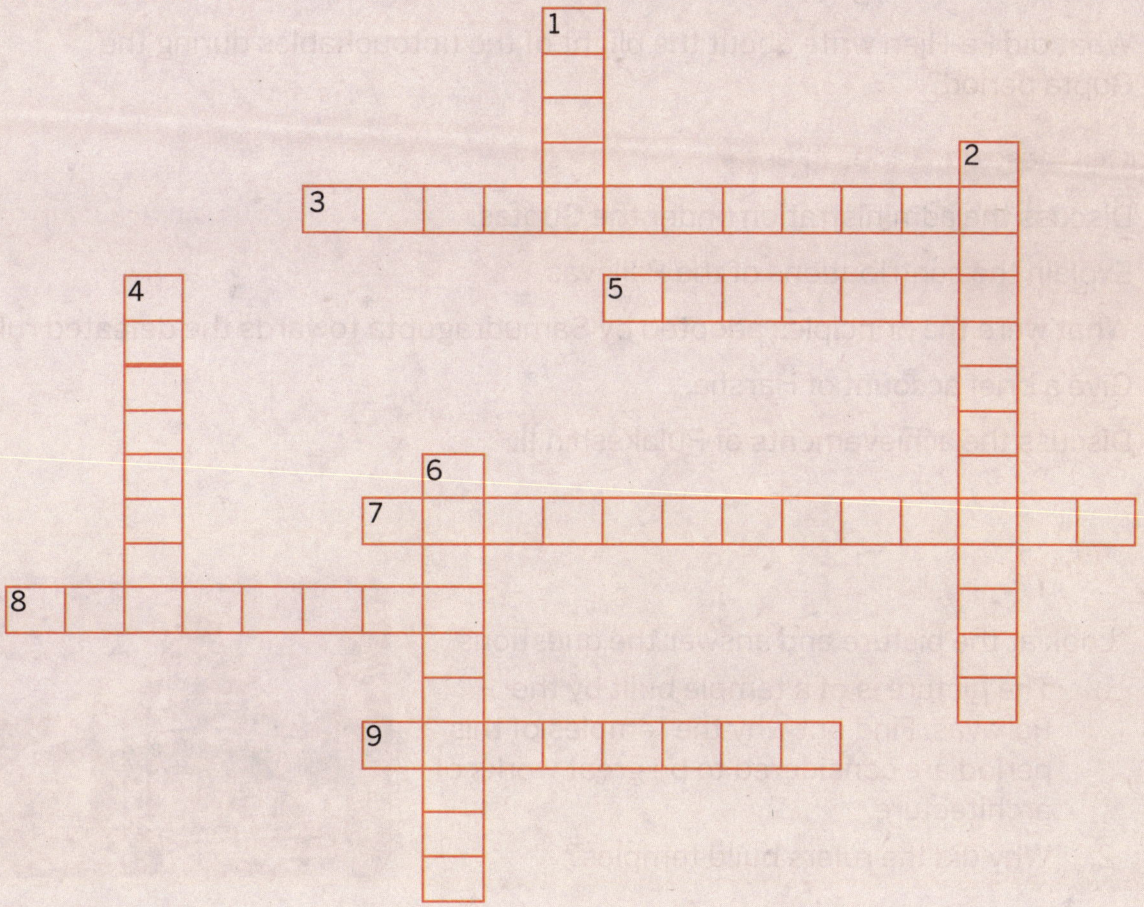

**Across**

3. Chandragupta II took on this title
5. Provinces during the Gupta period was known by this term
7. The place where the rock cut temple is situated
8. A dynasty ruled by Pulakesin II
9. A local tribe whose capital was Kaveripattanam

**Down**

1. The musical instrument played by Samudragupta
2. He was the ruler who moved his capital from Thanesar to Kanauj
4. He lived in the court of Chandragupta II and was a Sanskrit poet
6. He was the one who wrote a biography of Harshavardhan

D. Answer these questions in brief.

1. Who was Chandragupta I and whom did he marry?
2. Which Gupta ruler was known for his military achievements?
3. What do coins tell us about Samudragupta?

4. What were the religions that existed during the Gupta period?
5. What did Fa-Hien write about the plight of the untouchables during the Gupta period?

E. Answer these questions in detail.

1. Discuss the administration under the Guptas.
2. Explain the contributions of the Pallavas.
3. What were the principles adopted by Samudragupta towards the defeated rulers?
4. Give a brief account of Harsha.
5. Discuss the achievements of Pulakeshin II.

## Think

Look at the picture and answer the questions.

1. The picture is of a temple built by the Pallavas. Find out why the temples of this period are considered to be great works of architecture.
2. Why did the rulers build temples?

## Life skills and values

Why do you think the Gupta period is called the Golden Age of India? List at least three developments of this period to support your answer.

## Enjoy

A. Imagine yourself to be a student enrolled in the Nalanda University. Write about your experience as a diary entry.

B. Make a power point presentation on the magnificence of the Gupta Age with emphasis on trade and commerce. Compare it with the achievements of the Chola empire. Share it in the class.

## Web link

For more information, log on to:
https://knowindia.gov.in/culture-and-heritage/ancient-history/gupta.php

Last accessed on 30 September, 2019

# 12 Our Cultural and Scientific Wealth

### Take off

- The Gupta period is known as the ........................................ Age of India.
- Hiuen Tsang visited India during the reign of ........................................ .

### Warm up

Can you name some things that make India rich? List at least five of them in your notebook.

There are innumerable stories, buildings and innovations that reflect the collective heritage of India. Undoubtedly, our culture is rich, varied and diverse.

## Literature

Right from the composition of the *Vedas*, the *Upanishads*, the *Jataka Tales* and the *Panchatantra,* India has made tremendous contributions in the field of literature. The *Rig Veda*, which is nearly 4,000 years old, is one of the oldest literatures in the world. It, along with the three other *Vedas*, was composed in the Sanskrit language and were passed down orally, from one generation to another.

### Eco feat

Paper was first invented in China about 1900 years ago by a man named Cai Lun from plant fibres, cloth and the bark of trees. With improvements in technology and the invention of the printing press, the usage of paper has increased manifold. Over 30 million acres of forests are destroyed annually for producing paper.

### Panini's *Ashtadhyayi*

Between the 6th and 5th century BCE, the Indian grammarian Panini wrote *A Treatise on Sanskrit Grammar*. This work set the linguistic standards for classical Sanskrit. In the 4000 **sutras**, divided into eight chapters, the work sums up the science of phonetics and grammar,

**sutras:** a set of rules in Sanskrit literature, grammar, Hindu law or philosophy that had evolved during the Vedic Age. The *Ashtadhyayi* distinguishes between its usage in the spoken language and the usage that is proper to the language of the sacred texts.

## The Epics

An epic is a long poem narrating the deeds and adventures of heroic or legendary figures of the past. The *Ramayana* and the *Mahabharata* are two great epics of Indian literature. The *Ramayana* was composed by sage Valmiki. It is the story of Lord Rama, the ruler of Ayodhya and how he fought with the demon king, Ravana who had abducted his wife, Sita. The story ends with a moralistic lesson that good wins over evil. The *Ramayana* has over 24,000 verses. The *Mahabharata* was composed by sage Ved Vyasa. It is the story of the heroic war between the Kauravas and the Pandavas. It contains about 1,00,000 verses. It also contains the *Bhagwad Gita*, the sacred book of the Hindus.

**Fact quest**

Manusmriti, translated *Laws of Manu* or *Institutions of Manu*, is the most important and authoritative Hindu Law Book (Dharmashastra) which served as a foundational work on Hindu law in the ancient Indian society.

▲ Gita Stambha, a column with the text of the *Bhagvad Gita*

## Epics from Sangam literature

The *Panchkavyams* or the five great epics of Tamil literature are:

- *Cilappatikaram*: This Tamil epic was written by Ilango Adigal and is a non-religious literary work from the 1st century CE.
- *Manimekalai*: This was composed by Seethalai Sathanar and is a Buddhist religious work, probably written after the 1st century CE.
- *Valayapathi*: It is another Jain religious work from the 9th century CE.

These epics provide the historical verification of the cultural, social, religious and academic life of the people from that era.

## *Puranas*

The *Puranas* is a collection of legends and tales forming a part of the sacred literature of Hinduism. They were written in simple Sanskrit and were meant to be heard by everyone. The *Puranas* deal with the religious developments that occurred between 400 and 1500 CE. They detail how rituals and ceremonies should be performed. There are 18 *Puranas* in total and each of them is dedicated to a God or Goddess.

▲ A relief sculpture of Durga in the Cave temples of Mahabalipuram

## Poems and Plays

One of the greatest playwrights of Sanskrit literature was Kalidasa who lived during the reign of Chandragupta II. *Meghaduta, Kumarasambhava* and *Raghuvamsa* are few of his classical poems. He also wrote plays such as *Abhijnanashakuntalam* and *Malavikagnimitram*. His works form the cornerstone of Indian mythology. Other playwrights whose works give us a glimpse of the lives of the people include *Mrichchhakatikam* of Shudraka and *Kiratarjuniya* of Bharavi.

## *Panchatantra* and *Jataka Tales*

*Panchatantra* were tales written by Vishnu Sharma. These stories are centred around animals and in many stories, animals play the role of people. Each story has a moral or lesson attached to it. The tales of *Panchatantra* have been translated into Arabic and Persian.

The *Jataka Tales* tell us about the previous births of Lord Buddha in both human as well as animal form. Originally written in the Pali language, the *Jataka Tales* have been translated in different languages of the world. Self sacrifice, morality and honesty are a few values that the *Jataka Tales* preach to the people.

## Non-religious literature

This type of literature was secular in nature. Chanakya, who was Chandragupta Maurya's minister, wrote the *Arthashastra* which laid down rules for good governance. Accounts of foreign travellers such as the *Indika* written by Megasthenes, a Greek Ambassador, also provide us with details of the lifestyle of the people.

**Fact quest**

The Iron Pillar in Delhi was built during the Gupta period and has not rusted yet.

**Investigate**

*'That person alone is fit to nurse or to attend the bedside of a patient, who is cool-headed and pleasant in his demeanor, does not speak ill of any body, is strong and attentive to the requirements of the sick, and strictly and indefatigably follows the instructions of the physician.'*

—*Sushruta Samhita* Book 1, Chapter XXXIV

List the ancient qualifications of a nurse, as mentioned in the extract given.

Are the qualities of the nurse described in the *Sushruta Samhita*, relevant even today?

# Science

## Aryabhatta

Aryabhatta was a great mathematician and astronomer. His famous works the *Aryabhatiyam* and the *Aryabhattasiddhanta* were written in Sanskrit. He lived in Kusumapura near

Pataliputra, during the Gupta period. He studied in the famous Nalanda University. He was the first scientist to discover that the Earth was spherical in shape and that it rotated on its axis causing day and night. He gave valuable contributions in the fields of Science and Mathematics.

▲ Aryabhatta

## Varahamihira

Varahamihira was an Indian philosopher and scientist who lived in Ujjain during the Gupta period. His works include the *Brihat Samhita* and the *Pancha Siddhantika*. Varahamihira was convinced that there existed a force that pulled us towards the ground. We now call this force 'gravity'. He also stated that the Earth revolves around the Sun, and the Moon revolves around the Earth. He was an excellent astrologer and was one of the gems in the court of Chandragupta II.

# Art and Architecture

The Ashokan Pillars were some of the best examples of architecture of this period. Each structure stood between 40 and 50 feet tall, weighted up to 50 tons and each had carved edicts. Today, 19 pillars bearing the carvings survive. Metallurgy or the scientific study of metals had reached an advanced stage during the Gupta period. The Iron Pillar at Mehrauali in Delhi (near Qutab Minar), is an example of the metallurgical skill of those times. Although it was constructed in the fourth CE and is fully exposed to the elements, it is yet to gather rust.

Mathura, Pataliputra and Sarnath were the important centres of art during that period. The early temples consisted of a small central room, called the *garbhagriha*, where the image of the god was kept. Gradually, the number of rooms increased and the temples became larger. The temples were built of brick, stone and mortar. The Vishnu temple at Deogarh near Jhansi, the brick temple at Bhitargaon near Kanpur and temples at Sanchi are the best examples of Gupta architecture.

Many Buddhist monasteries were built during this period. Some of them were in caves, carved out from hills. The seated Buddha at Sarnath and the standing image of Buddha kept at the Mathura museum are the best specimens of sculpture of this period. Many images of Mahavira have been found at Mathura and Gorakpur.

The Golden Age of Indian architecture spanned from 230 CE to 1200 CE. Various empires began constructing temples. The Chola king, Rajaraja Chola constructed the Brihadishvara Temple complex. The Pallavas built a number of stone temples in the 7th and 8th centuries. The most famous temple of the Pallavas is the seven **ratha** temple.

**ratha:** (in Hindu architecture) a facet or vertical offset projection on the tower

## Paintings

▲ Ajanta caves

Go back to the earlier chapters of your textbook. What did you read? How did the early humans find expression to his thoughts? The answer is simple. The early humans found expression in painting. Some examples are the Bhimbetka cave paintings and the murals painted at Ajanta and Ellora near Aurangabad which reflect the life of Buddha. Many scenes from the *Jataka Tales* are also shown in these cave paintings. Natural colors were used to make these paintings.

### Case Study

**The Gandhara School of Art**

During the rule of Kanishka in the first century CE, there was a lot of influence of the Greeks and the Romans on Indian art. This Graeco-Roman style of art flourished in the north-western region in Gandhara and came to be known as the Gandhara School of art. Life-like statues of Buddha and their followers have been made in the Gandhara style.

**The Mathura School of Art**

The Mathura School of art is famous for the headless statue of Kanishka, a Kushan ruler. Under this school, life-size statues of Mahavira and Buddha and their followers have been made in red sandstone. This school also showed Graeco-Roman influence in its art.

Q. What kinds of artwork were made in these two schools?

### World Connect

Hellenistic art developed during the classical period from the time of Alexander the Great till the emergence of ancient Rome in 31 BCE. When Alexander the Great conquered the Persian Empire in 331 BCE, his domain extended from Greece to **Asia Minor**, Egypt, the Near East, and India. This contact with distant cultures exposed Greek art and artists to new and exotic influences. Vast quantities of gold was recovered from the Persian Empire. This gold was used to create fashionable gold jewelry such as earrings, necklaces, pendants, etc. The Hellenistic jewellery consisted of intricate designs, particularly, animal and plants motifs. The figures of gods and goddesses were also popular designs used in making jewellery. With the expansion of trade and the establishment of new trade routes, new precious and semi-precious stones were becoming available for inlay work in jewellery. This increase in trade, and exchange of cultures during the Hellenistic period led to the establishment of *koine,* or the common language, throughout the Hellenistic world.

**Asia minor:** the Asian part of modern Turkey and the Armenian highland

## Recall

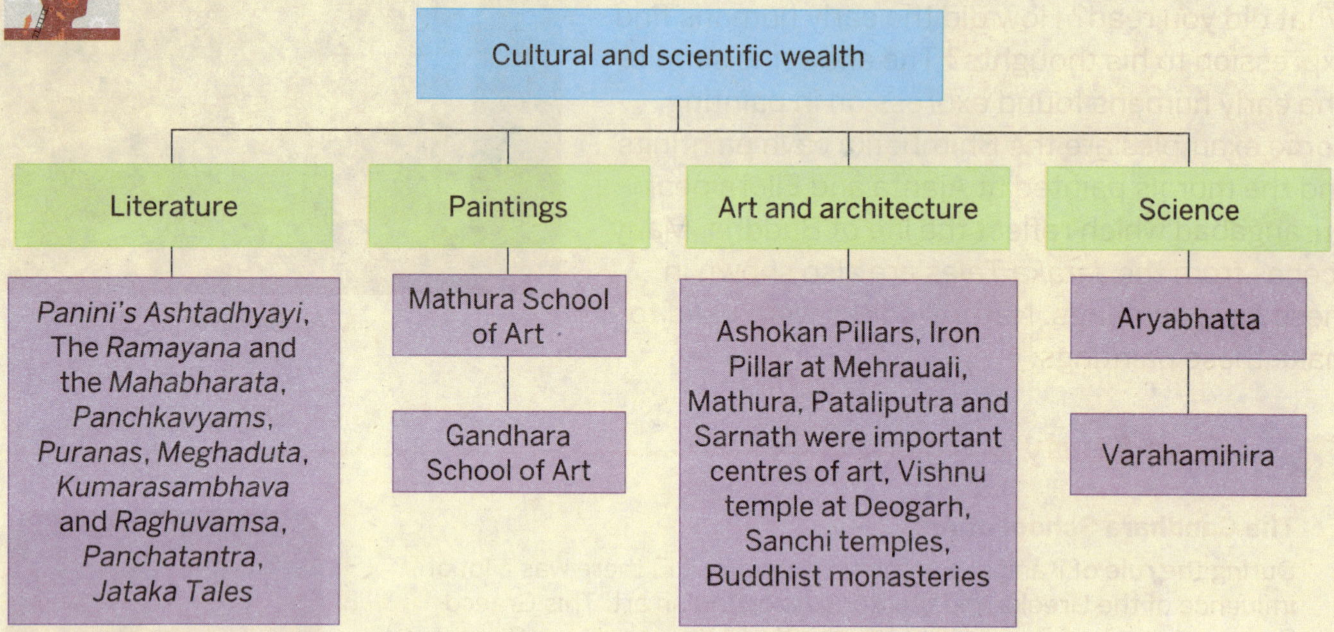


## Work out

A. Fill in the blanks with the correct answers.

1. The Sanchi Stupa was associated with the .................................... .
   a. Mauryas b. Guptas c. Chalukyas d. Pallavas
2. The science of studying metals is known as .................................... .
   a. history b. archaeology c. biology d. metallurgy
3. Aryabhatta was associated with .................................... .
   a. philosophy b. astronomy c. archaeology d. pottery
4. .................................... was written by Kalidasa.
   a. Meghaduta b. Cilappatikaram c. Indika d. Panchtantra
5. The Ramayana and the Mahabharata were rewritten during the period of the .................................... .
   a. Cholas b. Mauryas c. Sakas d. None of these.

B. Fill in the blanks.

1. A perfect example of metallurgy during the Gupta period is the .................................... .

2. The most popular work of Kalidasa were .................................... and .................................... .
3. Rock cut temples are found in .................................... .
4. .................................... are the caves in which the paintings that depict the life of Buddha are found.
5. The Mauryans built many monuments like .................................... .

## C. Write T for true and F for false.

1. Varahamihira was an Indian philosopher and scientist ☐
2. The Bhimbetka cave paintings were made during the Gupta period. ☐
3. Aryabhatta wrote the *Aryabhatiyam*. ☐
4. Chanakya was 'Ashoka the Great's' minister. ☐
5. *Panchatantra* were tales written by Vishnu Sharma. ☐
6. The *Jataka Tales* tell us about the previous births of Lord Buddha in both human as well as animal form. ☐

## D. Answer these questions in brief.

1. Who was Varahamihira?
2. Name the main characters that the *Panchtantra* revolves around.
3. Which is the oldest *Veda*?
4. Who wrote the *Mahabharata* and the *Ramayana*?
5. Gandhara school of art flourished under which ruler?

## E. Answer these questions in detail.

1. Give examples of the legacy left behind by our ancestors.
2. State the developments made by Aryabhatta in the field of Mathematics.
3. Trace the development in architecture during each of the following periods.
   a. Mauryan period  b. Gupta period
4. Who was Kalidasa and in whose court did he live?
5. Science and literature were very advanced during the Gupta period. Explain this with examples.

## Think

Look at the given picture of the Great Stupa at Sanchi and answer the questions that follow.

1. What do you think the dome of the stupa symbolizes?
2. Which ruler built this stupa?
3. Suggest ways to protect this monument and other similar monuments of ancient times.

## Life skills and values

Family traditions and cultures are fast disappearing. Do you or do you not agree? Support your answer with reasons.

## Enjoy

A. Divide the class into four groups. Let each group enact a story from the *Jataka Tales*. Allow all students to judge the stories on the basis of selection of story, dialogue delivery and performance.

B. Collect pictures of art and architecture of Ancient India and make a collage. Display it in the class.

## Web link

For more information, log on to:

https://knowindia.gov.in/culture-and-heritage/lifestyle-values-and-beliefs.php

Last accessed on 30 September, 2019

Info Time

## Major Milestones in History

5,00,000 BCE to 10,000 BCE
Palaeolithic Age

10,000 BCE–8000 BCE
The Mesolithic Age

5000–7000 BCE
The Neolithic Age

4,000 BCE–2,000 BCE
Chalcolithic Age

3300 BCE
The Bronze Age

1500 BCE
The Aryans migrated to the Indian subcontinent

600 BCE
The formation of janapadas and mahajanapadas

540 BCE
Vardhamana Mahavira was born

566 BCE
Gautama Buddha was born

322 BCE–185 BCE
The Mauryan Dynasty was in power

300 BCE
The second urbanization and the first traces of Hinduism developed

399–412 BCE
Fa Hien travelled to India

261 BCE
The Kalinga War

200 BCE
Development of urban centres; trade with other countries was established

320–500 CE
The Golden Period in India

543 CE
The Chalukyas came to power

275 CE–897 CE
Pallava Dynasty

606 CE
Harshavardhana assumed power in the north

630 CE
Hieun Tsang arrived in India

# 1 The Solar System

## Take off

- The ........................................ is the only planet which supports life.
- The ........................................ protects us from the harmful rays of the Sun.

## Warm up

'That's one small step for man, one giant leap for mankind.'

Who was the first man to set foot on the Moon?

Since ancient times, human beings have gazed at the dark sky and wondered about all the shining objects. Why do some stars twinkle? What holds them up there? Where do they go during the day?

The origin of the universe has its root in the **Big Bang**, a single massive explosion that occurred 12 billion years ago. All the matter of the universe, packed into a small superdense mass, was hurled in all directions by an explosion. As the fragments slowed down, the **galaxies** and stars evolved but the universe is still expanding.

The **Milky Way galaxy**, which is the home of the Earth and the solar system, was formed. The Sun, which is a star, was formed 4.6 billion years ago. The Earth and the other planets that revolve around the Sun, evolved from the Sun's debris, that is, gas and dust particles moving around the Sun.

▲ Milky Way

## Celestial Bodies

All objects that exist in the sky are called **celestial bodies**. Sometimes, celestial bodies are also called heavenly bodies. Celestial bodies that we know about include, the Sun, the Moon, asteroids, meteors, the planets and the stars.

## Fact quest

A light year is a unit of distance used in astronomy, equal to the distance travelled by light in one year. It is used to measure the vast distances between celestial bodies in the universe.

**galaxy:** an extremely large group of stars and planets that extends over many billions of light years

## Stars

**Stars** are huge celestial bodies. They look small because they are far away from us. They are made of burning gases. When these gases burn, they emit a temendous amount of heat and light. The star nearest to the Earth is the **Sun**. There are millions of stars like the Sun. The second nearest star is Proxima Centauri, which is 4.25 light years away from the Earth.

▲ Hydra

▲ Ursa Major

A **constellation** is a group of stars which form a pattern in the sky. Some constellations are Ursa Major, Ursa Minor, Orion, Canis Major and Hydra. Ursa Major is also known as *Saptarishi* in Hindi. The brightest star in the sky is the Pole Star or the North Star. It appears almost directly above the North Pole of the Earth. People in the ancient times used to determine the north direction at night by looking at the North Star.

## Solar System

The Sun, the eight planets, the asteroids, and comets form the **solar system**.

▲ The Sun and the eight planets

### Sun

Like all stars, the Sun is made up of intensely hot, burning gases. It is the main source of heat, light and energy for the Earth. The Sun lies at the centre of the Solar System and its gravity keeps the planets in their orbits.

The light from the Sun takes about 8 minutes and 20 seconds to reach the Earth's surface. This light is reflected by planets and their satellites which is why we can see them in the night sky despite the fact that they do not have their own light. The Sun's energy drives the weather and climate on Earth and supports almost all life on Earth.

## Planets

The word planet comes from the Greek word *planasthai* which means 'to wander'. These celestial bodies are made up of solid materials. Since they are not made of burning gases, they do not have heat and light of their own. They only reflect the light which they receive from a star. They move around the Sun along a fixed path called an **orbit**. There are eight planets in the Solar System and all of them revolve around the Sun.

In order of their distance from the Sun, the planets are Mercury, Venus, Earth, Mars, Jupiter, Saturn, Uranus and Neptune. Mercury, Venus, Earth and Mars are the **inner planets** or the **terrestrial planets**. The four giant planets farthest from the Sun—Jupiter, Saturn, Uranus and Neptune are the **outer planets**.

**Mercury:** This planet is closest to the Sun. It has the shortest orbit and it takes about 88 days to complete one revolution around the Sun. As it is closest to the Sun, it is very hot. Mercury has no atmosphere and hence, there is no life on it.

**Venus:** This is the brightest of all planets, as seen from the Earth. About the same size as the Earth, it is also called the Earth's twin. It is also called the **morning star** or the **evening star**.

**Earth:** This is the fifth largest planet in the Solar System. It is also called the **blue planet**, or the watery planet. The Earth is the only planet that supports life making it a unique planet.

**Mars:** It is also called the **Red Planet** because of the presence of iron oxide on its surface which makes it appear red. It is the closest planet to the Earth. It does not support life as the atmosphere contains 95 per cent carbon-dioxide. White polar caps that are visible through the telescope seem to be made up of water, ice and carbon dioxide.

**Jupiter:** It is the largest planet of the Solar System. It has a gaseous surface of hydrogen and helium. The most striking feature of Jupiter is the Great Red Spot, which is a rotating storm system that has lasted for more than a hundred years.

**Saturn:** It is the second largest planet in the Solar System. It is characterized by spectacular rings which are made up of ice and ice-covered dust particles.

**Uranus:** This planet rotates on its axis from east to west. Its atmosphere consists mainly of hydrogen with traces of helium, ammonia and methane. It has at least ten thin uniform black rings made up of dust.

**Neptune:** It is the most distant gas planet. The atmosphere consists of mainly hydrogen and helium. It has three rings made up of dust.

**Find out**

Why is Neptune the coldest planet of the Solar System?

## The Blue Planet

The Earth is the only planet in the Solar System which has water on its surface and enough oxygen to breathe comfortably. About 70 per cent of the Earth's surface is covered with water. The Earth's oceans, along with the atmosphere surrounding it, give it a blue **hue** when viewed from space hence the name, blue planet.

▲ The Earth as viewed from the Moon's surface

Since the Earth is the third planet from the Sun, it is neither too far from the Sun nor too near, making the surface temperature neither too hot nor too cold.

The atmosphere that surrounds the Earth, contains gases such as oxygen, nitrogen, carbon dioxide and argon. All these are required to sustain life on Earth.

Sunlight is another factor which makes the Earth a unique planet. While all planets receive light from the Sun, no other planet uses it as beneficially as the Earth. Plants need sunlight to grow and in return produce oxygen through the process of photosynthesis.

## Satellites

The word **satellite** means follower or an attendant. Satellites are spherical bodies that move around a planet, just as the planet moves round the Sun. Like planets, satellites have no light of their own but shine with the reflected light of the Sun. Almost all the planets have satellites except Mercury and Venus.

## The Moon

The **Moon** is the only natural satellite of the Earth. Its diameter is about one fourth of the Earth's diameter. It has no light of its own and refects the light of the Sun.

**Fact quest**

The largest of Jupiter's many Moons is named Ganymede and that of Saturn is named Titan.

The Moon revolves around the Earth in about 29 days and 8 hours. This is called a **lunar month**. It takes exactly the same time for it to complete one rotation around its axis. That is why we see only one side of the Moon. There is no air or water on the Moon, and it is very hot during the day while the nights are very cold.

Space satellites have been launched by various countries for meteorological information, telecommunication and disaster warning. The first Indian space satellite, *Aryabhatta* was launched in 1975.

**hue:** a colour or shade

## Asteroids

**Asteroids** (planetoids) are a group of small bodies made up of rock and metal which revolve around the Sun, between the orbits of Mars and Jupiter. This region is called the **asteroid belt**. Asteroids have different sizes and are also known as minor planets. The larger bodies are roughly spherical in shape while the smaller ones are **elongated**—best described as potato-shaped. Ceres, Pellas, Juno and Vesta are the four largest asteroids.

## Meteors and Meteorites

When celestial bodies collide with one another, fragments of rocks break-off. These pieces may find their way towards the Earth. Such objects are called **meteors**. Meteors are usually small and burn up before they can reach the Earth's surface. They emit light due to the heat produced by friction upon entering the atmosphere with high velocity. When meteors are large and do not burn up completely, they land on the Earth's surface and are known as **meteorites**. A meteor shower is a celestial event where a number of meteors, most not larger than a grain of sand, create streaks of light in the night sky as they enter the Earth's atmosphere at extremely high speeds. Intense meteor showers are known as meteor outbursts or meteor storms.

▲ Meteor Crater, Arizona

**Fact quest**

Halley's comet is a periodic comet visible from Earth every 75-76 years and can be viewed by the naked eye. It last appeared in 1986 and is expected to reappear in the year 2061.

Meteorites have struck the Earth in the past. The most famous site is that of the Meteor Crater in Arizona. The crater is 1.2 km wide and 170 metres deep. It appears that **impact** occurred within the last 20,000 years. Most scientists believe that a meteorite impact on the Earth caused dinosaurs to become extinct.

## Comets

**Comets** (from the Latin words *stella cometa* meaning 'hairy star') are **luminous** heavenly objects made up of clumps of ice which revolve round the Sun. These have a bright head and a tail which always points away from the Sun. They move around the Sun in regular orbits but these orbits are elongated so that it takes hundreds or thousands of years to complete one revolution around the Sun. They are made up of frozen gases, for example water vapour, ammonia, methane and carbon dioxide. They become visible only when they travel closer to the Sun, when the ice on these comets melt and the gas and dust is swept back into a tail.

---

**elongated:** long and thin; lengthened; impact: the force with which one object hits another; **luminous:** an object that emits light; bright or shining

## Explore

In 1609, Galileo Galilei heard of an invention from Holland known as the telescope. This object could make distant objects appear much closer. He decided to build his own telescope. He made great improvements to the telescope and began to use it to view the planets. Soon, Galileo's version of the telescope was being used throughout Europe. Galileo made many discoveries using his telescope including the four large Moons around Jupiter and the phases of the planet Venus. He also discovered the sunspots and learned that the Moon was not smooth, but was covered with craters.

Have you ever tried looking through a telescope? Imagine what Galileo Galilei saw and felt when he looked through the telescope for the first time and write a paragraph about it.

▲ Galileo

## World Connect

The Kepler Mission was launched by NASA to discover inner planets that have liquid water in the Milky Way and are habitable. NASA's Kepler mission has confirmed the existence of the first near Earth-size planet, in the 'habitable zone' around a Sun-like star. The newly discovered Kepler-452b is the smallest planet till date to be discovered orbiting in the habitable zone — the area around a star where liquid water could pool on the surface of an orbiting planet — of a G2-type star, like the Sun.

## Recall

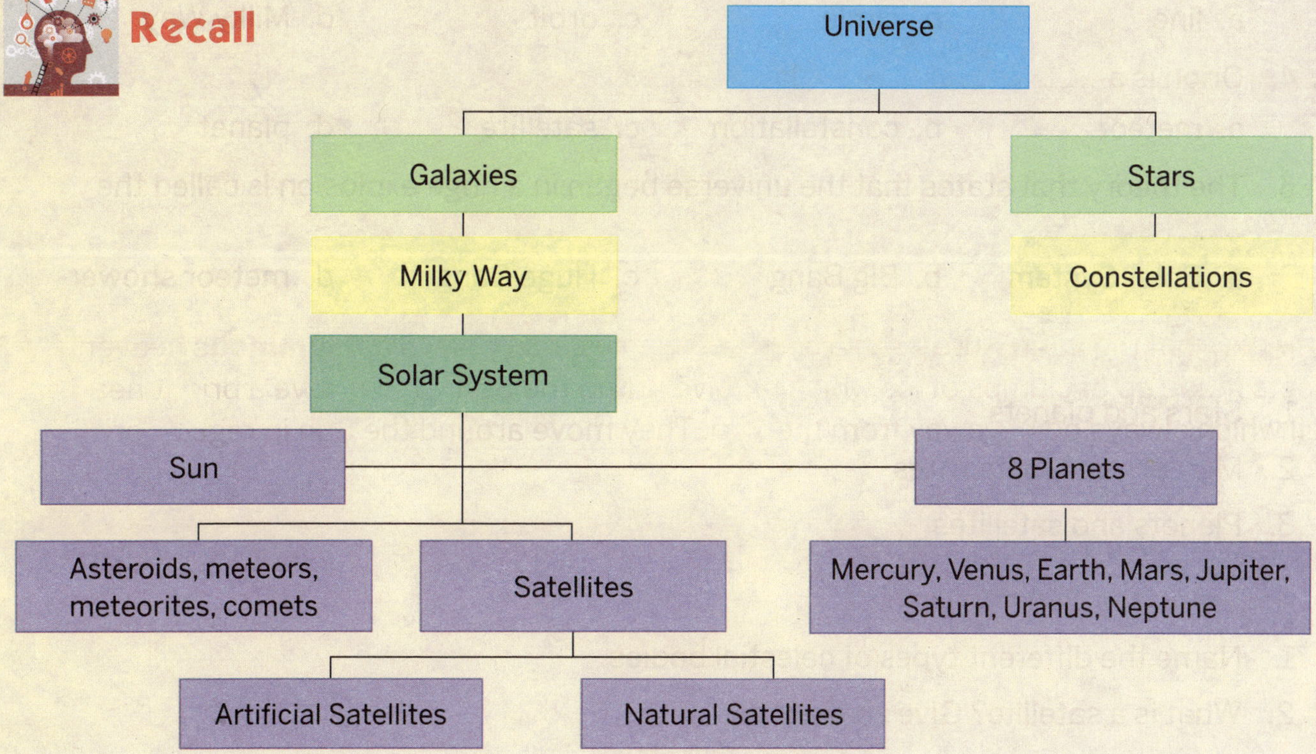

## Work out

A. Fill in the blanks.

1. Scientists have calculated the age of the Universe to be about .................... billion years.
2. The Milky Way is also called the .................... .
3. .................... is also known as the 'morning star'.
4. .................... is also called the 'Red Planet.
5. Meteors are commonly known as .................... stars.
6. .................... appear as beautiful shining bodies with long tails in the sky.

B. Fill in the blanks with the correct answers.

1. The system where eight planets and other celestial bodies move round the Sun is called the .................... .

   a. Sun System  b. Solar System  c. Celestial System  d. Universe

2. The fiery ball of gas and dust that provides the Earth with energy is called the .................... .

   a. Sun  b. Moon  c. Planets  d. Comet

3. The path of a planet around the Sun is called .................... .

   a. line  b. circle  c. orbit  d. Milky Way

4. Orion is a .................... .

   a. meteor  b. constellation  c. satellite  d. planet

5. The theory that states that the universe began in a huge explosion is called the .................... .

   a. Solar System  b. Big Bang  c. Huge Bang  d. meteor shower

C. Distinguish between these terms.

1. Stars and planets
2. Meteors and meteorites
3. Planets and satellites

D. Answer these questions in brief.

1. Name the different types of celestial bodies.
2. What is a satellite? Give an example.

3. Why do you always see the same face of the moon?
4. What are shooting stars?

E. Answer these questions in detail.

1. Explain why is the Earth called a unique planet.
2. Describe the composition of the Solar System.
3. Write a short note on the Moon.
4. Name the inner planets and write a short note on them.
5. What are the features of the outer planets?

## Think

Look at the picture and answer the questions.

1. What do you see glittering in the sky?
2. Do you see these often in the region where you live?
3. Why can't we see them very often in large cities?

## Life skills and values

In a mixture of flour and dry chocolate milk, drop marbles to form craters. You will see craters with elevated edges, and some with a series of splashed out materials centered on the crater. This is what the surface of the Moon looks like.

## Enjoy

Conduct a star gazing activity in school. Try to:
Spot the constellation, the Great Bear and the North Star.
Try to distinguish the twinkling of the stars from the planets.

## Web link

For more information, log on to:

https://spaceplace.nasa.gov/starfinder2/en/

Last accessed on 30 September, 2019

# 2 Globes: Latitudes and Longitudes

## Take off

- .............................................. is visible by the naked eye every 75–76 years.
- The universe came into existence after a gigantic explosion called the ............................ .

## Warm up

Why do you think it takes so long to travel from one place to another even by air? How do you think the lady in the picture missed a day?

We have already learnt that in the ancient times, people thought that the Earth was flat. As the new discoveries were made, people came to realize that the Earth was not flat but round. Today, we are able to see satellite images of the Earth from space depicting its shape and size. Its shape has been described as **oblate spheroid** which means that it bulges in the middle and is slightly flattened at the poles. This fact established by the Greek astronomers in the 3rd century and soon afterwards, a globe was constructed which proved to be the most accurate model of the Earth.

## Globes

A **globe** is a spherical model of the Earth. Globes come in various sizes and types. We all know that the Earth tilts on its **axis**. Similarly, a globe tilts on its **axle**. It can be rotated on its axle in the same manner as a top is spun. The axis of the Earth is tilted at an angle of 23½ degrees. Similarly, a globe tilts on its axle at the same angle. In a globe, the axle joins the two poles of the globe. It can represent the surface features, directions and distances of the Earth accurately.

▲ **Globe, a spherical model of the Earth**

As the Earth is spherical, it does not have corners, sides, a top or a bottom. At the ends of the axis are the **poles**. The **North Pole** is at

**axis:** an imaginary line through the middle of something; **axle:** a bar or shaft on which a wheel or other rotating member revolves the northern end and **South Pole** is at the southern end. Hence, it becomes difficult for us to locate places on the Earth. Therefore, we use certain lines and points of reference called latitudes and longitudes.

## Latitudes

**Latitude** is the distance, measured in degrees, north and south of the **equator**. It is measured with 180 imaginary lines that form circles around the Earth. Lines of latitude circle the globe in an east-west direction parallel to the equator. The distance between lines of latitude is always the same. They are also known as **parallels of latitude**. Each parallel of latitude is a circle. As the circumference of the Earth gets smaller toward the poles, the lines of latitude are shorter near the poles.

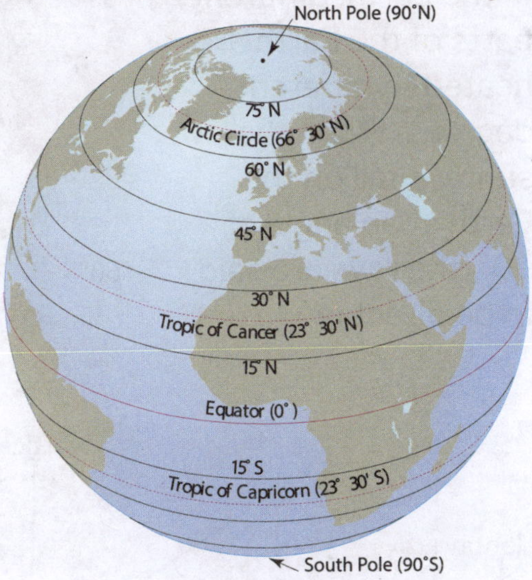

▲ Latitudes

The **equator** is at 0° latitude. It divides the Earth into two halves, the **Northern Hemisphere** and the **Southern Hemisphere**. All lines of latitude have numbers between 0° and 90° and a direction, north or south of the equator. The North Pole is at 90°N and the South Pole is at 90°S.

### Important Lines of Latitude

- **Tropic of Cancer(23½° N):** It marks the northernmost limit of the overhead Sun. It lies in the Northern Hemisphere.
- **Tropic of Capricorn(23½° S):** It marks the southernmost limit of the overhead Sun. It lies in the Southern Hemisphere.
- **Arctic Circle(66½° N):** It marks the northernmost point at which the Sun appears above the level of the horizon on the winter solstice.
- **Antarctic Circle(66½° S):** It marks the southernmost point at which the Sun appears above the level of the horizon at the winter solstice.

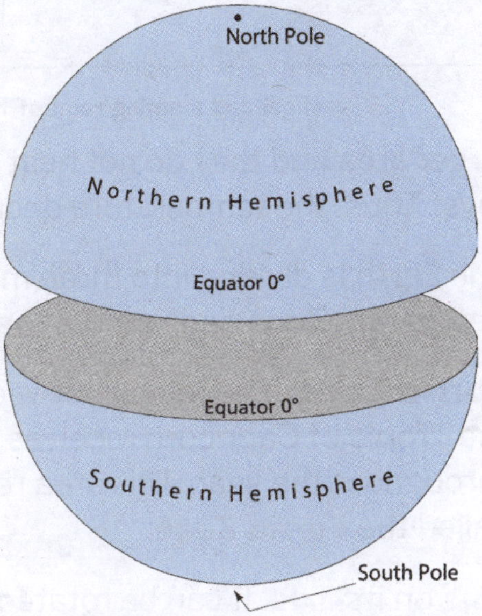

▲ Northern and Southern Hemisphere

## Climatic Zones of the Earth

Hold a torch and shine it once vertically on the floor and then at a slant, that is, at an angle. You will notice that vertical beam is bright and slanted beam spreads over a larger area and its brightness decreases because the same amount of light is now distributed over a larger surface.

This also explains why the vertical rays of the Sun are hotter than the slanting ones. Due to the spherical shape of the Earth, different parts of the Earth are heated to different degrees. When the sunrays fall on the Earth at an angle of 90°, the rays are said to be direct or **vertical**.

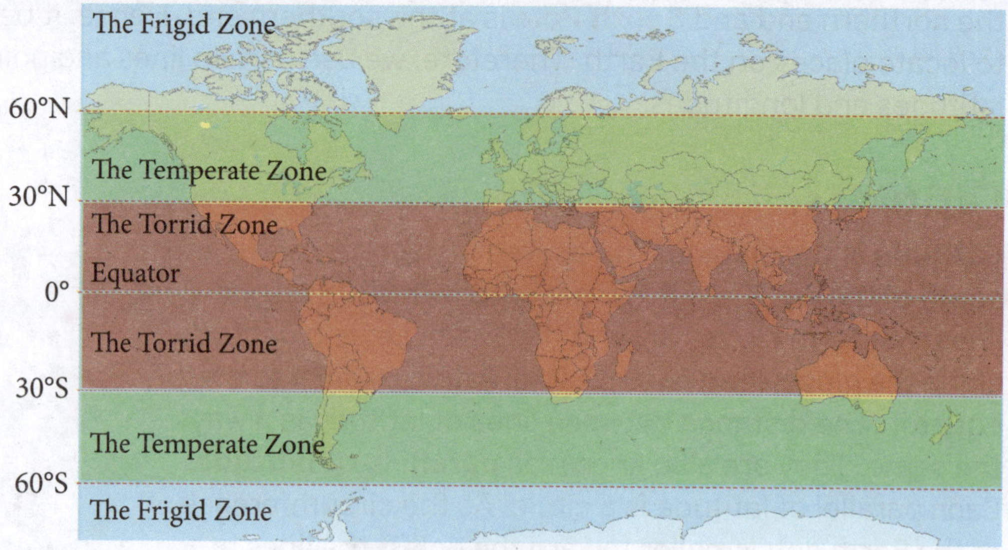


▲ **Climatic Zones of the Earth**

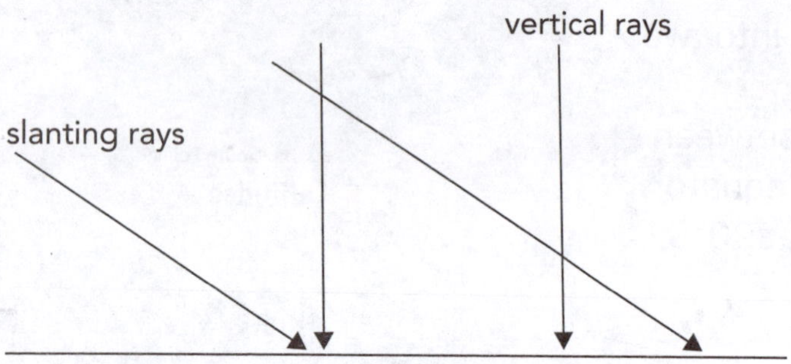


▲ **vertical and slanting rays of the Sun**

When the sunrays fall on the Earth at an angle less than 90°, the rays are said to be **slanting**. The region near the equator gets more direct rays. The direct vertical rays are concentrated over a smaller area so it heats up the Earth more. As we go away from the Equator, the Sun's rays reach the Earth's surface at an angle due to the curvature of the Earth. The slanting rays spread over a larger area and they do not heat the surface of the Earth to the same extent as do the vertical rays. Thus, the temperature decreases with the increasing distance from the equator.

The Earth is divided into three main Climatic zones—Torrid Zone, Temperate Zone and Frigid Zone.

**Torrid Zone:** The region between the Tropic of Cancer and the Tropic of Capricorn receives direct rays of the Sun almost throughout the year. This area receives maximum heat and is called the **Torrid Zone**.

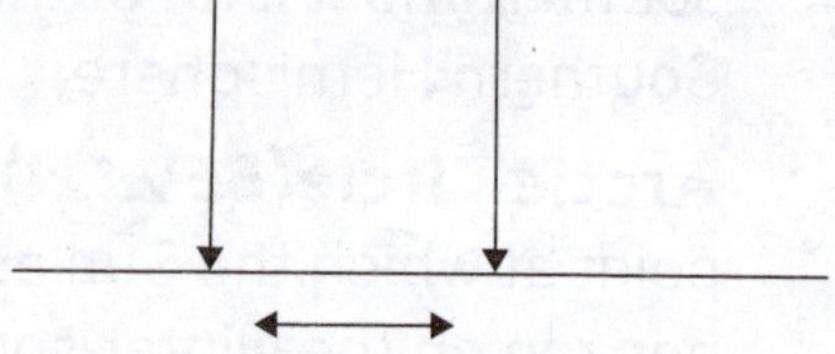

▲ **The rays of the Sun fall directly on the Torrid Zone**

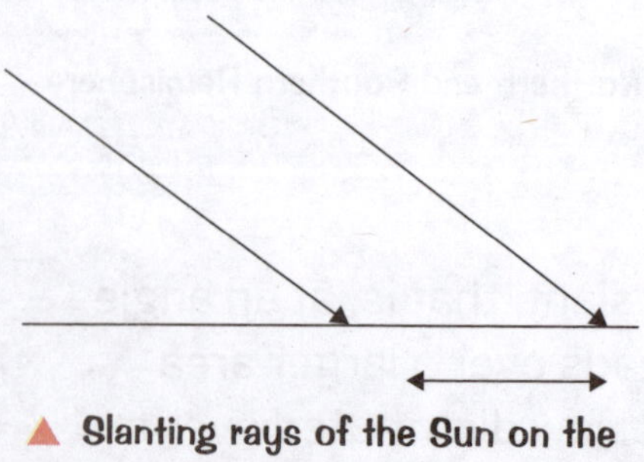

▲ **Slanting rays of the Sun on the Temperate Zone**

**Temperate Zone:** The regions between the Tropic of Cancer and the Arctic Circle in the Northern Hemisphere, and the Tropic of Capricorn and the Antarctic Circle in the Southern Hemisphere, are moderately hot. This is because the angle of the Sun's rays decreases as we move towards the poles. These areas have moderate temperatures and are called the **Temperate Zones**.

**Frigid Zone:** Near the Polar Regions, the rays of the Sun are very slanted and it is very cold. The regions between the Arctic Circle and the North Pole in the Northern Hemisphere, and in the Southern Hemisphere, between the Antarctic Circle and the South Pole are called the **Frigid Zones**.

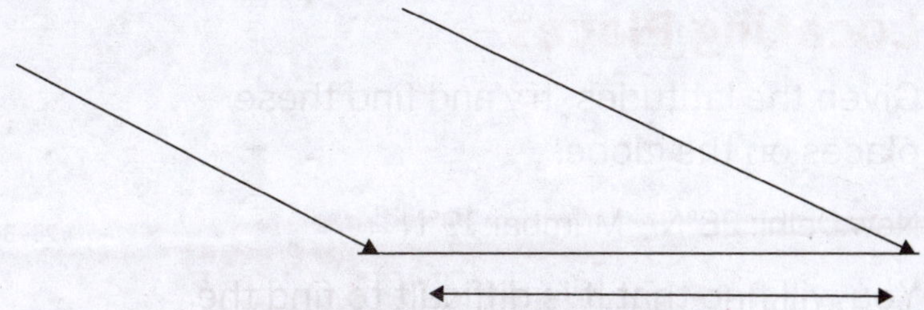

▲ Slanting rays of the Frigid Zone

## Longitudes

Longitudes are the imaginary lines that join the poles in a north-south direction. They are also called **meridians**, and are used to measure how far east or west the location of a place is. They measure the angular distance of a place on the surface of the Earth. The **prime meridian** is the line of longitude, corresponding to 0°and passing through Greenwich, England, from which all the other lines of longitude are calculated. On the opposite side of the Earth is the 180° meridian, which is the **International Date Line**. All lines of longitude have numbers between 0° and 180° and a direction, east or west of the prime meridian. The prime meridian divides the Earth into two halves, the **Eastern Hemisphere** and the **Western Hemisphere**.

### Fact quest

The word 'meridian' is derived from the Latin word meridanium, meaning noon. AM stands for ante meridiem meaning before midday or noon. PM stands for post meridiem meaning after midday or noon.

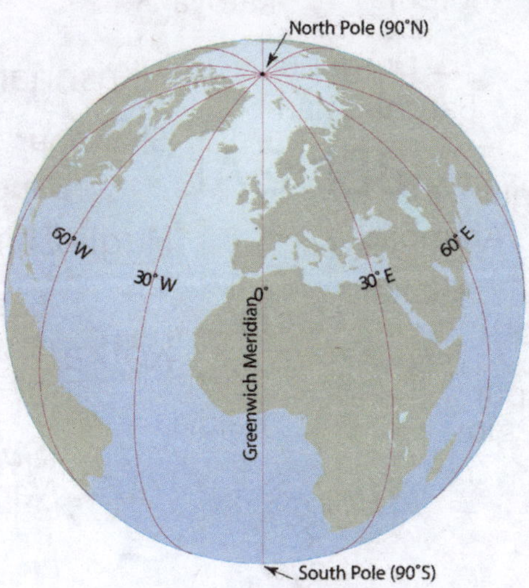


▲ Longitudes

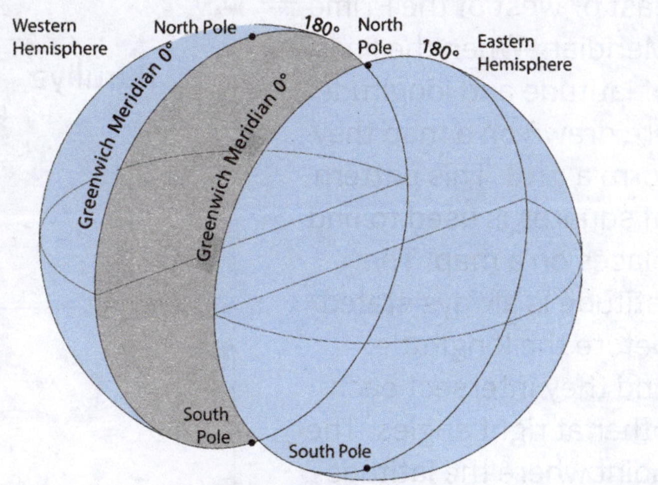


▲ Western and Eastern Hemisphere

As longitudes join the poles, they are always the same length, but are farthest apart at the equator and closest together at poles.

## Locating Places

Given the latitudes, try and find these places on the globe.

New Delhi: 28°N    Mumbai: 19°N

You will find that it is difficult to find the exact location with the help of the latitudes only. New Delhi can be anywhere along the latitude of 30° N, and Mumbai can be anywhere along the latitude 19° N. You need to know something else to fix its position. It will be easy to locate New Delhi on the globe knowing that the longitude of New Delhi is 78° E, and that of Mumbai is 72° E.

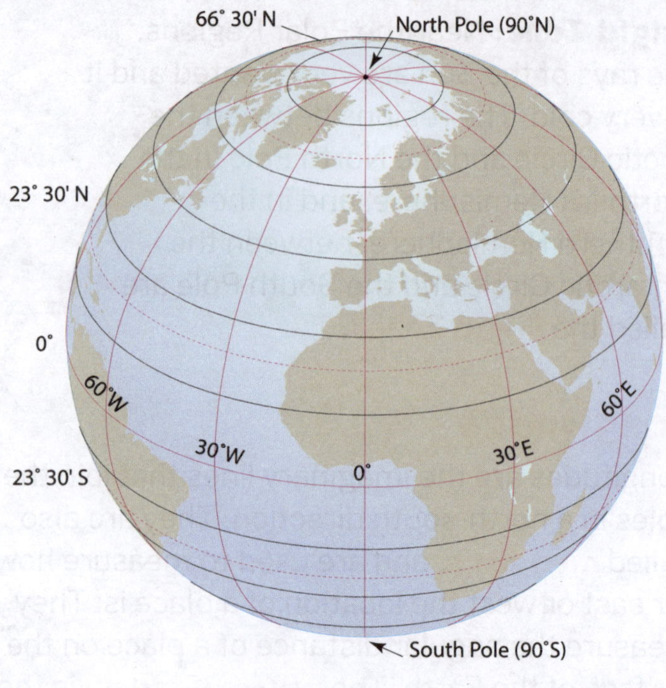


▲ Earth's grid

Look at the map and find out the geographical coordinates of point A.

Lines of latitude help us to locate places on the Earth, north or south of the equator. Similarly, longitudes help us to locate places on the Earth east or west of the Prime Meridian. When the lines of latitude and longitude are drawn on a map they form a **grid**. This pattern of squares is used to find places on a map. The latitude is always stated before the longitude, and they intersect each other at right angles. The point where the latitude and longitude of a place intersect gives us the exact location or the geographical **coordinates**

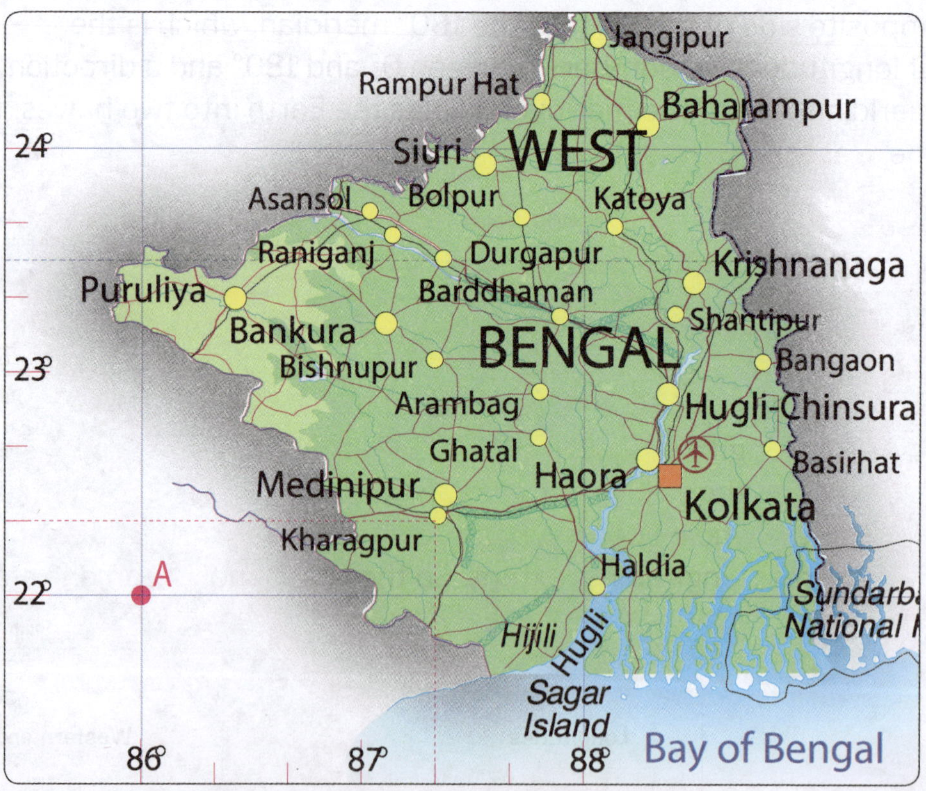


▲ Geographical coordinates of point A

of a place. The geographical coordinates are used to tell the exact location of a ship or an aircraft. To be even more accurate in locating a place, each degree of latitude and longitude is further divided into smaller units called **minutes**. There are 60 minutes in each degree.

## Longitude and Time

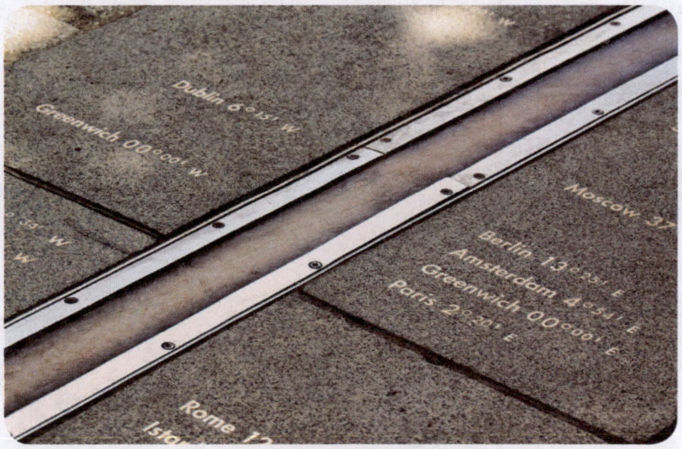

▲ Greenwich meridian

A relationship exists between the lines of longitude and time. In order to maintain uniformity, a standard time, corresponding to the location of the Prime Meridian is adopted by all countries. Every place in the world calculates time based on the **Greenwich Mean Time (GMT)**. Zone Times are the Standard Times kept on land and sea compared with 12 hours(noon) GMT. Every 15 degrees east or west of the Greenwich Meridian the time changes by 1 hour. East is ahead and west is behind Greenwich Mean Time. A time zone is a region throughout which the same standard time is used. There are 24 time zones in the world, demarcated approximately by meridians at 15° intervals, an hour apart.

**Local Time:** All places on the same meridian of longitude have noon at the same time. This is called the local time of that particular place. Places located on different meridians have different local time. The Earth takes 24 hours to complete one rotation, that is, it takes 24 hours to complete 360° of its rotation.

In 1 hour, the Earth rotates 360°/24 = 15° longitudes

If the Earth takes 60 minutes to rotate 15°, for 1° the Earth takes 60mins/15 = 4 mins

Hence, a difference of 1° longitude, creates a time difference of 4 minutes.

**Standard Time:** India has about 30 local times. To make a railway time table or a flight time table considering so many local timings will create lots of confusion. To avoid this confusion, the local time of a central meridian is taken as the standard time for the whole country. In India, the longitude of 82˜° E (82° 30'E), which passes through Mirzapur in Uttar Pradesh is treated as the standard meridian. The local time at this meridian is taken as the standard time for the whole country. It is known as the **Indian Standard Time (IST)**. Some countries have a great longitudinal extent. So they have more than one standard time. For example, the United States of America has five time zones.

### International Date Line

**The International Date Line (IDL)** is an imaginary line of longitude, on the Earth's surface. It is 180 degrees east or west of the Prime Meridian. The IDL separates two calendar days. The date towards the east of the IDL in the eastern hemisphere is one day earlier. As one crosses the IDL towards the west the time zone changes and a day is added.

**Find out**

Find out why does one say Sun rises in the east.

▲ Time zones of the world

## Explore

1. Which are the continents through which the Equator passes?
2. Which island lies at the intersection of 15° S latitude and 45° E longitude?
3. India lies between latitude and longitude.
4. Name two countries through which the Prime Meridian passes.

## World Connect

In 1675 the Royal Observatory was built at Greenwich to help ships find their bearings at sea. The Greenwich Mean Time (GMT) began as a standard time. Now, all places on earth are divided into standard time zones and UTC (Coordinated Universal Time) is the time standard of the world. All other parts of the world are offset (plus or minus) according to their longitudes.

Many countries follow daylight saving time, which is designed to allow people to enjoy more waking hours during daylight. In most of the United States, clocks are brought one hour forward in the spring. They fall back one hour in the fall.

## Recall

**Imaginary Lines**

- **Parallels of Latitudes** — Circle the Earth in east-west direction
  - **Heat Zones of the Earth**
    - Torrid Zone
    - Temperate Zone
    - Frigid Zone
  - **Important Latitudes**
    - Equator (0° )
    - Tropic of Cancer (23½°N)
    - Tropic of Capricorn (23½° S)
    - Arctic Circle (66½° N)
    - Antarctic Circle (66½° S)
- **Meridians of Longitudes** — Join the poles in north-south direction
  - **Important Longitudes**
    - Prime Meridian (0°)
    - International Date Line (180°)
  - **Time Zones**
    - 0° Greenwich Mean Time (GMT)
    - 82° E Indian Stamdard Time (IST)

## Work out

**A. Fill in the blanks.**

1. The Earth rotates on its .................................... .
2. The .................................... divides the Earth in the Northern and the Southern Hemispheres.
3. The line joining the North Pole and the South Pole is called the .................................... .
4. The 66½°N latitude is called the .................................... Circle.
5. Maximum heat is received in the .................................... zone.

**B. Fill in the blanks with the correct answers.**

1. We have a total of .................................... parallels of latitudes.
   a. 180° b. 90° c. 80° d. 181
2. The Arctic Circle and the Antarctic Circle are situated at .................................... and .................................... .
   a. 23½°N and 23½°S b. 66½° N and 66½CS c. 0° N
3. The network of criss-cross lines is called a .................................... .
   a. parallel b. longitude c. grid d. hemisphere
4. The Standard Meridian of India is .................................... .
   a. 82½°W b. 82½°E c. 180° d. 66° N
5. The most important meridian is the Prime Meridian, which is the .................................... longitude.
   a. 180° b. 0° c. 90° d. 23½°

**C. Distinguish between.**

1. Latitudes and longitudes
2. Local time and Standard Time
3. Torrid Zone and Frigid Zone
4. Northern Hemisphere and Southern Hemisphere

**D. Answer these questions in brief.**

1. What do you mean by the lines of latitude?
2. Name the important lines of latitude.

3. Define a longitude.
4. What is local time?
5. What is Greenwich Meridian

E. Answer these questions in detail.

1. Describe the climatic zones of the Earth.
2. What is the relationship between longitude and time?
3. Why do we use standard time?
4. Explain with the help of a diagram, how the vertical rays of the Sun cover a smaller area as compared to the area covered by the same amount of slanting rays.
5. Where does frigid zone located and why is it called so?
6. How do latitudes and longitudes help to locate places?

## Think

A Wimbledon match is being played at 2:00 pm in England. When can the viewers in India watch it?

## Life skills and values

Carefully study the position of five places on the Earth's surface and then answer the questions:

1. Which place is nearest to the Greenwich Meridian?
2. Which place is closest to the equator?
3. Which place is closest to the North Pole?
4. Which place is closest to the International Date Line?
5. Which place lies closest to the Tropic of Cancer?

| Station | Latitude | Longitude |
|---|---|---|
| A | 75° E | 100° W |
| B | 20° N | 120° W |
| C | 15° S | 25° E |
| D | 25° N | 88° E |
| E | 40° S | 148° E |

## Enjoy

List five countries and note down the time difference between all these countries. Then make clocks for each of these countries.

For the clocks, you will need two paper plates, glue, markers, cardboard paper and a small nail.

1. Stick the two plates together using glue one on top of the other so your clock has a rim that is a different color from the face.
2. Stick the numbers (or write them) in their proper places.
3. Write the minutes with the marker.
4. Cut out the hour and minute hands and fasten them to the center of the plate with a small nail.

## Web link

For more information, log on to:
https://www.nationalgeographic.org/media/understanding-time-zones/

Last accessed on 30 September, 2019

# 3 Motions of the Earth

## Take off

- The shape of the Earth is called an ..................................................... .
- ..................................................... was the first explorer who proved that the Earth was round.

## Warm up

How do you think the movement of the Earth affects the seasons?

In ancient times, people believed that the Earth was stationary, and the heavenly bodies moved around it. In 1530 BCE, **Nicolaus Copernicus**, a Polish astronomer, proposed that the Earth spins on its axis once every day and also revolves around the Sun once in a year. He was right. Not only does the Earth rotate on its axis but it also revolves around the Sun. The Earth is in constant motion. The movement of the Earth around its axis is called **rotation**. The movement of the Earth around the Sun is called **revolution**. Both these movements take place simultaneously.

## Rotation of the Earth

The Earth spins on its axis from east to west. The axis of the Earth is inclined at an angle of 23½° vertically and 66½° from the plane of the Earth's orbit. The tilt of the Earth's axis is called the **inclination** of the Earth's axis. This inclination of the axis causes the unequal duration of day and night at different places. It also causes a difference in temperature between different regions of the Earth. Without the inclination of the Earth's axis, there would be no distinct change of seasons. It is due to the inclination of the Earth's axis that the poles have six months of daylight

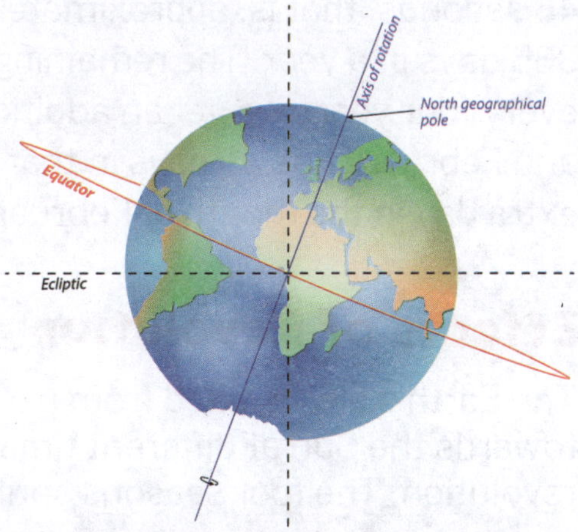


▲ Inclination of the Earth's axis

and six months of night. It takes about 24 hours to complete one rotation. One rotation is equivalent to one Earth day.

### Effects of Rotation

The rotation of the Earth has the following effects:

- It causes the daily cycle of day and night. At any one given moment in time, one half of the Earth is in sunlight, while the other half, facing away from the Sun, is in darkness. As the Earth rotates it also creates the apparent movement of the Sun from east to west across the sky.
- The rotation of the Earth causes tides.
- The rotation of an Earth exerts an outward force near the equator creating an **equatorial bulge** and flattening of the Earth near the poles.

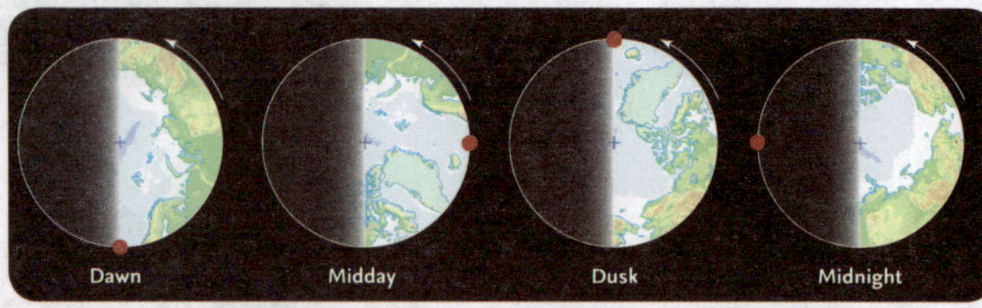

▲ Day and night

Due of the Earth's spherical shape, only one half of the Earth faces the Sun at a time and receives sunlight. The imaginary line that divides the part of the Earth which has day from the part of the Earth which has night is called the **circle of illumination**. Different places on the Earth get varying amounts of sunlight at different times of the day. This is why in a day we have dawn, sunrise, mid-day, sunset, dusk and midnight.

**Find out**

What are the 'Northern Lights' and where can we see them?

## Revolution

The movement of the Earth around the Sun, is called revolution. The Earth moves around the Sun along an elliptical path called the orbit. As the orbit is **elliptical**, the distance between the Sun and the Earth changes with motion.

The Earth completes one revolution in 365 days 48 minutes and 45 seconds, that is, approximately 365.25 days. we count only 365 days in a year. The remaining six hours are added up and after every four years we get an additional day. Such a year has 366 days and February has 29 days in that year and is called a **leap year**. The extra day in the month of February is called a leap day.

**Find out**

Why has an extra day been added to the month of February only?

## Effects of Revolution

The Earth's axis is tilted from perpendicular therefore different parts of the Earth are oriented towards the Sun at different times of the year. The change of seasons is a direct effect of revolution. The four seasons spring, summer, autumn and winter are a result of this.

**elliptical:** has the shape of an ellipse which is an oval shape similar to a circle but longer and flatter

**Solstices:** Twice in a year, the Earth is at a maximum distance from the Sun. The days on which this phenomenon occurs are called **summer solstices** or **winter solstices**. In the Northern Hemisphere, the summer solstice occurs on the 20 June or 21 June. The winter solstice in the Northern Hemisphere occurs on 21 December or 22 December. The situation is exactly the opposite in the Southern Hemisphere. Therefore, the summer solstice in the Southern Hemisphere occurs on 21 December or 22 December. On 20 June or 21 June the Southern Hemisphere experiences the winter solstice. During solstices, the rays of the Sun shine directly on one of the two tropics. During the June or the summer solstice, the rays of the Sun fall directly on the Tropic of Cancer and during December or the winter solstice, the Sun's rays fall directly on the Tropic of Capricorn.

**Fact quest**

Near the poles, the Sun does not set for six months. That is why the areas around the poles are called **Land of the Midnight Sun.** Hundreds of tourists flock to Norway in summer to see the Sun shining at midnight.

**Equinoxes:** Twice in a year, the Sun shines directly above the equator. These days are called the equinoxes. During the equinoxes, the lengths of the days and nights are equal. The **vernal equinox** marks the beginning of the spring in the Northern Hemisphere. It occurs on 21 March. The **autumnal equinox** occurs on 23 September. Look at the diagram to understand the solstices and equinoxes.

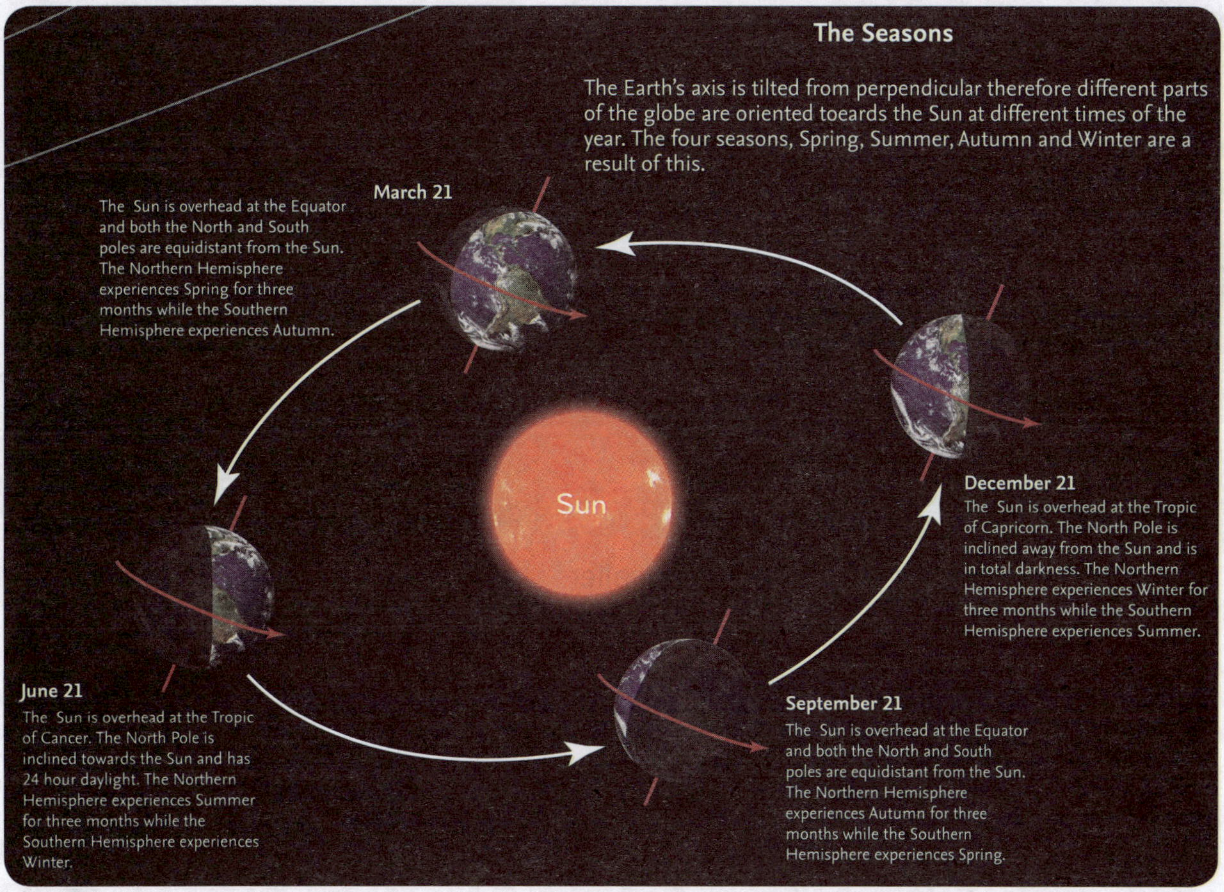


▲ Changing seasons

## Explore

There are many places on Earth that experience little or no change in seasons throughout the year. Find out five places on Earth that have more or less the same weather throughout the year and state the reason behind this phenomenon.

## World Connect

The Kyoto Protocol is an international agreement linked to the United Nations Framework Convention on Climate Change, which commits its Parties by setting internationally binding emission reduction targets. The Kyoto Protocol was adopted in Kyoto, Japan, on 11 December 1997 and began to be enforced only from February 2005.

Recognizing that developed countries are principally responsible for the current high levels of Greenhouse Gases (GHG) emissions in the atmosphere as a result of more than 150 years of industrial activity, the Protocol places a heavier burden on developed nations under the principle of "common but differentiated responsibilities."

The Kyoto Protocol is seen as an important first step towards a truly global emission reduction regime that will stabilize greenhouse gas emissions, and can provide the architecture for the future international agreement on climate change.

*–Source: United Nations Climate Change*

## Recall

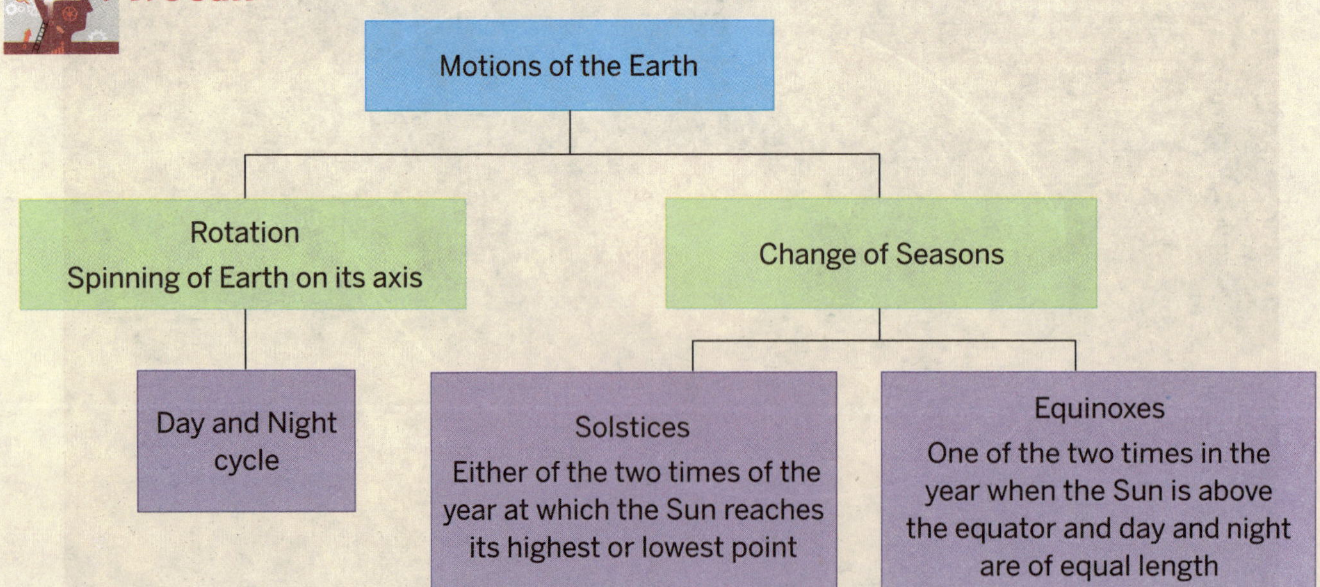

## Work out

A. Fill in the blanks.

1. The Earth rotates from .......................... to .......................... .
2. The axis of the Earth is inclined at an angle of .......................... degrees.
3. At the .......................... the length of days and nights are always equal.
4. The Earth tilts on its .......................... .
5. On 21 March the Sun's rays fall vertically at the .......................... .

B. Distinguish between the following.

1. Solstice and Equinox
2. Day and Night
3. Rotation and Revolution

C. Answer these questions in brief.

1. Name the two motions of the Earth.
2. List any two effects of rotation.
3. What do you mean by the summer solstice?
4. What is a leap year?
5. When are days and nights equal?

D. Answer these questions in detail.

1. What causes the changes in the seasons.
2. The Northern and the Southern hemispheres experience different seasons at the same time of the year. Give geographical reasons for this phenomenon.
3. With the help of a diagram explain the cycle of seasons.

## Think

David and Susan live in Argentina in South America. On which dates of the year will they experience

1. equal days and equal nights
2. the longest day and
3. the shortest day.

## Life skills and values

What would life on the Earth be like if it did not tilt on its axis?

## Enjoy

The places around the poles and equator do not witness seasonal changes as seen in the other regions on the Earth. Different seasons only lead to a change in the amount of sunlight and darkness in these areas. Collect more information on it and make a Power Point presentation.

## Web link

For more information, log on to:

https://www.nationalgeographic.org/media/earths-tides/

Last accessed on 30 September, 2019

# 4 Understanding Maps

## Take off

- We use .................................. maps when we want to know about the physical features of a place.
- The needle of a compass always points to the .................................. .

## Warm up

What kind of symbols would you use if you were to make a map for a treasure hunt?

We have already learnt that the Earth is a sphere, and the most accurate model of the Earth is a globe. Globes are round and provide the truest possible view of the entire Earth. But can you find out all about the Earth by looking only at a globe? Can you find out information about the city in which you live by looking only at a globe? No, to find out such detailed information we would need an extremely large globe. So, when we want to find out information about places on the Earth we use a **map**.

The word 'map' comes from the Latin word *mappa*, meaning cloth, as many of the earliest maps were drawn on skins, **parchment** and cloth. A map gives information about the Earth's surface in a simple and graphic manner and helps us to understand where we are in relation to other people and places.

A map is a representation of the Earth or a part of it on a flat surface. A map is a better representation of the Earth than a globe because a map can show large areas on a single piece of paper making it easy to compare cities, countries and other places. Also, a map can be rolled or folded and stored or carried around easily.

## Fact quest

The most famous ancient maps of the world were made in the second century CE by the Greek scholar, Claudius Ptolemy. He based his drawings on mathematical calculations, along with information provided by sailors and explorers.

**parchment:** a material that was used in that past for writing

## Types of Maps

There are different types of maps. The three categories of maps are—**political**, **physical** and **thematic**. These maps are categorized according to their function.

> **Find out**
>
> What is the art of making maps called?

**Political map:** Political maps show the countries of the world. It can also show parts of nations, such as states, and the borders between the states.

**Physical map:** Physical maps are small-scale maps, which show the surface of the Earth, or specific parts of it. Mountains, valleys, rivers, plains, and many other features that depict the topography of a place are shown on these types of maps.

**Thematic map:** 'Thematic' comes from the word 'theme' meaning an idea or a topic. Such maps are also called distribution maps. Distribution means 'dividing into parts or shares'. Thematic maps represent particular features, such as weather, roads, distribution of population, rainfall, crops and minerals.

▲ Physical Map

▲ Political Map

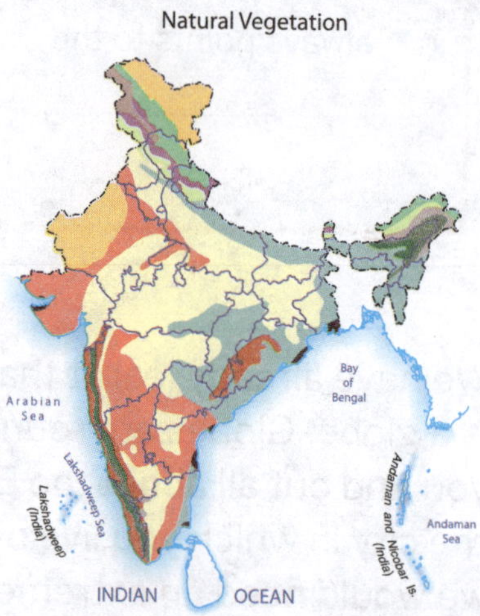


▲ Thematic Map

## Components of a Map

There are three main components of maps—**distance**, **direction** and **conventional symbols**.

### Measuring Distance on Map

Distance between any two points on a map may be measured in centimetres using a **scale**. The scale of a map may be used to calculate the actual distance between the two points on the ground. For example, if the distance between two points P and Q on a map, is 2.5 cm, and the scale of the map is 1 cm to 2 km, then the distance between the two points on ground will be 2.5 × 2 = 5.0 km.

A map can be drawn to many different scales depending on its purpose.

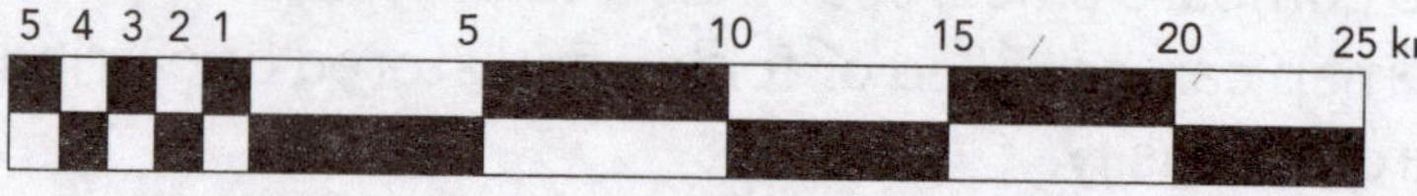


▲ Map scale

**Small-scale maps** represent large areas of the Earth. They are used to show a small amount of detail about a large area. A political map and most maps in an atlas are examples of small scale maps.

**Large-scale maps** cover a small area of the Earth. They are used to show a large amount of information about a small area. City guide maps are examples of large scale maps as they show streets and important buildings of a neighbourhood.

### Explore

Take a look at any thematic map from an atlas. Write a report on it. You can base your report on the following observations:

1. Type of map
2. Information given in the map
3. Scale of the map
4. Conventional signs and symbols used and what they represent
5. Colours used in the map and what each colour represents

## Directions on a Map

The four directions—north, south, east and west are known as the four **cardinal directions.** You already know that the Sun rises in the east and sets in the west. If we face the Sun in the morning we are facing east and west is behind us. If we spread out our hands sideways, our left hand points towards the north and our right hand points towards the south. Earlier, sailors would follow the Pole Star for heading northwards. Now they use a compass wherein the needle always points to the north.

Using the cardinal directions we can find out the intermediate directions. For example, you can mark the direction between north (N) and east (E) as north-east (NE). Finding directions on a map is not difficult. On a map, the 'north line' (↑) points to the north. If the north line is not shown, the top of the map is considered as the north direction.

## Conventional Signs and Symbols

**Conventional** signs and symbols on maps are especially used in large-scale maps. Certain relief features and human activities can be shown, with the help of conventional signs and symbols. These signs and symbols are usually small pictures of the objects that they represent. With the help of these symbols, we get maximum information about the place.

Map makers or cartographers use symbols on a map for the following reasons:

- They give plenty of information in a small space.
- There is an understanding among the nations of the world regarding the use of these symbols. As the conventional symbols are followed throughout the world there is no confusion.

**conventional:** established by accepted usage or general agreement

- Maps can be drawn easily, quickly and are simple to read.

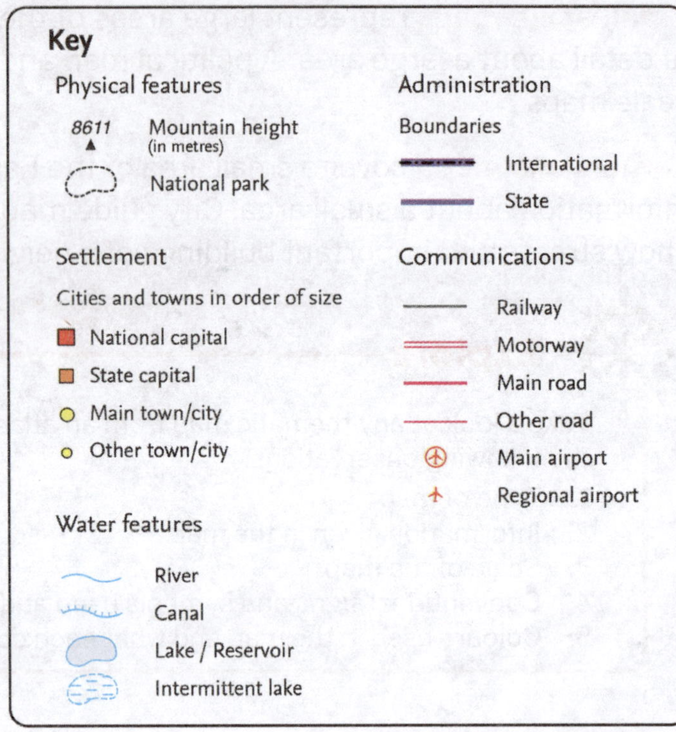


A **map legend** explains the symbols used on a map. It is called a legend because it tells the story of the map. It is also called a **map key** because it explains the meaning of the maps symbols.

Some common colour patterns used on small scale maps:

1. yellow—cultivated area
2. green—wooded land, covered with forest
3. black—dry rivers, streams, tank, well
4. blue—all perennial water bodies
5. red—roads, buildings, settlements
6. white—barren land
7. brown—**contour** lines, stony waste, sand features

An **atlas** is a collection of maps of the world, the continents or selected countries. Besides maps, an atlas may also include information and diagrams of the Earth in space, geographical features and population data.

## Sketches and Plans

Some maps are drawn hurriedly. They are not drawn according to scale. Such maps are called sketches**.** Sometimes maps are drawn at a very large scale. Such maps are called plans**.**

▲ **A sketch**

**contour:** a line joining points of equal height indicating hills, valleys, and the steepness of slopes on a map

## World Connect

**Cartography** has developed with technology. Technology has continually changed in order to meet the demands of new generations of mapmakers and map users. While scientists have long developed complete topographic maps of the Earth, the United States Geologic Survey, along with some prominent research institutions, released the first complete topographical map of Mercury. The map is **courtesy** of NASA's Mercury Surface Space Environment Geochemistry and Ranging (MESSENGER), the first spacecraft to ever orbit Mercury. MESSENGER was launched in 2004, and has orbited the planet 4,104 times, stitching together more than 100,000 images to form the final complete picture.

## Recall

- Understanding maps
  - Types of Maps & Components of a Map
    - – Political Map
    - – Physical Map
    - – Thematic Map
    - Scale
      - Used to calculate the actual distance between the two points on the ground
    - Directions
      - Cardinal Directions
      - Intermediate Directions
    - Signs and Symbols
      - Small pictures of the objects they represent
    - Map Key
      - Explains the symbols used on a map

## Work out

A. Fill in the blanks.

1. The Earth is .................................... in shape but .................................... at the poles.

---

**cartography:** the art of drawing maps; **courtesy:** doing something free of cost

2. The scale represents the ratio between the distances measured on .................................. with respect to the distance on the .................................. .
3. .................................. lies between north and east.
4. .................................. maps show the countries of the world.
5. Sometimes, the symbol on a map that shows direction, is called a .................................. .

B. Give a single technical term for the following.
1. A collection of maps, bound into a book.
2. Instrument used to find directions on the Earth.
3. Map showing mountains, plateaus, plains, rivers etc of an area.
4. The four directions of the compass—north, south, west and east

C. Write T for true and F for false.
1. Maps give plenty of information in a small place. ☐
2. If we face the Sun in the morning, we are facing west. ☐
3. The needle of the compass always points to the north. ☐
4. In small scale maps, the green colour represents wooded land covered by forests. ☐
5. Large-scale maps are more detailed than small-scale maps. ☐

D. Answer these questions in brief.
1. Name the types of large-scale maps.
2. What do you mean by the 'scale of a map'?
3. Name the four intermediate directions in map reading?
4. Name the basic elements of a map.

E. Give geographical reasons for the following.
1. Although the globe is the most accurate model of the Earth, a map is often preferred to a globe.
2. Mapmakers use symbols on a map.
3. A compass is a very important instrument for travellers.

## Think

Look at the picture and answer the questions.

1. Would you say this is a new map or an old map?
2. Is it a correct map of the Earth?
3. What are the differences that you see between this map and the one on your atlas?

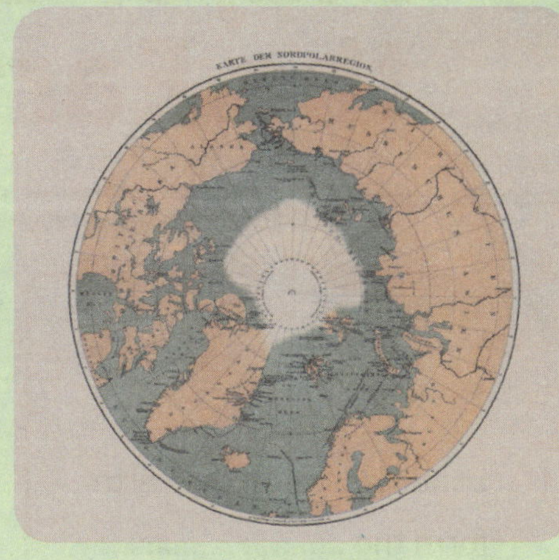

## Life skills and values

You have to invite your friends to your birthday party. Make a plan of the route to your house from the main bus stop. Make a sketch of your house.

## Enjoy

Using a map of India, answer these questions.

1. Which country borders India on the north-eastern side?
2. Which states does the Brahmaputra river flow through?
3. Which islands are located in the Arabian Sea?
4. Where are the Himalayan mountains located?
5. Which is the northern-most state?

## Web link

For more information, log on to:

https://www.nationalgeographic.org/encyclopedia/compass/

Last accessed on 30 September, 2019

# 5 Major Domains of the Earth

## Take off

- Landmasses on the Earth form the ...........................
- The vast expanse of air that surrounds the Earth is called the ....................................

## Warm up

What causes this difference in seasons between the countries in the Northern Hemisphere and those in the Southern Hemisphere?

We have already learnt that the Earth is the only planet in the solar system that sustains life. Life on the Earth is possible because of the presence of land, water and air.

The environment can be divided into two groups—**physical environment** and **biological environment**. The physical environment is made up land, air and water. It is essential for the existence of different forms of life. The biological environment, made of living things such as plants and animals is important for survival as it provides food.

Our environment consists of four realms or parts—the **lithosphere**, the **hydrosphere**, the **atmosphere** and the **biosphere**. The lithosphere is the solid surface of the Earth—the landmasses on which humans, animals and plants live. The oceans, seas, rivers and the other water bodies constitute, the hydrosphere. The atmosphere is a mixture of gases that surround the Earth.

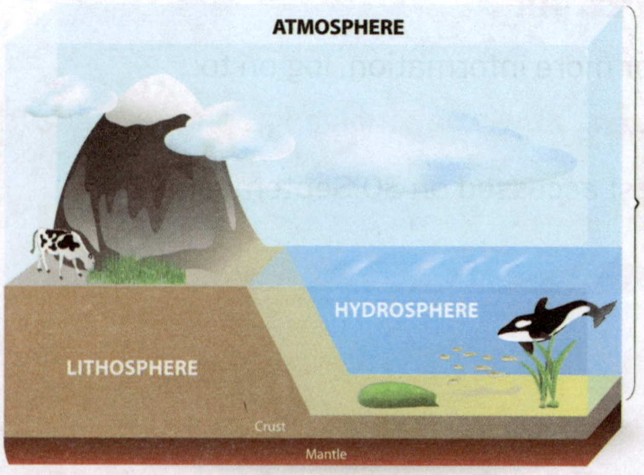


▲ Realms of the Earth

The part of the Earth where land, air and water meet and where plants and animals can live is called the biosphere.

## Lithosphere: The Realm of Rocks

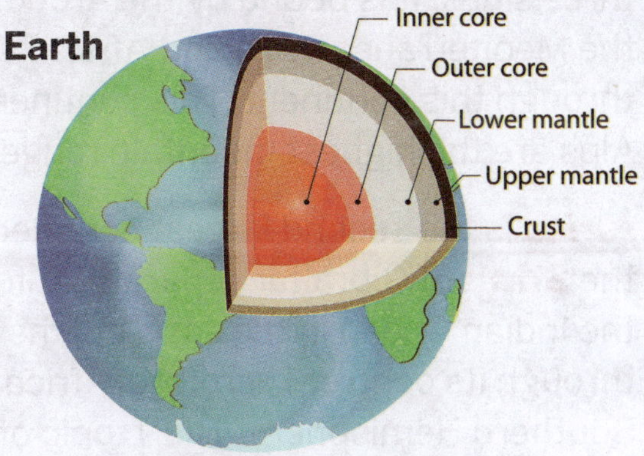

Layers of the Earth

The Earth is made up of different layers. The inner most layer of the Earth is called the **core**. It is the hottest layer of the Earth. The **mantle** is a layer of molten rock that surrounds the core. The crust is the upper-most part of the Earth, it is solid and rocky. The **crust** and the rigid upper layers of the mantle together form the **lithosphere**. Continental lithosphere forms the land and oceanic lithosphere forms the sea floor.

The lithosphere is not just one single continuous layer but made up of fragments called **lithospheric plates**. These plates float on the molten part of the mantle and often keep colliding or scraping with one another.

The lithosphere is important as it comprises of the land on which the human beings live. It consists of different rocks and minerals, including coal, precious stones and minerals used in production of energy.

### Continents

The huge landmasses on the Earth are called the **continents**. The Earth has seven major continents—Asia, Africa, Europe, North America, South America, Australia and Antarctica.

**Asia** lies in the Northern Hemisphere and covers one-third of the Earth's surface. It is the largest and the most populous continent in the world. It shares its borders with Africa and Europe in the west, the Pacific Ocean in the east and the Arctic Ocean in the north.

Himalayas

Asia is located entirely in the Northern Hemisphere. It is located to the east of the prime meridian in the Eastern Hemisphere and the Tropic of Cancer passes through it. Asia is separated from Europe by the Ural Mountains, the Black Sea and the Caspian Sea. The major geographical features of this continent are the Himalayas and the Ural Mountains.

The Grand Canal, Venice

**Europe** is the sixth largest continent in the world. It lies to the west of Asia. The continents Europe and Asia are together called **Eurasia**. Europe is a **peninsula** with water bodies surrounding it on

**peninsula:** a narrow strip of land projecting into a sea or lake from the mainland three sides. It is bound by the Arctic Ocean in the north, the Atlantic Ocean in the west and the Mediterranean Sea and Africa in the south. The prime meridian and the Arctic Circle pass through this continent. This continent is surrounded by high mountains and vast plains. The Alps are the highest mountain range of Europe. Mount Blanc is the highest peak of the Alps.

**Africa** is the second largest continent in the world. The Suez Canal separates it from Asia and the **Strait** of Gibraltar separates it from Europe. The Atlantic Ocean borders it in the west, the Indian Ocean in the east and the Mediterranean Sea in the north. The equator passes through its centre. Therefore, Africa lies partly in the Northern Hemisphere and partly in the Southern Hemisphere. The Tropic of Cancer passes through northern Africa and the Tropic of Capricorn passes through southern Africa. The Sahara Desert, the largest hot desert in the world is located in this continent.

**North America** is the third largest continent in the world, and it lies entirely in the Northern Hemisphere. It is bordered by the Atlantic Ocean in the east and the Pacific Ocean in the west. In the south, it is connected to South America by the **Isthmus** of Panama. About seventy-five per cent of North America is comprises of Canada and the USA. The Caribbean Islands also called the West Indies, and Greenland cover the rest of North America. The geographical features of North America include deserts, temperate forests, taiga vegetation and grasslands.

**South America** is the fourth largest continent in size and the fifth most populated continent in the world. Most of the continent lies in the Southern Hemisphere. The equator passes through the northernmost part of this continent. It is surrounded by the Atlantic Ocean in the east and the Pacific Ocean in the west. The geography of South America is dominated by the Andes Mountain Range, which is the longest mountain chain in the world and the Amazon River, which is the largest river in the world. South America is situated in the Western Hemisphere.

▲ Peru, South America

**Australia** lies entirely in the Southern Hemisphere. It is the smallest continent and is also called the **island continent**. It is located to the southeast of Asia. It is bordered by the Indian Ocean and the Pacific Ocean. New Zealand, New Guinea and several other islands in the Pacific Ocean together are known as Australasia. In terms of geographical features, Australia has rainforests, deserts, savannah vegetation and temperate forests. Some of the important geographical features are the Great Dividing Range, the Central Lowland, the Western Desert and the Great Barrier Reef.

**isthmus:** a narrow piece of land connecting two very large areas of land

## Explore

On 14 May 1501, Amerigo Vespucci set on what would be his most successful voyage. His ships travelled along the South American coast down to Patagonia. Along the way, he encountered the present-day Rio de Janeiro and Rio de la Plata. During this voyage, Vespucci realised that parts of the world that were considered a part of Asia, actually belonged to an entirely new continent. He proved this by sailing 400 miles south of Tierra del Fuego, the southernmost tip of South America. This confirmed that he had found a new continent that extended further south than anyone had guessed. During his voyage, Vespucci wrote letters to a friend in Europe describing his travels and identifying the New World as a separate continent from Asia.

- Which continent did Vespucci discover?
- What was the new continent that Vespucci discover named?

**Antarctica** is the fifth largest continent. It is the windiest, driest and iciest place on the Earth. It is located around the South Pole. Because of the thick ice cover that covers most of the continent, it is also known as the 'white continent' or the **frozen continent**.

▲ Nuuk, Greenland

Antarctica is surrounded by the Pacific Ocean, the Atlantic Ocean and the Indian Ocean. The continent has provided great scope for the scientific study of weather and lends itself as an ideal base for the establishment of scientific stations to several nations of the world. India's two research stations in Antarctica are named **Maitri** and **Dakshin Gangotri**.

## Hydrosphere: The Realm of Water

The Earth looks blue and watery when seen from the space. All the water on the surface of the earth, including oceans, lakes, glaciers, water vapor and clouds comprise the hydrosphere.

We know that two-thirds of the surface of the Earth is covered with water in the form of seas and oceans. Oceans are vast expanses of water, seas are comparatively smaller.

Let us learn about the oceans of the world.

## Oceans

There are five major oceans—the Pacific Ocean, the Atlantic Ocean, the Indian Ocean, the Arctic Ocean and the Southern Ocean. The world's largest seas are the South China Sea, the Caribbean Sea, the Mediterranean Sea and the Bering Sea.

The **Pacific Ocean** is the deepest and the largest ocean the world. It is bounded on the west by Asia and Australia. It is bounded on the east by North and South America. The Pacific Ocean covers nearly one-third of the Earth's surface. The ocean was named by the Portuguese explorer, Ferdinand Magellan and it means calm or **tranquil**. The **International Date Line** passes through the Pacific Ocean. The Mariana Trench, the deepest part of the world's oceans is located on this ocean.

### Fact quest

When the coastline is indented, deep water comes close to the harbour and provides a large entrance for ships.

A harbour sheltered in an indented coast is protected from strong winds and dangeroucs currents. Also, there is not a lot of silting.

The **Atlantic Ocean** is the second largest ocean. It is S-shaped and stretches longitudinally from the north to south. Its coastline is **indented**, which provides good sites for sheltered **harbours.** The shipping routes across the North Atlantic Ocean connect the two major manufacturing regions—North America and Western Europe. It is the busiest ocean for trade and commerce.

Scale 1 : 83 000 000  Eckert IV projection

**tranquil:** calm, peaceful or quiet; **indented:** uneven edges or surface with parts which have been worn away or cut away; **harbour:** a sheltered port

The **Indian Ocean** is the only ocean named after a country. It is bordered by Africa in the west, Asia in the north and Australia in the east.

**Arctic Ocean** is the smallest ocean. It lies within the Arctic Circle. The Bering Strait connects it with the Pacific Ocean. Most of the Arctic Ocean remains frozen for most of the year.

The **Southern Ocean** encircles the continent of Antarctica. It comprises the southern portions of the Pacific, the Atlantic and the Indian oceans.

## Atmosphere: The Realm of Air

The surface of the Earth is surrounded by a blanket of gases called the **atmosphere**. The atmosphere appears to be very thin but there are actually five distinct layers in the atmosphere—each with its own characteristics.

### Structure of the Atmosphere

The atmosphere has a layered structure. Layers form in the atmosphere as a result of temperature changes that occur at various altitudes. There are five distinct layers. They are the **troposphere**, the **stratosphere**, the **mesosphere**, the **thermosphere** and the **exosphere**.

The troposphere is the lowest layer of the atmosphere. It is the layer nearest to the surface of the Earth and helps the human habitation. It is the most important layer of the atmosphere. It contains almost ninety per cent of the total air of the atmosphere. The temperature in this layer decreases by one degree for every 165 m of elevation. Clouds, lightening and other weather **phenomena** occur in this layer.

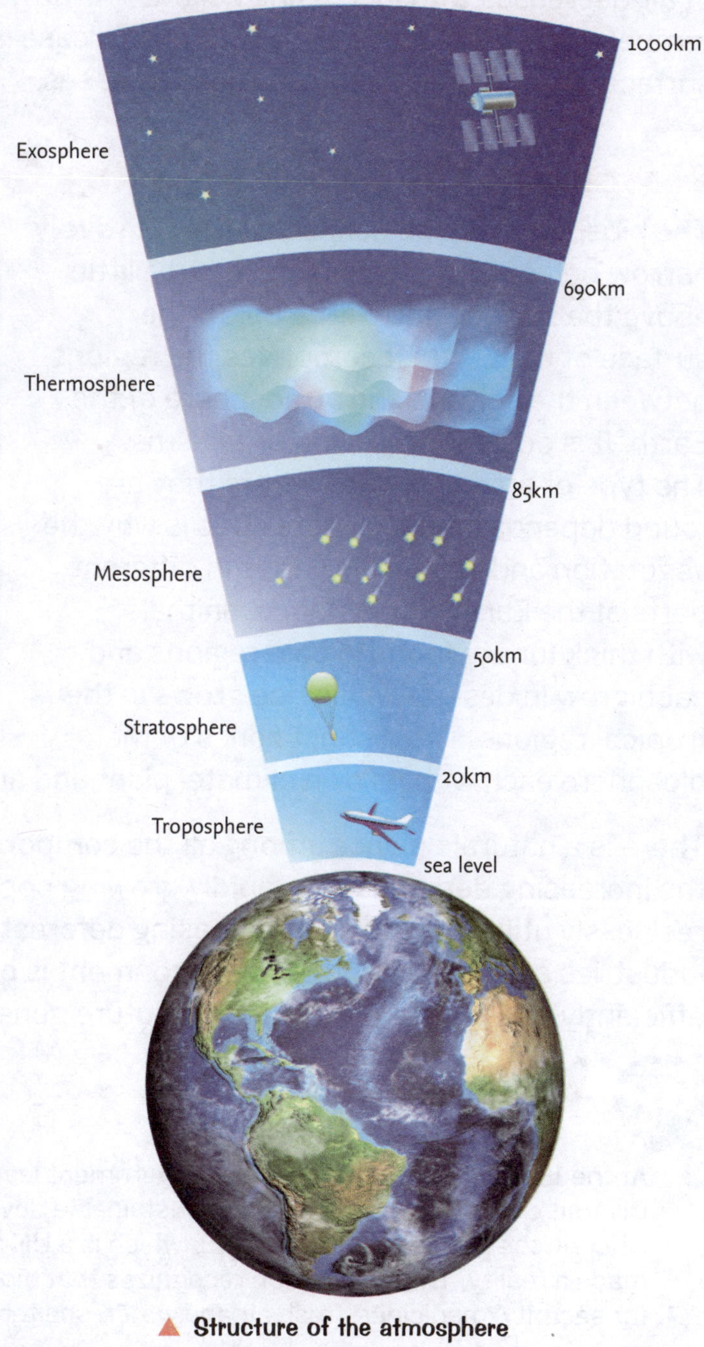


▲ Structure of the atmosphere

**phenomena:** a fact or an event in nature

## Importance of the Atmosphere

The atmosphere contains ozone, which shields us from the harmful ultraviolet radiation of the Sun. It is thin enough to allow the warmth of the Sun's rays to reach us and it also prevents the internal heat from escaping the Earth. Therefore, it helps to maintain an even temperature. It contains oxygen (21%), which is essential for respiration. The nitrogen (78%) present in the air, is a source of proteins for the living organisms. The carbon dioxide present in the air is used by green plants to make food (carbohydrates). The water vapour present in the air prevents our body from drying up and is the source of drinking water. The density of air decreases with increasing height. The atmosphere is densest near the surface. The temperature decreases evenly with an increase in height. Air pressure is maximum at the surface, it decreases as the altitude increases.

## Biosphere: The Realm of Living Organisms

The biosphere can be defined as the **relatively** narrow belt of living organisms found a little above the surface and a little below the surface of the Earth. It comprises the regions between the surface and atmosphere of the Earth. It is occupied by living organisms. The type of organisms and where they are found depends on the climate. This is why the vegetation and animal life varies in different parts of the Earth. For instance, animals with thick fur are found in cold regions and cacti grow in deserts, while rice grows in the tropical regions. The distinct zones of the biosphere each with its own climate, plant and animal life are called **ecosystems**.

▲ Ecosystem

There is a natural balance among all the components of the biosphere. However, to meet the increasing demands of a rapidly growing population, the natural resources are being recklessly utilised. With ever increasing deforestation to make away for agricultural lands, industries and settlements, the environment is being polluted. So, we must use our resources efficiently and preserve them for our future generations.

### World Connect

At the 1992 Rio Earth Summit, 150 government leaders signed the Convention of Biological Diversity, which aims at promoting sustainable development. It was formulated as a realistic device, wherein the principles of Agenda 21, which is a UN action plan on sustainable development, are made a reality. This convention recognizes that biological diversity involves people, and the need for security, medicines, fresh air and water, shelter and a clean and healthy environment.

**relatively:** in comparison or relation to something else; not absolutely

## Recall

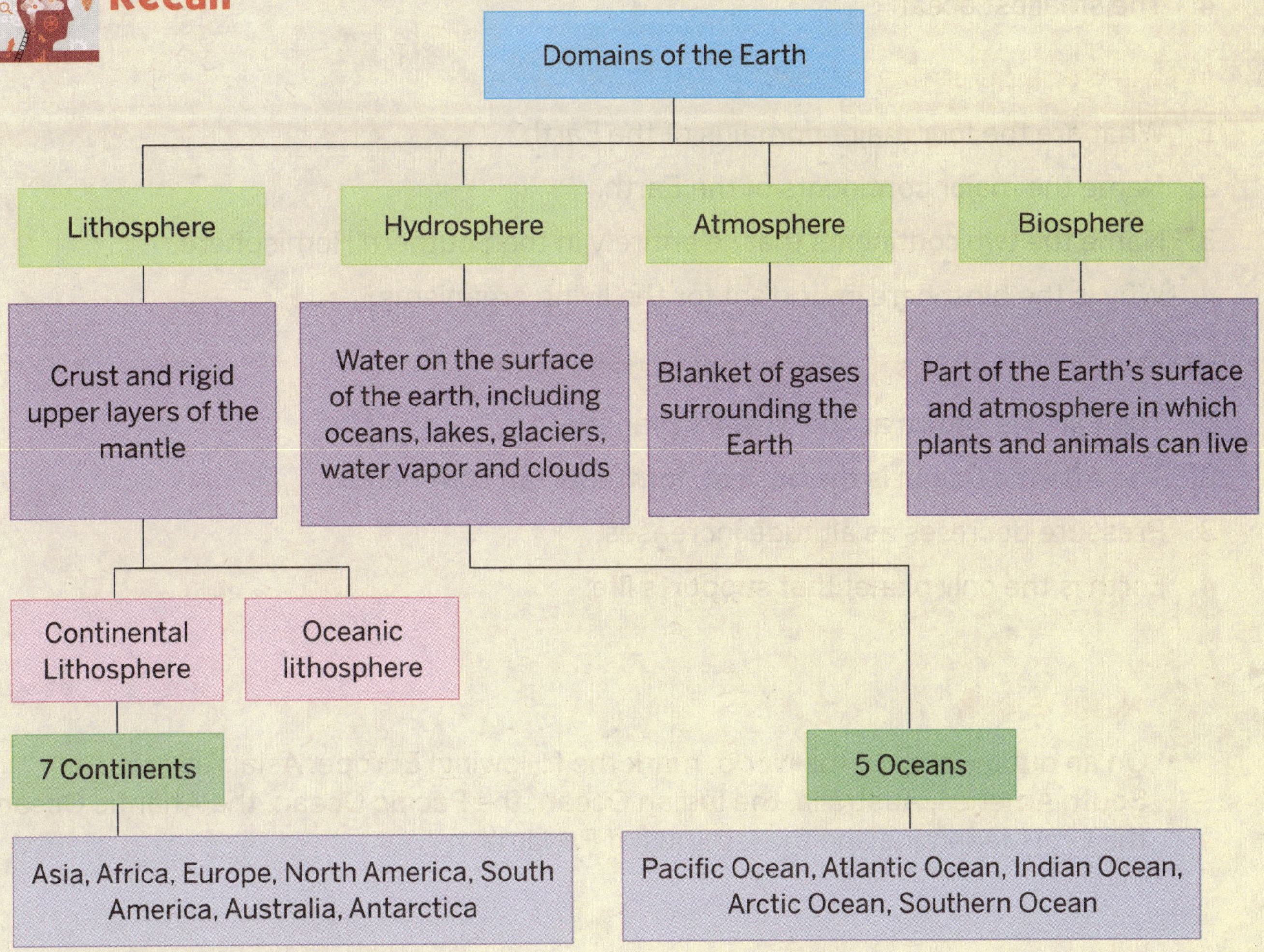


## Work out

A. Fill in the blanks.

1. The .................................. Ocean is the deepest ocean.
2. The .................................. Ocean is the second largest ocean in the world.
3. Distinct areas with their own climate, soil, plants and animals are called .................................. .
4. The .................................. Ocean is the only ocean named after a country.

B. Name the following.

1. The Blue Planet
2. The largest ocean in the world

3. Realm of water
4. The smallest ocean

## C. Answer these questions in brief.

1. What are the four major domains of the Earth?
2. Name the major continents of the Earth.
3. Name the two continents that lie entirely in the Southern Hemisphere.
4. Why is the biosphere important for the living organisms?

## D. Give geographical reasons for the given statements.

1. The Earth is known as the 'Watery Planet'.
2. The Atlantic Ocean is the busiest, for trade and commerce.
3. Pressure decreses as altitude increases.
4. Earth is the only planet that supports life.

## Map work

On an outline map of the world, mark the following: Europe, Asia, Antarctica, South America, Australia, the Indian Ocean, the Pacific Ocean, the Atlantic Ocean, the Ural Mountains and the Isthmus of Panama.

## Think

Look at the picture and answer the questions.

1. Identify the continent shown on the map.
2. How many countries does it have?
3. Who discovered this continent?

## Life skills and values

Make a list of the water-saving tips that you have learned. Which ones can you start using today?

## Enjoy

Make a model of the layers of the atmosphere using coloured paper. You can paste the paper as shown in the illustration.

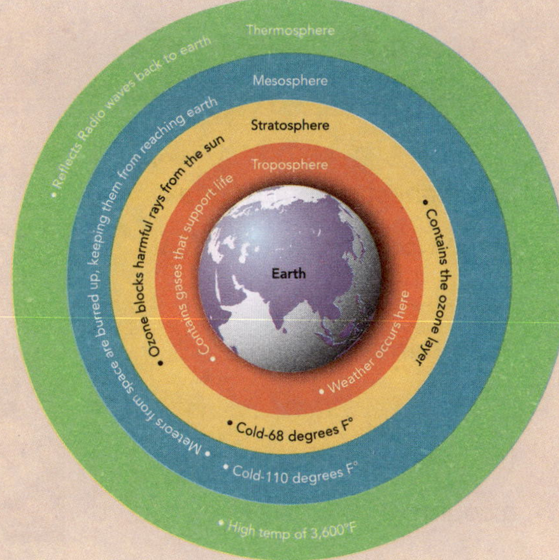


## Web link

For more information, log on to:

https://www.nationalgeographic.org/encyclopedia/atmosphere/

Last accessed on 30 September, 2019

# 6 Major Landforms of the Earth

## Take off

- The highest mountain peak in the world, lies in the .................................. mountain range.
- .................................. is the only ocean named after a country.

## Warm up

Make a list of the various features of the Earth mentioned in this dialogue and give one example of each from India.

Have you ever noticed, that the surface of the Earth is not the same everywhere? In some places it is flat and elevated in other places. These natural features of the Earth's surface are called **landforms**.

Landforms are the result of two opposing forces. The forces that uplift areas of the Earth's crust or cause it to sink forming cracks or depressions on the Earth's surface are called **internal forces**. Forces that wear down or rebuild the landforms formed on the Earth are called **external forces**. They have two components—**erosion** and **deposition**. These processes are carried out by running water, moving ice, winds and sea waves.

The Earth has a variety of landforms. On the basis of their height, they are classified into **mountains**, **plains** and **plateaus**.

## Mountains: Landforms of High Relief

A **hill** is a landform that extends above the surrounding area. It is often, smaller in height. A mountain is a landform which is higher and steeper than a hill. It rises high above the surrounding **terrain** in a limited area. Mountains have a broad base, narrow peaks, steep

**erosion:** the gradual destruction and removal of rock or soil; **deposition:** a process in which layers of a substance are formed inside something or on its surface over a period of time; **terrain:** ground slopes and deep valleys. Some mountains constitute single isolated mountain tops, or peaks, like Mount Kilimanjaro in Africa. Some mountains are arranged in a line and are known as mountain ranges, like the Jura mountain ranges in Europe. A whole series of long narrow ranges that stretch for hundreds or even thousands of miles is called a **mountain chain**. The Himalayas in Asia, the Andes in South America and the Rockies in North America are examples of mountain chains.

Broadly, there are three types of mountains. They are **fold mountains**, **block mountains** and **volcanic mountains**.

## Fold Mountains

Fold mountains are mountains formed because of the compression of the Earth's crust. They are formed by the folding of rock layers into a series of wave-like **anticlines** (upfold or troughs) and **synclines** (downfolds or ridges) without breaking or fracturing the rock layers.

▲ Fold mountains

The fold mountains which have formed recently are known as the **young fold mountains**, and the fold mountains which had formed earlier than these are known as **old fold mountains**.

The Rockies of North America, the Himalayas in Asia and the Atlas Mountains are examples of some young fold mountains. The Urals in Russia, the Appalachains in North America and the Aravalli in India are examples of some old fold mountains.

- The upfold is called the anticline
- The downfold is the syncline.

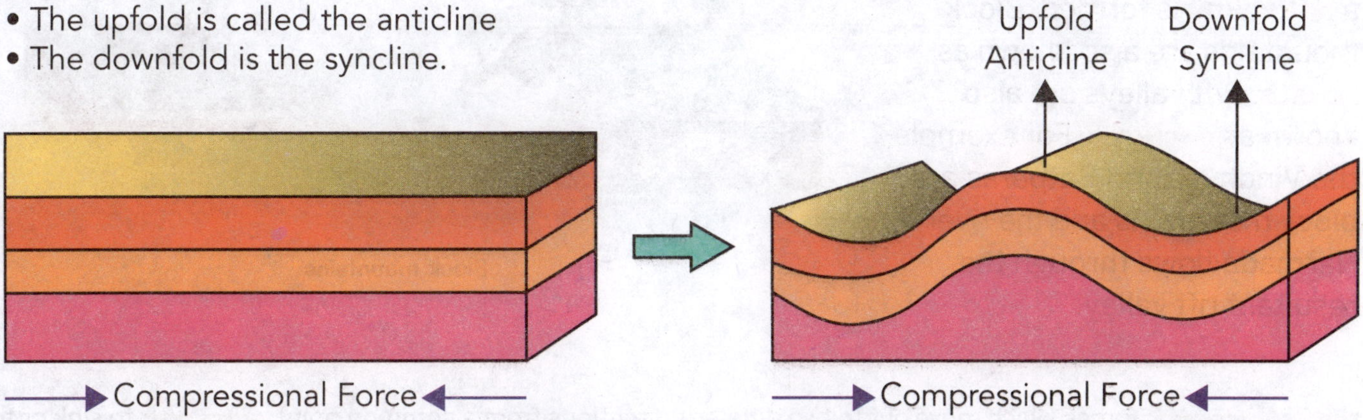


▲ Formation of fold mountains

## Explore

Fold mountains

You will need three hand towels of different solid colours, folded into narrow lengths and a partner

1. Place the hand towels on top of each other on a table.
2. Now you and your partner should each take one end of the towels.
3. Slowly push the towel ends toward the middle.
4. As the towels start to fold, they form a fold mountain shape. Layers of rocks pushed together can form fold mountains.

Let's see how do the young fold mountains differ from the old fold mountains.

| Young fold mountains | Old fold mountains |
|---|---|
| 1. Recently formed | 1. Formed a long time ago |
| 2. Higher than the old fold mountains | 2. Shorter in height than the young fold mountain |
| 3. Peaks are pointed | 3. Peaks are rounded |
| 4. Steep slopes | 4. Gentle slopes |

## Block Mountains

Block mountains are formed by the **tensional forces** which cause cracks or faults on the Earth's crust. These faults can break the crust into blocks. When these blocks are raised, block mountains are formed. Block mountains have flat tops and steep slopes. Sometimes, a section of the crust rises above or **subsides** under the surrounding area. When it rises above, **block mountains** are formed, and when it subsides, a **rift valley** is formed. Block mountains are also known as **horsts**. Rift valleys are also known as **grabens**. For example, the Vindhyas and Satpuras are block mountains and the river Narmada flows through the resultant rift valley.

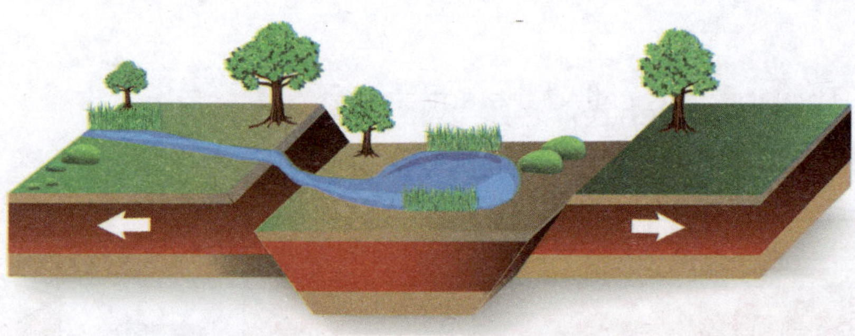

▲ Block mountains

**tensional forces:** forces which move out to two different directions from a common point; **subsides:** to sink or to fall to a lower level

### Volcanic Mountains

Volcanic mountains are formed by volcanic activity. Materials like cinder, ash, dust and liquid mud accumulate and solidify to form volcanic mountains. Some examples of volcanic mountains are Mauna Kea and Mauna Loa in Hawaii, Mount Vesuvius in Italy, Mount Fujiyama in Japan and Mount Kilimanjaro in Tanzania.

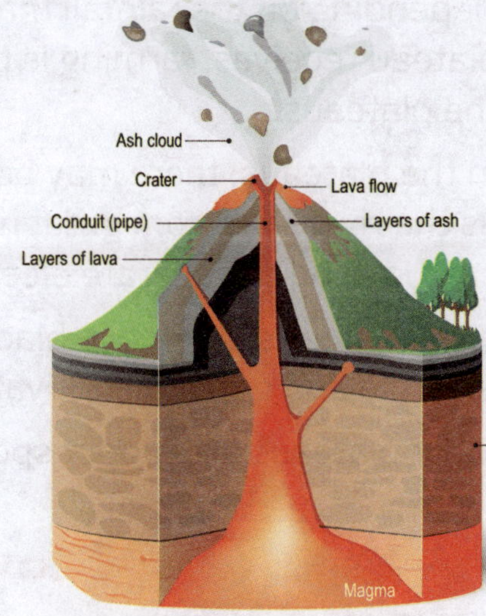


▲ Volcanic mountain

### Importance of Mountains

- Mountains act as barriers from winds. They influence the climate by causing rainfall.
- Glaciers found in the mountains are a source of perennial rivers. For example, the river Ganga originates from the Gangotri glacier. These rivers are navigable and provide water for irrigation and for generating hydroelectricity.
- Mountain slopes are ideal for rearing cattle due to the presence of green pastures. The dense vegetation of mountains is home to many animals and birds. Large reserves of timber and medicines are also found in these forests.
- Mountainous regions are terraced for cultivating a variety of crops such as tea, fruits and rice.
- Mountains are also known for scenic beauty. They make for an ideal tourist destination.

**Fact quest**

The Alps in Europe are the youngest of the world's great mountain ranges.

The Andes in South America are the world's longest range of mountains on land. The chain stretches for 7,200 km.

## Plateau: Landform of Medium Relief

Plateaus are highlands, with a broad and flat surface. They are sometimes referred to as **tablelands**. They rise abruptly above the surrounding plain. Most of them cover thousands of square kilometres in area. Some plateaus are quite high but they do not have high pointed peaks like the mountains. The Tibetan Plateau is the highest plateau of the world. The Deccan Plateau in India and Ethiopian Plateau in Africa were formed from solidified volcanic lava. The Bolivian Plateau in South America is located in between the Andes.

**Find out**

What are Piedmont plateaus and where are they located?

### Importance of Plateaus

- Plateaus made up of old rocks have rich mineral deposits. Mining is an important occupation of the people living in the plateaus of Australia and the Chhota Nagpur plateau of India.

- Depending on the rainfall that the plateau receives, farming is possible in the plateaus.
- In the plateaus, there may be waterfalls as the rivers fall from great heights. This can be used to generate electricity.
- Lava plateaus are rich in black soil, that is fertile and good for cultivation.
- Most plateaus are tourist spots.

▲ The Tibetan Plateau lies between the Himalayan range to the south and the Taklamakan Desert to the north

## Plains: Landform of Low Relief

A plain is a flat and relatively low-lying land. Some are extremely flat while some are slightly rolling or **undulating**. Plains are mainly formed by rivers flowing down mountains. While flowing down a slope, rivers erode and transport a lot of materials, which they deposit on their course to form plains. The Northern Plain of India and the Yangtze Plain of China were formed by the deposition by rivers. Plains may be formed by deposition of lava flow too, for example, the Hell's Half Acre Lava Field in Idaho, United States. Sometimes, rivers deepen and widen the valleys they form, until in due course of time the entire area is reduced to a low surface or a plain, for example, the Nullarbor Plain in Australia.

### Importance of Plains

Plains make up one-third of the world's land, but support three-fourths of the world's population. This is because they have the most favourable conditions for human settlement.

- Plains are fertile and the climate is suitable for agriculture.
- The flat land makes transportation easy.
- The rivers flow slowly over the plains and can be used for navigation.

### World Connect

Drumlin hills, found commonly in North America and Europe, are shaped like upturned boats and lie clustered together in great numbers. They are believed to be footprints of massive sheets of ice that developed during the Ice Age. Geologists have been baffled by these landforms for more than a century. It was unclear whether these hills developed gradually over a period of time or they were carved out of older sediment by the effects of weather and climate. Today, researchers are beginning to understand the origin of these hills by the use of satellite laser imagery and LiDAR, which is a detection system that works on radar, but uses light from a laser. These have helped geologists and researchers literally see the surface of the planet.

**undulating:** having a wavy form or appearance

## Recall

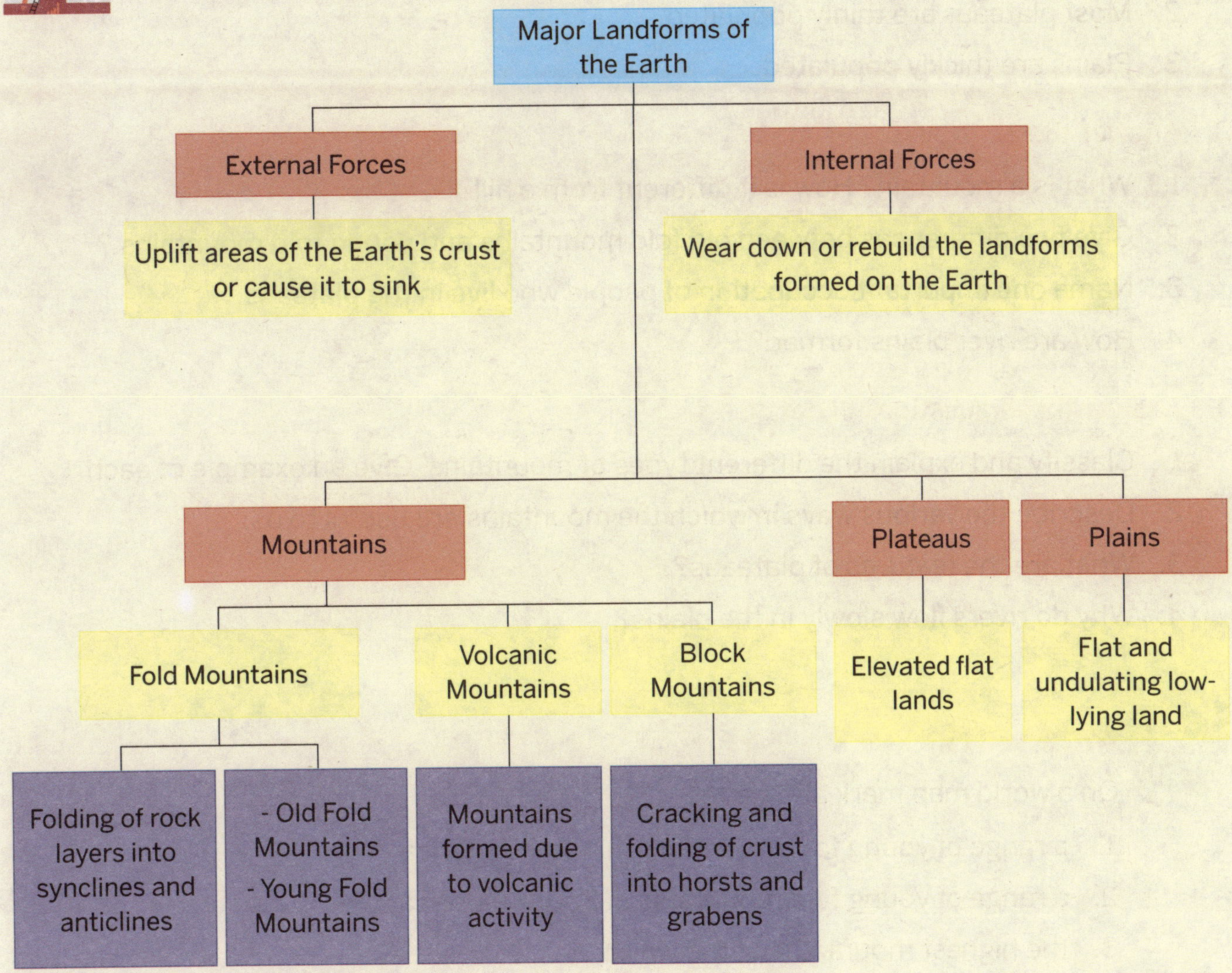


## Work out

**A. Fill in the blanks.**

1. The Aravalli is a .............................. mountain.
2. A plateau is called a .............................. .
3. Plateaus are rich in .............................. .
4. The Himalayas are an example of .............................. mountains.
5. Rivers in the .............................. flow slowly.

B. Give reasons.

1. Farming is not always possible on the mountains.
2. Most plateaus are thinly populated.
3. Plains are thickly populated.

C. Answer these questions in brief.

1. What is a mountain? How is it different from a hill?
2. Give two differences between old fold mountains and young fold mountains.?
3. Name one important occupation of people who live in the plateaus.
4. How are river plains formed?

D. Answer these questions in detail.

1. Classify and explain the different types of mountains. Give an example of each.
2. Describe the various ways in which the mountains are useful to us.
3. What are the features of plateaus?
4. Why do rivers flow slowly in the plains?

## Map work

On a world map mark and name:

1. a range of young fold mountains in North America
2. a range of young fold mountains in South America
3. the highest mountains of the world
4. the highest plateau of the world
5. the Indo-Gangetic Plain

## Think

Look at the picture and answer the questions.

1. This is highest plateau in the world. Which plateau is it?
2. In which country is this plateau located?
3. Which continent is this plateau located in?

## Life skills and values

Make a list of the things you would need to go on a camping trip to the hills. You can only carry a few items that would fit in your backpack, so don't make the list too long.

## Enjoy

Make a model of a mountain

You would require a wooden or heavy cardboard base, paper, pencil, aluminium foil, paper packing tape, a gallon of warm water, large plastic bin, newspapers, scissors, blender, large bowl, sieve, white craft glue, 1/4 cup table salt, plastic bag, acrylic craft paints, paintbrush, elements from nature (twigs, pebbles, etc.), hot glue gun

1. Find a sturdy base made of wood or cardboard, that is wider than the size you want your finished mountain to be.
2. Crumple large sheets of aluminum foil loosely and shape them in the form of a mountain. Remember to add peaks and valleys to make it seem real. Then, glue the foil to the base.
3. Cover the entire foil mountain with a layer of tape.
4. In a container of water, add small pieces of paper, and mix it till it becomes soapy. You can blend it if you want. When done, drain off the excess water.
5. Mix the papier mâché with glue and salt.
6. Spread the mixture on to the mountain shape. Make sure the paper layer is as thin as possible, and leave it overnight to dry.
7. The next morning, your mountain is ready to be painted.

## Web link

For more information, log on to:

https://www.nationalgeographic.com/science/earth/surface-of-the-earth/plateaus/

Last accessed on 30 September, 2019

# 7 Our Country—India

## Take off

- Land surrounded by water on three sides is known as a .................................................. .
- India is the .................................................. largest country in the world.

## Warm up

Can you identify some of the characters in the picture? What do they all have in common?

India, officially known as the **Republic of India**, is a country of South Asia, bordered by the Arabian Sea and the Bay of Bengal, between Myanmar and Pakistan. It is the seventh largest country in the world, with an area of about 3.28 million sq km. The distance between the northernmost part and the southernmost part of India is approximately 3,200 km. The east (easternmost point in Arunachal Pradesh) to west (western most point in Gujarat) extent measures about 2,900 km.

## India's Location and Neighbours

India lies entirely in the Northern and Eastern Hemisphere. It extends from 8° N to 37° N latitude. The Tropic of Cancer that divides India into almost two halves lies between 68° E and 97° E longitudes. The longitude of 82°30'E, which passes through the middle of India, is taken as the **Standard Time Meridian** of India. India is bounded by the Himalayas in the North, the Indian Ocean in the South, the Arabian Sea to the west and the Bay of Bengal to the East.

The country's boundaries measure the length of 15,200 km. To the north lies China and the small nations of Nepal and Bhutan are also located along our northern borders. To the east lies Myanmar. India's borders with Bangladesh mostly correspond to the delta of the Ganga

**republic:** is a country where power is held by the people or the representatives that they elect. Republics have presidents who are elected, rather than kings or queens.

and the Brahmaputra rivers. To the west, Pakistan and Afghanistan India's neighbours. The Maldives and the island of Sri Lanka lie to the south of India, separated by the Palk Strait and the Gulf of Mannar. India has a fairly regular coastline. The Gulf of Kuchch and the Gulf Of Khambhat are found along the coast of Gujarat. Lake Chilka is found along the eastern coast of Odisha. India occupies a strategic position on the international trade route, linking the eastern and western countries.

## Political and Administrative Divisions

For administrative purposes, and considering a large number of factors like local cultures and languages, India is divided into 28 states and 9 Union Territories. Rajasthan is the largest

▲ Political map of India

state and Goa is the smallest state in terms of area. The states are further divided into districts and tehsils.

**Explore**

Look at the political map of India and locate the 28 states and seven union territories, with their respective capitals. Write down the names of the states that have a common boundary with Pakistan, China, Nepal, Bhutan and Bangladesh.

## Physical Features of India

India can be divided into six major physical divisions:

- The Northern Mountains
- The Northern Plains
- The Peninsular Plateau
- The Great Indian Desert
- The Coastal Plains
- The Islands

### The Northern Mountains

Towards the northern part of India stand the highest mountains in the world. The Northern Mountain Ranges in India include the Himalayan Mountain Ranges. These mountains stretch from the Indus River in the west to the Brahmaputra River in the east. The word **Himalaya** is **derived** from the two words. *Him* means snow and *alaya* means the abode. Thus, together, Himalaya means 'the abode of snow'. The length of the Himalayan Range is about 2400 km and the breadth, on an average, is 240 km. The Himalayas consist of three parallel ranges which are classified on the basis of their height. They are the **Himadri**, the **Himachal** and the **Siwaliks**.The Northern Mountains have many **passes** which are low points that allows easy access to climbers.

▲ Northern Mountains

**The Himadri:** Also known as the **Greater Himalayas** or the Inner Himalayas, this range makes up the highest part of the mountains. The average elevation of the Himadri is 6,000 m and it is permanently covered with snow. The world's highest peaks, many of them over 8000 m, are found in the Himadri. Mount Everest (8848 m), the highest part of the Himalayas, is located here. Other peaks are the Nanga Parbat (8123 m) and the Kanchenjunga (8598 m).

**derived:** to draw or be drawn from source or origin; to trace or be traced

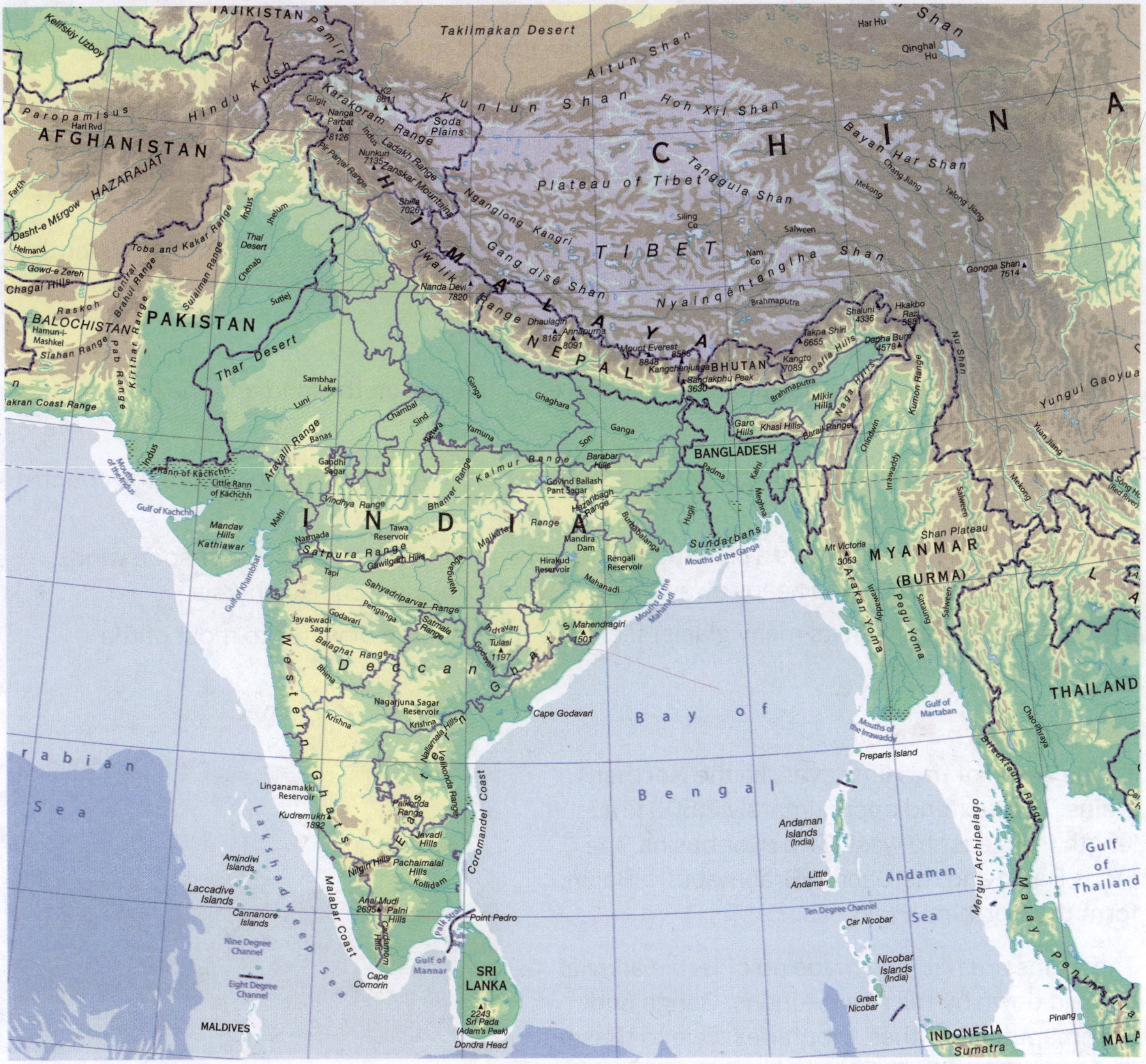


▲ Physical map of India

Some of the important passes on the Himadri Himalayas are Baralacha, Shipki La (Himachal Pradesh), Niti, Lipulekh (Uttaranchal), Nathu La, Jelep La (Sikkim) and Burzil (Kashmir).

**The Himachal:** The Himachal is known as the **Middle or the Lesser Himalayas**. This comprises a number of ranges, running in different directions. These ranges lie to the south of the Himadri and have an elevation of about 4500 m. Most of the well-known hill stations in India are located on the southern slopes of the Himachal. The notable ranges of the Himachal Himalayas are the Dhauladhar, the Pir Panjal, the Nag Tibba and the Mahabharata (located in Nepal).

**Find out**

Locate two Himalayan passes in the physical map of India.

**The Siwaliks:** The Siwalik Mountains, also known as the **outer Himalayas**, lie to the north of the Indo-Ganga-Brahmaputra Plain. This range stands at an elevation of 1200 m, and extends south-east from the Jammu hills of Kashmir to Arunachal Pradesh. The Siwaliks break in a stretch, between the eastern boundary of Nepal and the Torsa River in Bhutan, but rise gradually northward from the North Indian Plain to a height of about 620 m. There are flat valleys in between the Himachal and the Siwalik ranges. These have been called duns, for example, Dehra Dun, Patli Dun and Kothri Dun.

The **Purvanchal range** lies along the eastern boundaries of India. These mountains cover the states of Assam, Manipur, Tripura, Nagaland, Meghalaya and Mizoram.

## Importance of the Himalayas

The Himalayas are very important and have a great influence on the land and the people of India.

- The Himalyas act as a physical barrier from the rest of Asia helping to secure the country against invasions.
- The Himalayas also act as a climatic barrier. The mountains traps the monsoon winds within the country, and keeps away the cold wind, blowing from North Asia.
- The Himalayas, with its many glaciers, are the main source of water to most of the perennial rivers.

## The Northern Plains

To the south of the Himalayas, lie the Northern Plains. They extend approximately 2,500 km in length from east to west. Two river basins, the Indus Basin and the Ganga–Brahmaputra Basin, form the Northern Plain.

▲ Northern Plains

The plains are flat, and made up of fertile alluvial soil laid down by the rivers—Indus, Ganga and Brahmaputra and their tributaries. Due to these factors, the Northern Plains of India are densely populated. The Northern Plains can be further divided into the Indus Valley Plains and the Ganga-Brahmaputra Basin.

**The Indus Valley Plains:** This area is drained by the river Indus and its tributaries—Chenab, Jhelum, Ravi, Beas, and Sutlej. A major part of this plain lies in Pakistan now. This fertile area was the cradle for one of the earliest civilizations—the Indus Valley Civilization which was established around 4000 years ago.

**Fact quest**

The Sarasvati River was a river which flowed between the Yamuna in the east and the Sutlej in the west. Although this river has dried up and does not exist today, we know about it from studying the *Rigveda*.

**The Ganga-Brahmaputra Basin:** The Ganga-Brahmaputra Basin is drained by the river Ganga and its tributaries—Yamuna, Ghaghara, Gandak, Kosi, Son and Damodar, and also by the river Brahmaputra and its tributaries—Tista, Subansiri, Barali, Dhansiri and Dihing. Most of these rivers emerge from the snow covered Himalayas.

**Eco feat**

The Sundarbans are the largest natural tidal mangrove forest region in the world. It lies in the Ganga-Brahmputra basin. This area spans across India and Bangladesh. On the Indian side, it is a biosphere reserve and a national park.

## The Peninsular Plateau

The Peninsular Plateau lies to the south of the Northern Plains. This plateau is the oldest part of the Indian subcontinent. It is made up of hard rocks which are rich in mineral resources. It is divided by the Narmada River into two parts—the **Malwa Plateau** and the **Deccan Plateau**.

The important rivers of this region are the rivers Narmada, Tapi, Mahanadi, Godavari, Krishna and Kaveri. Except for the Narmada and the Tapi, the other rivers flow towards the east. The rivers Narmada and Tapi flow towards the west.

**The Malwa Plateau:** The Malwa Plateau is bounded by the Vindhyas in the south, the Aravallis on the west and the Chhota Nagpur Plateau in the east. It is drained by the rivers Betwa, Son, Chambal, Sindh and Damodar. These rivers are not perennial.

**The Deccan Plataeu:** The Deccan Plateau lies to the south of the river Narmada. It is triangular in shape. It is bordered by the Satpuras in the north, the **Western Ghats** in the west and the **Eastern Ghats** in the east.

The Western Ghats are continuous hills, rising steeply from the coastal plains, along the west coast of India. Also known as the Sahyadri, these hills cause heavy rainfall in the western coastal plains, as they intercept the south-west monsoon winds from the Arabian Sea. Mount Anaimudi is the highest peak of the Western Ghats.

▲ The Deccan Plataeu

The Eastern Ghats are low hills along the eastern edge of the Deccan Plateau. They are not continuous as rivers cut through them to drain the region. The Eastern Ghats do not cause much rain. Both the Western and the Eastern Ghats meet at the Nilgiri hills in Tamil Nadu.

## The Great Indian Desert

The Great Indian Desert lies to the west of the Aravalli Range. It occupies a major part of the state of Rajasthan and extends into Sindh, Pakistan as the Thar Desert. The land is generally flat and covered with sandy soil. It is a dry region with hardly any rivers. The rivers that are present in the region do not have enough water to reach the sea. They dry up, or disappear into the sand. The river Luni is the only large river in this region.

▲ The Great Indian Desert

## The Coastal Plains

The Deccan Plateau has two narrow slips of coastal plains along the Bay of Bengal ,**Eastern Coastal Plains** and the Arabian Sea ,**Western Coastal Plains**.

The Eastern Coastal Plains lie along the Bay of Bengal. It is known as the **Northern Circars** to the north of the river Godavari and the **Coromandal Coast** to its south. This comprises the fertile deltas of the rivers Mahanadi, Godavari, Krishna and Kaveri. The Eastern Coastal Plains are broader and more level than the Western Coastal Plains. The coastline is regular.

The Western Coastal Plains lie along the Arabian Sea. It is known as the **Konkan Coast** in Maharashtra, the **Kanara Coast** in Karnataka and the **Malabar Coast** in Kerala. The Western Coastal Plains are is narrow and uneven with a broken coastline.

## Islands

Two groups of islands also form a part of India. The Andaman and Nicobar islands and the Lakshadweep Islands. The **Andaman and Nicobar Islands** are a group of more than 300 islands located in the Bay of Bengal. Most of the islands are volcanic in nature. India's only active volcano erupted in Barren Island in the Andamans. The **Lakshadweep Islands** are a group of 36 coral islands in the Arabian Sea. These islands are located 300 km to the west of the coast of Kerala. Lakshadweep means 'a hundred thousand islands'.

▲ The Lakshadweep Islands

India is called a subcontinent, as it is vast, and a more or less self-contained subdivision, of a continent.

### World Connect

The Indian plate lies in the Eastern Hemisphere. Originally a part of the Gondwana supercontinent, it now includes most of South Asia, parts of South China, Indonesia and some part of the Indian Ocean. Millions of years ago, when it collided with the Eurasian plate, it gave rise to the mighty Himalayas, and the Tibetan Plateau.

## Recall

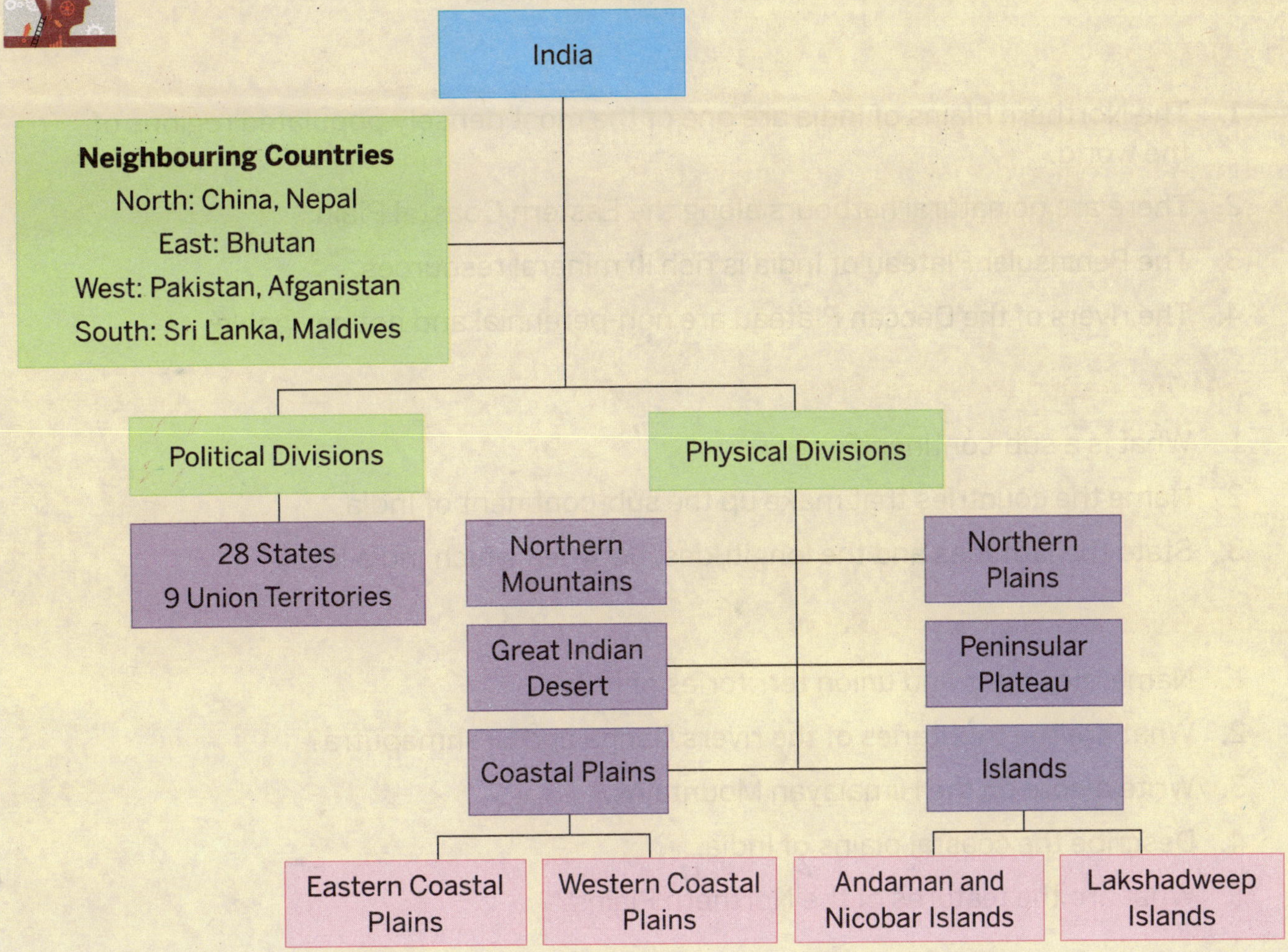


## Work out

**A. Fill in the blanks.**

1. India has an area of .................................. million square kilometres.
2. The Andaman and Nicobar Islands lie in .................................. .
3. India's only volcano lies in .................................. Island in the Andamans.
4. The .................................. Ocean lies to the south of the country.

**B. Name the following.**

1. States that have a common border with Bangladesh
2. States that are part of the Peninsular Plateau

3. States that lie completely in the Himalayas
4. States that are made up of hills, in North-East India

C. Give reasons.

1. The Northern Plains of India are one of the most densely populated regions of the world.
2. There are no natural harbours along the Eastern Coastal Plain.
3. The Peninsular Plateau of India is rich in mineral resources.
4. The rivers of the Deccan Plateau are non-perennial and not navigable.

D. Answer these questions in brief.

1. What is a sub-continent?
2. Name the countries that make up the sub-continent of India.
3. State the latitudes and the longitudes, between which India lies.

E. Answer these questions in detail.

1. Name the states and union territories of India.
2. What are the tributaries of the rivers Ganga and Brahmaputra?
3. Write a note on the Himalayan Mountains.
4. Describe the coastal plains of India.
5. What are the features of the Northern Plains?

## Map work

1. On a political map of India, mark the following:
   Himachal Pradesh, Rajasthan, Mizoram, Chhattisgarh
2. On a physical map of India, mark the following:
   The Deccan Plateau, the Eastern Coastal Plain, the river Brahmaputra, the river Ganga

## Think

Look at the picture and answer the questions.

1. Who do you think this person is?
2. What is he doing?
3. Why is the person wearing a mask and goggles?

## Life skills and values

Imagine you are stranded in an island, while visiting any one of the Island groups. How will you pacify your fellow passengers? How will you manage your day, till you are rescued?

## Enjoy

Divide your class into five groups. Each group can pick any one region of India. Choose any two states from North, South, East, West and Northeast. Write in brief about their climate, natural vegetation, wildlife and landforms. Make a Power Point presentation and share with the class.

## Web link

For more information, log on to:

http://www.natgeotraveller.in/off-the-grid-in-the-andaman-nicobar-islands/

Last accessed on 30 September, 2019

# 8 India—Climate, Natural Vegetation and Wildlife

## Take off

- July and August are the months corresponding to the ............................... season in north India.
- The ................................. protect us from the cold wind blowing from the Arctic Region.

## Warm up

What mode of transport are the people in the picture using? Is it still in use today?

While travelling to different parts of India, one comes across different types of houses, trees, crops and even clothing. Weather pertains to the day-to-day changes in the atmosphere. Climate comprises the average weather conditions, which have been measured over many years. Climate influences the life of the people in a big way. In India, we see how the cllmatic differences between different regions, have influenced the life of the people living in particular areas.

India is a vast country, having varied relief features, that influence the climate. Climatic conditions vary from place to place. The interior part of the country experiences a **continental climate**. The coastal regions experience an **equable climate** and the people living in mountainous regions experience a cold climate.

The Tropic of Cancer passes through the centre of the country, and divides it into halves. The southern half lies in the Tropical Zone, and the northern half lies in the Temperate Zone. The monsoons give our country a climatic unity. Hence, the climate of India is known as the **tropical monsoon** climate**.** Monsoon a season of heavy is rainfall, caused by the difference in temperature, between a landmass and the adjacent ocean.

**continental climate:** very hot summers and extremely cold winters; **equable climate:** summers not too hot and winters not too cold

## Factors Affecting the Climate of India

Let us see the factors which affect the climate of a India.

**Latitudes:** The Tropic Of Cancer divides the country into the Tropical zone and the Temperate zone.

**Distance from the Sea:** All places near the sea coast have more equable climates than places in the interior. Water bodies comprising the Arabian Sea and the Bay of Bengal surround the peninsular India and make climatic conditions mild along the coastal areas.

**Altitude (height above the sea level):** Temperature decreases with height. Places high up on the mountains, are colder than the plains.

**The Northern Mountains:** The Himalayas prevent the cold wind blowing from the north, from entering into India. They trap the monsoon winds, and forces them to shed their moisture.

**Wind:** The most dominating factor of the Indian climate is the 'monsoon winds' as a result of which it is often called the monsoon climate. The complete reversal of the monsoon winds brings about a sudden change in the seasons. The south-west summer monsoons from the Arabian Sea and the Bay of Bengal bring rainfall to the entire country. The **retreating** monsoon winds in winter travel from land to sea and do not cause much rainfall except along the Coromandel coast after getting moisture from the Bay of Bengal.

## Seasons of India

India has four seasons in a year.

- The cold weather season
- The hot weather season
- The southwest monsoon season
- The **retreating** southwest monsoon season

**The Cold Weather Season:** This season starts in December and lasts till February. During this time, the Sun's rays do not fall directly on this region. The lowest temperature is found in the mountains and the Northern Plains since it is far away from the sea. The **Deccan Plateau** is warmer since it lies closer to the Equator. This season is dry and it does not rain in most parts of India, except the east coast and north-west region of the country.

**The Hot Weather Season:** This season starts in March, and ends in May. The temperature rises in most of India, except in the hills and the coastal areas. It is mostly dry, with occasional local storms.

**The South-West Monsoon Season:** This season starts in June, and lasts till September. The winds blow from the Arabian Sea, and the Bay of Bengal, towards the land. Every part

**retreating:** moving away

of India gets rainfall, except Tamil Nadu. The arrival of the monsoons is very sudden and its departure is usually unpredictable.

**The Retreating South-West Monsoon Season:** This season lasts through October and November. The temperature and moisture content in the air is very high. This is known as the 'October Heat'. This is a season of transition, from a hot rainy season to cold dry conditions. The east coast receives heavy rainfall during this time.

### Importance of the monsoons

- India is an agricultural country, and the monsoons are of great importance to the **economy** of the country.
- Delays and long breaks in the monsoon, are dangerous for the agricultural crops.
- Conservation programmes and rainwater harvesting are some of the modern methods, adopted by Indian farmers.

## Natural Vegetation of India

The grasses, the shrubs and the trees, which grow on their own, without interference or help from human beings, are called **natural vegetation**. The natural vegetation of any area, depends primarily on variations in rainfall and relief. Natural vegetation in India is extremely diverse, due to the diversity of rainfall and terrain. Unfortunately, the forests are now disppearing, due to the increasing demand for cultivation. In the hilly areas the forest cover has decreased to only about nineteen per cent.

Based on the different amount of rainfall and landforms available, there are five types of forests in India:

- The tropical evergreen forests
- The tropical deciduous forests
- The thorn forests
- Tidal Forests (Ganga-Brahmaputra Delta)
- Mountain vegetation (Himalayas)

### Tropical Evergreen Forest

The tropical evergreen forests, are found in areas with annual rainfall of 200–300cm. distributed throughout the year. These type of forests are found in the western slope of the Western Ghats, the hills of the northeastern states and, the Andaman and Nicobar Islands. They are dense forests where trees do not shed their leaves at the same time. Important trees are rosewood, ebony and mahogany.

▲ Tropical evergreen forest

**economy:** the management of the resources, finances, income, and expenditure of a country, community or a business enterprise

## Tropical Deciduous Forest

Most typical forests of the tropical region, are called tropical deciduous forests. That is why, these forests are also known as **monsoon forests**. These forests are found in regions with an annual rainfall of 100-200 cm. We can find such forests in Madhya Pradesh, Uttar Pradesh, Bihar, Jharkhand and Chhattisgarh. The trees in these forests shed their leaves, for six to eight weeks during summer, in order to survive the dry season. Important trees are sal, teak, peepal.

▲ Tropical deciduous forest

## Thorn Forest

▲ Thorn forest

Thorn forests are found in areas which receive under 50 cm of rainfall. Forests of this type, are scattered around the northwest region of India, which includes the state of Rajasthan, and drier parts of Punjab and Gujarat. They consist of stunted trees and bushes, which are widely scattered. The trees have long roots, which help them to obtain water from deep underground. They have sharp spines to reduce surface area, and thorns, which help them to conserve water. Common trees are babul, kikar, wild palms and different varieties of acacia.

## Tidal Forest

Also known as **mangrove forests**, or 'littoral', (means 'on a shore'), tidal forests are found in the Ganga-Brahmaputra delta (in West Bengal). The most important tree is the sundari tree, after which the Sundarbans are named.

▲ Tidal forest

## Mountain Vegetation

▲ Mountain vegetation

Vegetation in the mountains varies according to height, since temperature and rainfall changes with a change in altitude. At a height between 1500 metres and 2500 metres, most of the trees are conical in shape. These trees are called coniferous trees. Important trees are chir, pine and deodar.

## Importance of Forests

Forests are a very important natural resource.

- They provide us with a variety of forest products.
- They prevent soil erosion.
- They also help in checking floods.
- They provide a habitat for wildlife.

**Find out**

What movements have been undertaken for the conservation of forests?

**Explore**

1. What is the Beej Bachao Andolan or Save the Seeds Movement?
2. What are their aims and methods?

**Forest Products:** Timber, that is wood obtained from trees, is a major forest product. Also, resins, gum, lac and khus, are minor products. We need to conserve forest resources and use them moderately.

## Wildlife

Forests are home to a variety of wildlife. India has over 500 species of animals and 1,200 species of birds. There are a number of reptiles and species of fish as well. Different regions of India have different species of animals. For example, lions are found only in the Gir forest of Gujarat.

- Tigers, the national animal of India are found in the Sundarbans.
- Elephants are found in Kerala and Karnataka.
- The one-horned rhinoceros is found in the forest of Assam.
- Camels are found in the Thar Desert.
- Wild asses are found in the Rann of Kachchh.
- Wild goats, snow leopards and bears are found in the Himalayan region.

### Wildlife Conservation

Many **species** of animals are losing their natural homes in many regions, due to depletion of forests and **poaching**. As a result, a few species have been categorized as endangered animals. Wildlife is our heritage, and it is our duty to preserve every species of animal, for the future generations. It is important for us to conserve both the forests as well as its wildlife.

▲ A tiger in the Sundarbans

**species:** a class of plants or animals whose members have the same main characteristics; **poaching:** the illegal practice of trespassing on another's property to hunt or steal game without the landowner's permission

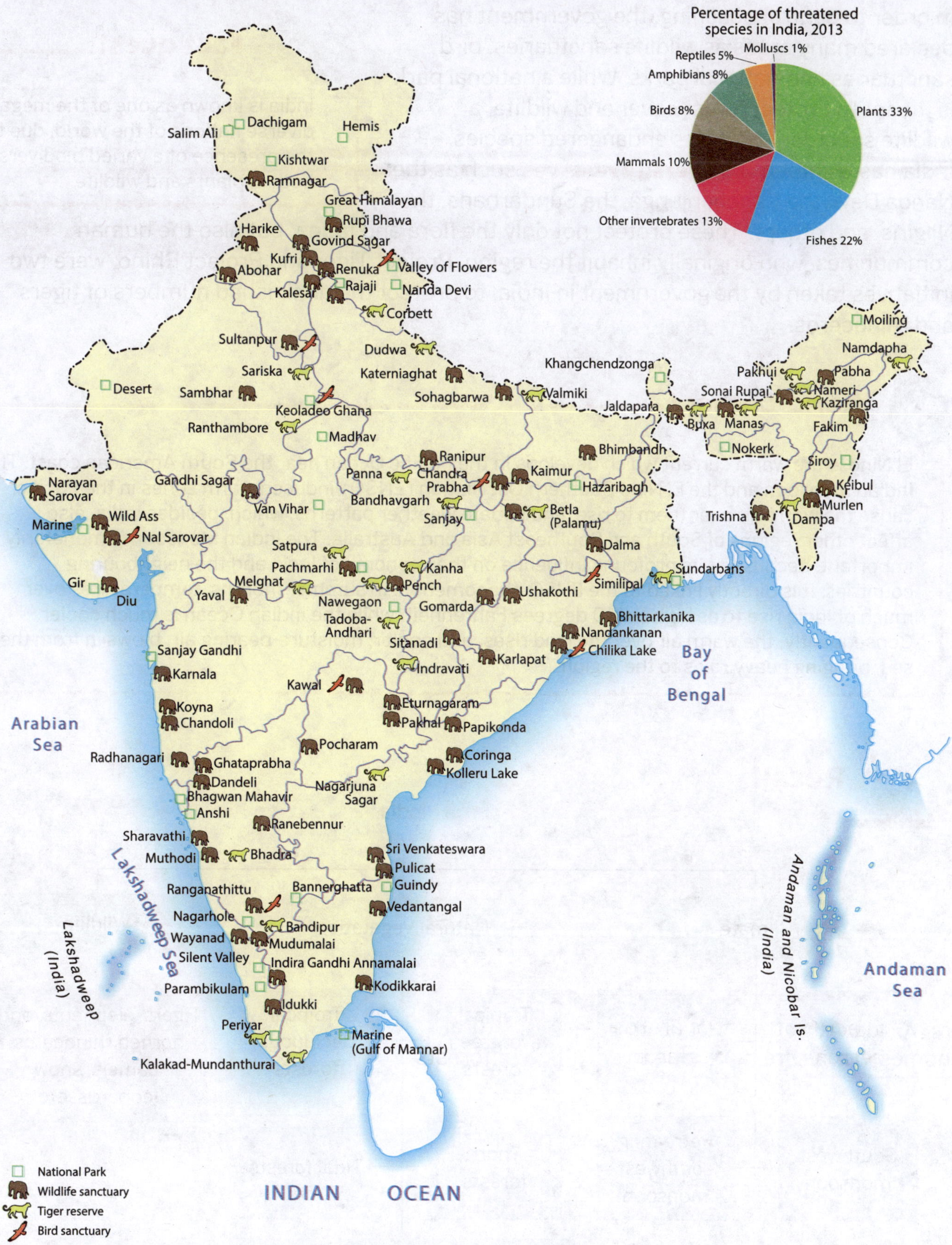


▲ **India: Wildlife and Protected Areas**

In order to control poaching, the government has declared many areas as wildlife sanctuaries, bird sanctuaries and national parks. While a national park is meant to protect forest cover and wildlife, a wildlife sanctuary protects endangered species. India has eighteen **biodiversity reserves** such as the Nanda Devi, the Kanchenjunga, the Sundarbans, the Nilgiris, and others. These protect not only the flora and fauna, but also the human communities, who originally inhabit the region. Project Tiger and Project Rhino, were two initiatives taken by the government in India, to protect the diminished numbers of tigers and rhinoceros.

### Fact quest

India is known as one of the mega-diverse nations of the world, due to the presence of a varied biodiversity, both in plants and wildlife.

### World Connect

El Nino is the warm current which develops in the Pacific Ocean near the South American coast. The Indian monsoon and the El Nino Southern Oscilliation (ENSO)-induced warm zones in the Pacific, cause the warm air over them to rise, and initiate weather patterns, which, besides India, also affect other regions of South and Southeast Asia and Australia. The Indian Monsoon is monetarily important, because of its profound influence on the economy of India and the neighbouring countries. It is directly linked to the ENSO phenomenon. In summer months, temperatures over much of India rise to as high as 110 degrees Fahrenheit, while the Indian Ocean is much cooler. Consequently, the warm air over the land rises, and cooler, moisture-bearing air, blows in from the sea, bringing heavy rains to the region.

### Recall

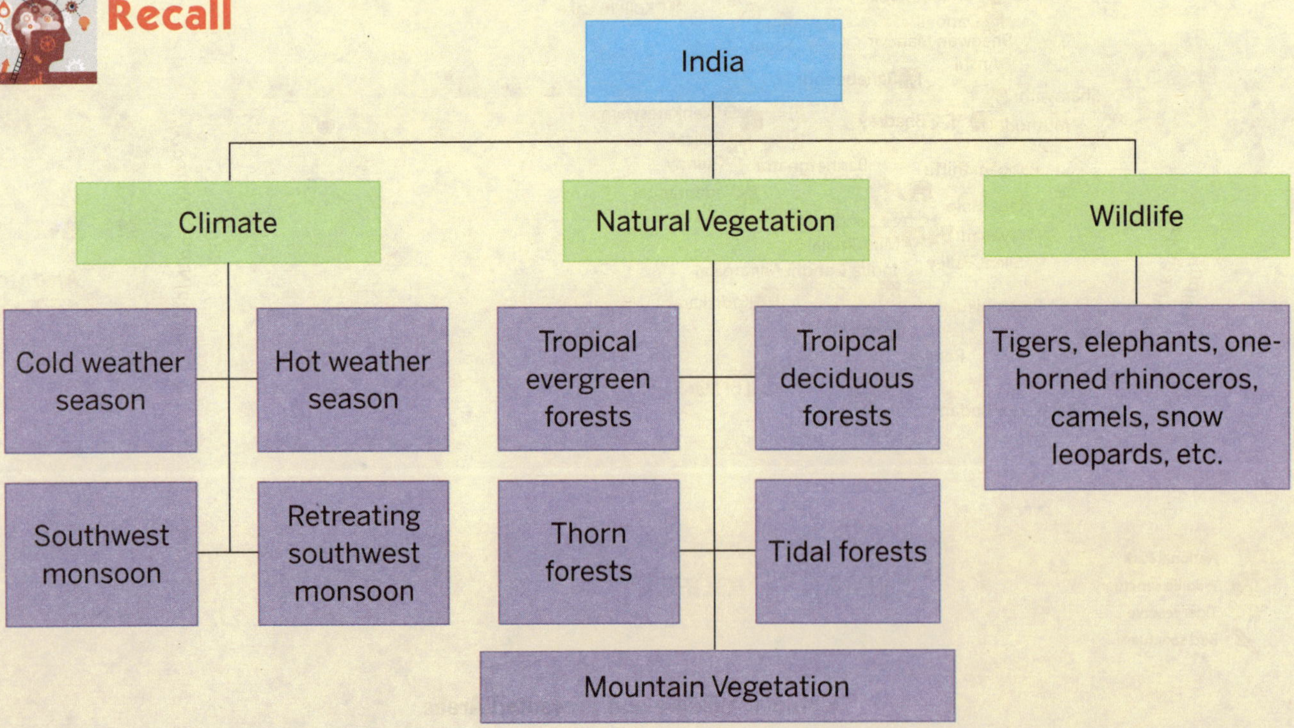

## Work out

A. Fill in the blanks with the correct answers.

1. The coastal regions in India experience .................................... type of climate.
   a. continental b. equable c. extreme cold d. dry
2. The retreating south-west monsoon season lasts from .................................... .
   a. February to March b. June to August
   c. October to November d. December to January
3. Based on the amount of rainfall, there are .................................... types of forests.
   a. five b. three c. two d. four
4. Forests are important as they prevent .................................... .
   a. soil erosion b. rainfall c. urbanization d. depletion
5. The biodiversity Parks in India are more in the .................................... .
   a. Eastern Ghats b. Dachigam c. Northern Plains d. Western Ghats

B. Name the following.

1. Two common plants of thorn forest
2. The main animal of the tropical deciduous forest
3. The main product of the tropical evergreen forest
4. Two local winds in India

C. Give geographical reasons for the following:

1. The Deccan Plateau is relatively warmer than the Northern Plains during winter.
2. Tamil Nadu does not get rain during the south-west Monsoon season.

D. Answer these questions in brief.

1. In which parts of India are the thorn forests found?
2. What are the tidal forests, in the Ganga-Brahmaputra Delta, called?

E. Answer these questions in detail.

1. Explain the factors that influence the climate of India.
2. Write a short note on the tropical deciduous forests in India.
3. Describe the wildlife in India.

## Map work

Mark five national parks and three wildlife sanctuaries on an outline map of India.

## Think

Look at the picture and answer the following questions.

1. What animal do you see in the picture?
2. In which regions of India are these animals found?
3. What human activities have caused these creatures to become endangered?

## Life skills and values

Project Tiger was a nationwide campaign, established in1973 to prevent the extinction of tigers. Collect some information on the progress made by the project till March 2016.

## Enjoy

Conduct a debate in the class about the topic 'The government of India is doing enough to conserve and protect forests and wildlife.'

## Web link

For more information, log on to:

https://www.nationalgeographic.org/encyclopedia/monsoon/

Last accessed on 30 September, 2019

Info Time

## Earth's Biggest Milestones

4.5 billion years ago
The Big Bang occurred

3 billion years ago
Continents began to form.

1 billion years ago
Organisms with mouths, limbs and sense organs came into being.

850–635 million years ago
Earth froze over, twice.

535 million years ago
Animals evolved.

465 million years ago
Plants began to grow on land.

460–430 million years ago
The first Ice Age began.

375 million years ago
Insects came into existence.

320 million years ago
The first reptiles appeared.

300 million years ago
All of Earth's continents came together and formed one supercontinent.

252 million years ago
Massive volcanic eruptions led to a mass extinction of species.

220 million years ago
Dinosaurs evolved.

160 million years ago
Birds evolved from feathered dinosaurs.

130 million years ago
Flowers came into existence.

65 million years ago
Earth was hit by asteriods which led to mass extinction of species.

60–55 million years ago
Dinosaurs became extinct.

13–7 million years ago
The first apes appeared in Africa.

200,000 years ago
Homo sapiens, our species, evolved.

# 1 Diversity in India

## Take off

- We celebrate many .................................... in India.
- Different .................................... are spoken in different parts of India.
- Different rulers of India have left a rich .................................... heritage..

## Warm up

Look how two boys are similar. State two similarities between you and your classmates?

Imagine you have moved to a new country, and are surrounded by many different people from different states, countries and cultures. How would you adjust to the new environment? Just as our natural environment has different flora and fauna, it has different people too. A **diversity** of things is a range of things which are very different from each other. Our societies, neighbourhoods and classrooms are diverse because people from different parts of the world live together in single communities. They all speak different languages, wear different clothes and follow different religions.

## Diversity in India

India is a vast country with diverse geography, cultures, religions, festivals, languages, dress, and food. People must respect these differences, and celebrate the diversity of India. India is known for its cultural, linguistic and religious diversity all over the world.

Have you ever wondered how India became a land with such diversity? If we look back in history, we can understand the factors that have contributed to this rich culture. Earlier, people from distant regions visited India for conquest, adventure or trade.

These people influenced India's food, clothes, language, buildings and culture. This fusion of diverse cultures came together to form the present India. Each period of history had a distinct influence on the lives and culture of India.

## Geographical Diversity

There are six physical divisions in India and each of them contribute to the geographical diversity of the country. These divisions are, the Northern Mountains, Northern Plains, Great Indian Desert, Peninsular Plateau, Coastal Plains and The Islands The fertile coastal plains and the Ghats along the coastlines of India have attracted traders who come for spices such as pepper and cardamom since the ancient times. The geographical diversity leads to diverse climatic conditions, fauna, flora and way of life. People living in different regions have different food habits, clothes, occupations and customs influenced by the region and the climatic conditions of the place. Different rulers in India influenced its culture greatly and introduced new dishes with potatoes, tomatoes and chillies.

### Eco feat

The dense forests of central and eastern India are home to a large variety of plants, animals and birds. The tribes in the forests have protected and nurtured the forests for all these years.

### Fact quest

The UN has declared 21 May as the World Day for Cultural Diversity for Dialogue and Development.

## Economic Diversity

The economic condition of people is determined by the region in which they live. Agriculture, which is the main occupation in the country is the basis of the livelihood of the people. In the plains, where food crops grow in plenty, people depend on farming for their **sustenance**. In areas which do not receive adequate rainfall, people cannot grow crops. Factories and industries provide jobs for people usually in areas which are rich in mineral resources. Many people make handicrafts or depend on other occupations such as livestock rearing and mining.

### Find out

How do you think has the history of India influenced its cuisine?

The history and geography of a region influences its economy and trade. For example, Kerala, a coastal state in south India is known for its spices. People cultivate spices and rice. Fishing and silk weaving are other occupations. Traders from Arab and Europe came for spice and silk. The economy of another region Ladakh, the desert state in north India, largely depends on livestock rearing as the geography is not suitable for agriculture. People rear sheep and produce wool which is bought by weavers from Kashmir. They also make woollen rugs and carpets. Traders from Arab and other countries travel through mountain passes to trade wool and carpets.

## Religious Diversity

India is not **homogeneous** in terms of religion. People follow different religions such as Hinduism, Islam, Christianity, Buddhism, Jainism, Sikhism, Zoroastrianism and many

---

**sustenance:** food and drink regarded as a source of strength; nourishment; **homogeneous:** of the same kind; alike others. India is a secular country and the Constitution of India ensures that all religions are treated equally.

## Cultural Diversity

India is an combination of various cultures and traditions. This reflects in the different monuments and in festivals celebrated by people from different states. Each state also has its own unique **cuisine**, architecture, music, dance forms, and traditions.

▲ The Basilica of Bom Jesus, Goa, Portuguese architecture

▲ Chhatrapati Shivaji Terminus, Mumbai, British architecture

▲ Taj Mahal, Agra, Mughal architecture

▲ Brihadeeswarar Temple, Tanjaore, Temple architecture

▲ Qutub Minar, New Delhi, Indo-Islamic architecture

▲ Church of our Lady of Good Health, Puducherry, French architecture

## Linguistic Diversity

India is home to people from different cultures. Favourable physiography and climatic conditions have brought about an **influx** of people from all around the world. This is a major factor which contributes to the linguistic diversity that exists in India. The different languages spoken by people from different regions, races and tribes adds to the diversity.

To see how diverse India is, let us take a close look at the eastern and the westernmost states in India.

**cuisine:** a style of cooking that is characteristic of that place; **influx:** the arrival or entry of many people or things in a place

## Case Study

| Gujarat | Arunachal Pradesh |
|---|---|
| Gujarat is the western-most state of India. The capital of Gujarat is Gandhinagar. Most people in Gujarat speak Gujarati as the main language thus it is a linguistic state. | Arunachal Pradesh is the eastern-most state of India where the Sun rises first. The capital of Arunachal Pradesh is Itanagar. Arunachal Pradesh is not a linguistic state. It is inhabited by diverse tribes, each having its own colourful and vibrant lifestyle. |
| Gujarat experiences moderate climate due to its location as a coastal state. The southern part of Gujarat receives rainfall but the northern regions have a desert type of climate. Mangrove forests, desert plains, salt marshes, and wetlands make up the topography of Gujarat. The Gir National park in Gujarat is home to the Asiatic Lion. The forest also supports a variety of birds and animals, such as deer, blackbuck, etc. | The region receives heavy rainfall. It experiences moderately hot to cold climate depending on the altitude of the place. The Eastern Himalayas extend into this state. The river Tsang Po enters India, and flows as Brahmaputra from here. Nature has endowed this state with bounties of rich flora and fauna. It has dense tropical forests, which are home to about 5000 species of plants and 500 species of birds and reptiles. |
| Navratri is a very important festival, which is celebrated with *Dandiya ras* dance. The International Kite flying festival is celebrated on 14 January to mark the movement of the Sun into the Northern Hemisphere. | Losar is the main festival of the Tawang district of Arunchal Pradesh. It is the celebrated as the new year, with much ceremony and pageantry by the people of the Monpa tribe who constitute a majority of the population here. |
| Men wear cotton dress, a traditional *chorno* and *kediyo*, with colorful turbans as headgear. Women wear a skirt with blouse, called *chaniyo choli* with an *odhni*. The dresses are vibrant with embroidered mirror and shell work. | Different costumes are worn by different tribes that reside in this state. The Monpas are famous for their skullcap, which is decorated with laces and fringes. The women wear a sleeveless chemise tied around the waist with a long narrow strip of cloth with an embroidered or woven full-sleeves jacket and a long skirt. |
|  ▲ Gujarati dress |  ▲ Arunachali dress |

Q. List two similarities and two differences between Gujarat and Arunachal Pradesh.

**equality:** same status, rights, and responsibilities for all the members of a society, group, or family

## Diversity and Equality

The Constitution of India treats all citizens of India as equal. In the view of India's diversity, the Consitution of India promotes and supports **equality** and national intergration in which all people from different races, religions, cultures, castes and backgrounds are treated equally. However, this has not been wholly achieved. There are still innumerable instances where people have been discriminated against. Developing an awareness and appreciation for diversity and guaranteeing access to opportunity and inclusion for all is an ongoing process.

## Unity in Diversity

The diversity of India has always been seen as a source of its strength. The phrase **unity in diversity** was first used by Jawaharlal Nehru, India's first Prime Minister, in his book *The Discovery of India*. Indians from different regional, religious and cultural backgrounds participated together in India's struggle for freedom despite attempts by the British to divide the nation. Despite the variety of cultures, India remains a united country. We take pride in the different cultures, respect them, and consider them at par with each other. People from diverse groups identify themselves as citizens of India. This unity, which binds us despite our differences is what makes India united amidst diversity. All citizens of India must appreciate and respect the diverse cultural traditions of people in different parts of India.

### Consider

Soon after independence from the British, Sardar Vallabhbhai Patel single-handedly undertook the most difficult task of bringing together over 565 princely states of India under the umbrella of a single Indian Union, which became the foundation of the Indian Republic. The diverse nature of the princely states was carefully preserved and it was ensured that all religions, languages, customs and culture of the people were able to flourish in the new set-up.

- Why is India called a union?
- Find out what a republic is.
- Why is it important to preserve diversity?

### World Connect

*'No culture in South Africa is pristine and no language is unaffected by the multi-lingual experience, that has been the melting pot that is South Africa. The Afrikaans diction has been heavily influenced by indigenous languages, which reflect English and Afrikaans influence in many respects.'*

This is an excerpt from a speech by the Deputy President Kgalema Motlanthe on the Heritage Day, calling on South Africans to unite in their diversity, to build a society based on democratic values, social justice and fundamental human rights. Like many other countries of the world, South Africa too has cultural diversity. The nation is also called the 'Rainbow Nation' as people of many different social background live there. It is now a collective responsibility of all the people to preserve this diversity.

## Recall

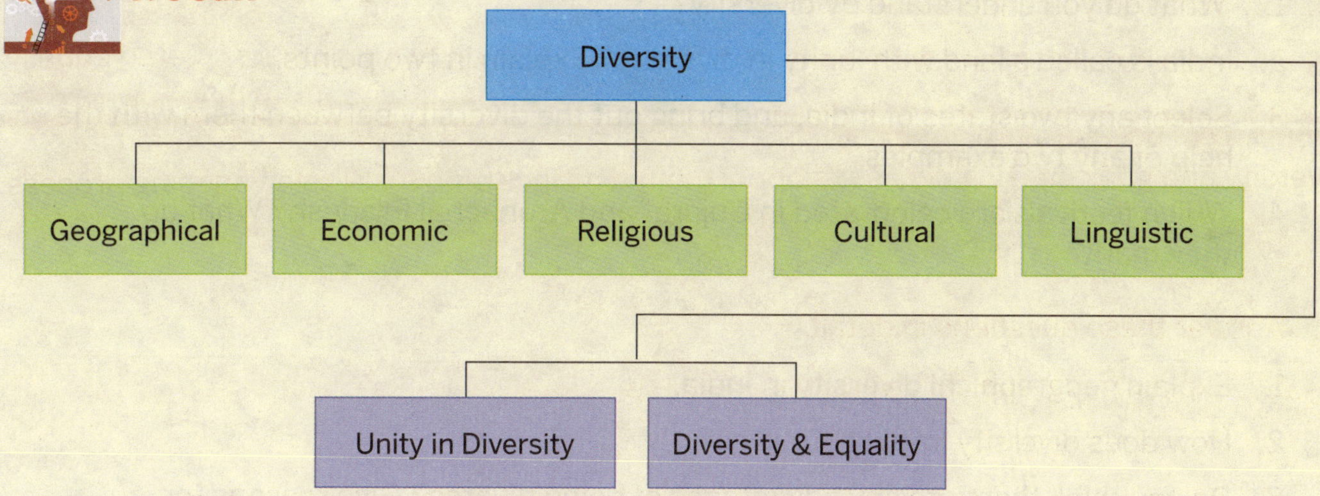


## Work out

**A. Fill in the blanks.**

1. .................................... is a vast country with diverse geography and cultures.
2. Each period of .................................... had a distinct influence on the lives of people.
3. The UN has declared 21 May as .................................... .
4. Religion, languages, food, festivals and rituals are called .................................... .

**B. Fill in the blanks with the correct answers.**

1. The phrase unity in diversity was coined by .................................... .
   Mahatma Gandhi
   a. Pandit Nehru   b. Sardar Patel   c. Dr B R Ambedkar
2. Victoria Memorial in Kolkata is an example of the architectural style of the .................................... .
   a. Portuguese   b. British   c. Mughals   d. French
3. States formed on the basis of language are called .................................... .
   a. artistic states   b. cultural states   c. linguistic states   d. diverse states
4. *Chorno* and *Kediyo* are examples of men's traditional clothing from .................................... .
   a. Assam   b. Gujarat   c. Arunachal Pradesh
   d. Rajasthan

C. Answer these questions in brief.

1. What do you understand by diversity?
2. India is called a land with 'unity in diversity'. Explain in two points.
3. Select any two states of India, and bring out the diversity between them with the help of any two examples.
4. Which festivals are celebrated in Gujarat and Arunachal Pradesh? What do they mark?

D. Answer these questions in detail.

1. Explain geographical diversity in India.
2. How does diversity impact our lives?
3. Do you think there are any advantages of being diverse? Give reasons for your answer.
4. Suggest any two ways in which we can preserve the diversity of this country.
5. Contact with the Arabs, the Persians, the Turks and the Europeans has made India's already diverse culture more diverse. Explain with examples.

E. Complete the crossword puzzle.

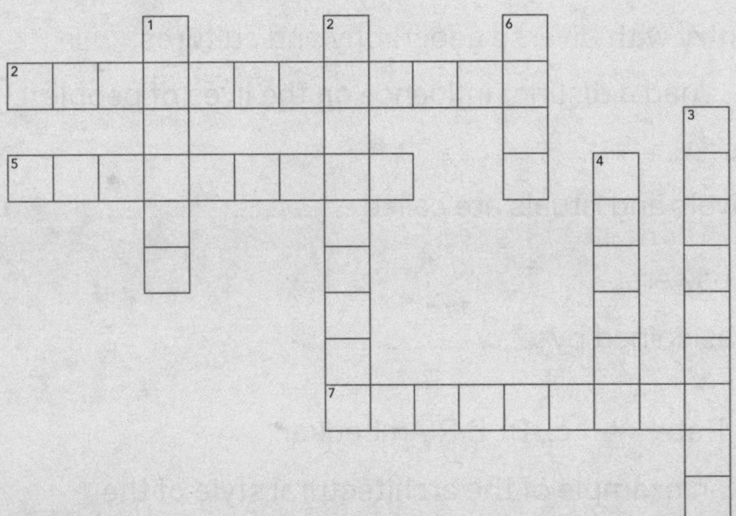

**Down**

1. A cold desert of India
2. A language spoken in Kerala
3. This is the newest state in India
4. The world famous Rath Yatra takes place in this state.
6. A hot desert of India

**Across**

2. A state in which the Maikal hills are situated.
5. Lofty and snowcapped mountain ranges in the northern part of India
7. The state which is called the home of clouds.

## Think

Look at the picture and answer the questions.

1. This is a picture of a girl from Nagaland in her traditional dress. Does she look different from you?
2. Have you met and interacted with anyone who looks like her?
3. Should you discriminate against people who are different from you?

## Life skills and values

There is a group of people who have been officially been recognized as the third gender. In India, we call them hijras and their rights are protected by law. How does society view them? Do they enjoy the same rights and privileges?

## Enjoy

Organize a food and culture festival in your school. You can bring any food that is characteristic of the state to which you belong, wear traditional clothes introduce yourselves in your home language and present dances or songs of your state.

## Web link

For more information, log on to:

https://www.india.gov.in/my-government/constitution-india

Last accessed on 30 September 2019

# 2 Diversity and Discrimination

## Take off

- ............................................ is the classical dance of Tamil Nadu.
- ............................................ is a famous drink from Kashmir, made with nuts, saffron and cinnamon to keep the body warm during extreme winters.

## Warm up

How would you treat a new student with a different cultural background in school?

We have already learnt that diversity constitutes the framework of the Indian society. Guided by the principle of secularism, tolerance and mutual respect, India has thrived with its diverse cultures and races. People from different cultures and regions make up the rich fabric of India. When the nation's diversity is not wholly accepted and appreciated, it might trigger negative attitudes and opinions amongst people. However, while diversity has enriched our nation manifold, it has also been the main reason for discrimination, prejudice, inequality and formation of stereotypes in the social fabric.

## Discrimination, Prejudice and Stereotypes

**Discrimination** is the practice of treating one person or group of people less fairly or less well than other people or groups. Discrimination refers to treating people differently on the basis of caste, creed, color, language, gender etc. We discriminate when we do not treat everyone equally.

Before the Constitution came into force in 1950, there was a lot of discrimination in the Indian society. Caste rules prevented some groups of people from using public facilities, accessing wells and mingling with the rest of the society.

After gaining independence, the Constitution declared everyone to be equal and also guaranteed fundamental rights to all the citizens without any discrimination.

**Prejudice** is an unreasonable dislike of a particular group of people or things, or a preference for one group of people or things over another. It is a **preconceived** opinion formed about someone or something that is not based on reason or actual experience or fact. Prejudice can lead to discrimination. For instance, children who are overweight are often believed to be below average in sport. Therefore, in some cases they are prevented from taking part in sports altogether. Prejudice can lead to many harmful effects on the society. It leads to conflicts between communities, creates disunity, causes racial arrogance and hampers the development of the nation.

A **stereotype** is a widely held but fixed opinion of a person or a group of people, which is often not true. It is a set idea about a particular type of person or a thing. When judgments are made about people without knowing them and without basing those judgements on facts, stereotypes are created. People generally unconsciously create stereotypes out of bias against a particular group of people or a religion. Women are usually expected to do household chores while men are expected to earn their daily bread. Just like prejudice, stereotyping can often lead to discrimination. For instance, boys who cry are often ridiculed for behaving like girls. It is the collective responsibility of both the people and the government to work towards deconditioning to challenge age-old beliefs and opinions.

▲ Today, women are breaking barriers and are employed in all kinds of fields which were earlier considered to be fit only for men.

Before forming pre-conceived notions about a person or a group of people we must stop to think whether it is based on a fact or if it is just what many people say. We must respect people and their individuality and not judge them on the basis of their economic background, race, religion or appearance.

## Discrimination and Inequality in India

Throughout the ages, India has been characterized by deeply-**entrenched** social hierarchies defined by caste, gender, region and religion. In the 21st century, these characterizations continue to be an enormous problem in the Indian society endorsing privilege and limiting opportunities for the poor and the backward sections of the society. Major concerns for the future include money-lending reforms, ensuring the breakdown of the worst aspects of the caste system and improving educational opportunities for women.

▲ Girls should be allowed to go to school and be educated

**preconceived:** ideas or opinions formed before having the evidence for its truth or usefulness;
**entrenched:** firmly established and unlikely to change

### Social Inequality

**Caste System**

In the ancient times in India, the Hindu society was divided into four castes on the basis of the work that people did. The caste system led to the lowest caste being treated in a highly unequal manner. They were denied the opportunity to be educated and earn money, and consequently remained backward and poor. The caste system discriminated among people on the basis of their birth and a person born in a particular caste had to perform the duties assigned to that caste. The Constitution of India finally abolished untouchability in the year 1950, and declared all people to be equal.

### Economic Inequality

**Being Rich and Poor**

Poor people have to face discrimination in all areas of life. They have to do menial jobs to earn their livelihood as they do not have proper education to get better jobs. There is a huge difference in the facilities available to them and those available to the rich in India. The rich enjoy facilities like good education, healthcare, shopping in malls, access to the best restaurants and hotels, holidays, visiting other countries, and other such things. The poor, on the other hand, have to struggle hard to make ends meet. They are hardly able to meet their basic needs of food, shelter and clothing. Poverty has become a major challenge for our country.

## Discrimination and Inequality in the World

Religious discrimination is common in different parts of the world. People often discriminate against religions. Religious groups often clash with each other over their beliefs.

Gender discrimination is another issue for which women struggles have taken place.

Women face discrimination and are subject to unequal laws all over the world even in the developed countries. They have to constantly fight to get their due place in society. Many protests were organised by different groups of women to get women suffrage.

**Fact quest**

London hosted the first Paralympics in 1948 and the sporting event for the differently abled people has grown ever since. It is now recognized throughout the world.

## Breaking Stereotypes

In the changing world, we must consciously try to break stereotypes and develop a broad-minded perception of people and situations around us. Events such as the Paralympics have significantly changed the prejudices and stereotypes associated with people facing any kind of physical disability. They have events ranging from athletics for para-athletes, to football matches between visually impaired teams. These events draw huge crowds and is very popular among sports enthusiasts. There is an increasing number of examples of breaking stereotypes from all around the world and all walks of life as a ray of hope that things are gradually changing.

▲ A person with an artificial limb running across the desert

## Case Study

**Discrimination on the Basis of Physical Disability**

Nine year old Gabi Shull was just like any other girl of her age very active, and had hobbies, like dancing, singing, reading and playing. She was a talented ballet dancer but her hopes of becoming a dancer came crashing down when she was diagnosed with cancer at the age of nine. Her condition required the lower part of her leg, knee down to be amputated. She now had to get an artificial leg. Her road to recovery was very tough but she never gave up hope. She is now back to dancing on her toes as is the requirement of ballet and she is a competition level dancer.

▲ Gabi Shull

Read about some other famous personalities who have overcome similar challenges.

## Consider

*Dr BR Ambedkar was the chief architect of the Indian Constitution. He had to face discrimination during life, on account of being from the lowest caste. Each incident of discrimination made him a stronger person and he decided to fight for the equal status of all people. He studied to become a lawyer and an economist and also became a social reformer. He said, 'If you ask me, my ideal would be a society based on liberty, equality and fraternity.... an ideal society should be mobile, should be full of channels for conveying a change taking place in one part, to other parts.' All these ideals are enshrined in our Constitution. He was awarded the Bharat Ratna in 1990, posthumously.*

*—Excerpt from Dr Babasaheb Ambedkar Writings and Speeches Vol. 1, compiled by Vasant Moon*

▲ BR Ambedkar monument

1. Who was Dr Ambedkar?
2. Why did he have to face discrimination?
3. What were his views on an ideal society?

## Towards Equality

The Preamble to the Indian Constitution is a statement of all the ideals that our country strives to achieve. It envisions a society, free from any discrimination, a society where all citizens are equal. The diverse character of the Indian society must be respected and allowed to grow. The term **fraternity** as used in the Preamble, encourages people to embrace the spirit of brotherhood. The fundamental rights given in the Constitution of India, safeguard people from discrimination and exploitation and promote equality and diversity. The right to vote is also extended to all citizens of India, who are 18 years and above without any discrimination. Government of India is making constant efforts through varied welfare schemes to end discrimination.

### Find out

Which words/phrases in the Preamble promote equality?

### Eco feat

Nature also supports diversity. The different kinds of ecosystems such as deserts, mountains, plains, plateaus and coasts support the biodiversity on the Earth and make life varied and rich.

## World Connect

### Racial Discrimination

For a very long time in South Africa, the practice of apartheid was followed by the white minority government leading to discrimination against the blacks. This was a policy of segregating the blacks and treating them in an inferior manner. They were not allowed to use public facilities and did not have the right to vote. The inhuman practices of apartheid came to an end due to the efforts of a leader of the African National Congress, Nelson Mandela. The blacks were given full political rights including the right to vote in 1994. He was awarded the Nobel Peace Prize for his contribution and is regarded as a respected world leader.

## Recall

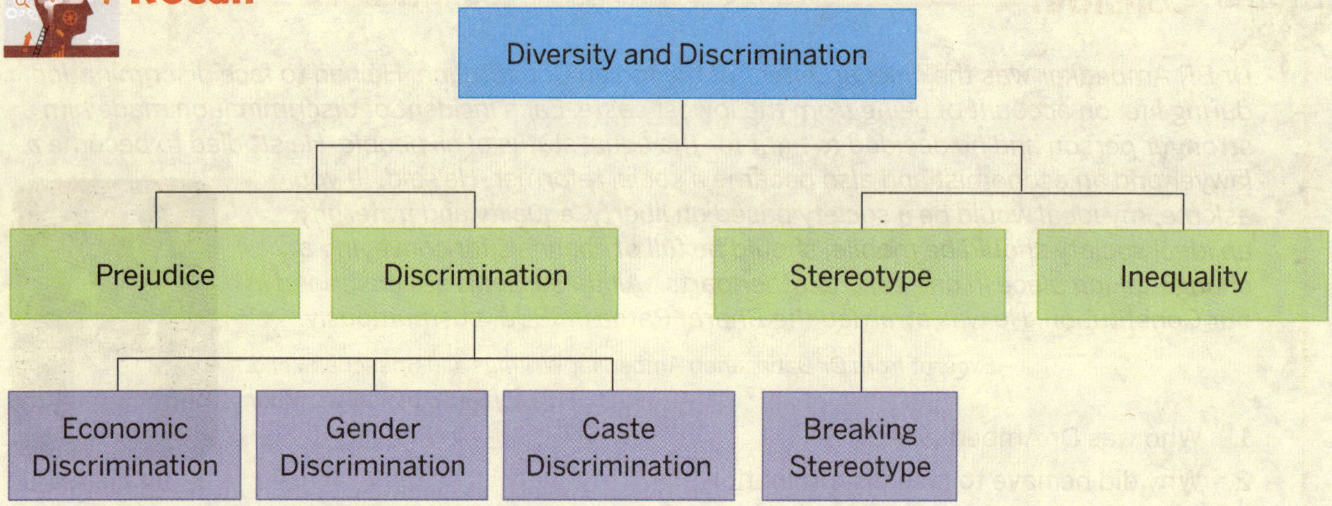


## Work out

A. Fill in the blanks.

1. .................................. was a practice of racial discrimination in South Africa.
2. .................................. refers to appreciating the differences among people.
3. .................................. was an unfair system in ancient India, which divided people.
4. The Constitution came into force in the year .................................. .

B. Write T for true and F for false.

1. Believing in prejudices makes our country progressive. ☐
2. Discrimination and inequality exist only in India. ☐

3. Stereotypes cannot be changed as they have become a part of society. ☐

4. Gabi Shull's story gives us hope. ☐

5. The Constitution treats everyone equally. ☐

C. Answer these questions in brief.

1. What do you understand by stereotypes?
2. What is prejudice? Why should we not believe in them?
3. What was the practice of apartheid? How was it brought to an end?

D. Answer these questions in detail.

1. Explain the reasons for discrimination in India.
2. What do you understand by religious discrimination? Explain with examples.
3. How can we say that caste based discrimination was an evil in the Indian society?
4. Give some examples of common stereotypes and prejudices from your day to day life.

## Think

Look at the picture and answer the questions.

1. Identify the lady in the picture. Which stereotype did she break?
2. What did she come to symbolize in the national struggle for freedom?

## Life skills and values

Read the following statements and write down which stereotypes are being broken in each.

1. Germany's first woman Chancellor, Angela Merkel, is considered one of the most powerful women in the world.
2. Women in India get permanent commissions in the Indian Navy.
3. The Chief Justice of India broke down in tears while addressing a gathering of dignitaries, on the shortage of judges in the country.

## Enjoy

Michelangelo, Isaac Newton, Mozart and Charles Darwin are world renowned personalities. They made remarkable contributions in their fields of art, science, music and evolution ary biology. Many psychologists believe thay they may have suffered from autism during their lifetime. Collect information on autism, which is a condition that makes people differently-abled from the rest. Also, think about whether there should be prejudices against differently-abled people?

## Web link

For more information, log on to:

https://www.india.gov.in/topics/social-development

Last accessed on 30 September 2019

# 3 Government

## Take off

- The Prime Minister and the .................................... are very high ranking and important officials in our country.
- Many facilities are required in every area like street lights, pavements, parks, hospitals, etc. These are provided by the .................................... .

## Warm up

What do you understand by the word a government?

Have you ever wondered what it would be like if there were no rules or laws? All regions in a country need proper **administration** to develop. The **government** of a country is the group of people who are responsible for governing it. A government determines the way in which a country, state, city or village is administered. At each level, the government formulates laws that the citizens have to follow and creates policies about everything connected with the daily life of a community.The government has to provide those conditions, which will help citizens of the country to make the best of their potential and realize their dreams. This means that the task of making and implementing laws and providing the city, state or nation with the proper facilities to function and develop, is the responsibility of the government.

## Functions of Government

A government performs many different functions and develops and elaborate system to do so. Its major functions are:

- Maintaining law and order
- protecting international boundaries of the country
- conducting foreign policy for peaceful relations with rest of the world
- provide facilities like railways, postal services, housing, healthcare and education to all its citizens

### Fact quest

The only place in the world, where there is no form of government, is Antarctica.

**administration:** a range of activities connected with organizing and supervising the way that an organization or institution functions

- collecting tax and revenue
- protecting citizens from natural disasters and managing disasters
- resolving interstate conflicts in case of federal structure

A government provides facilities and institutions to maintain law and order. It establishes agencies for facilities, collecting taxes and revenues. It maintains the armed forces for defence of the country and regulates its relations with other countries of the world. All these are the responsibilities of the government. It also provides healthcare facilities and constructs houses and buildings for people. The government also plays a crucial role in understanding the fast changing world, and takes decisions about the policies to be followed to adapt to these changes.

**Consider**

Read these questions carefully, and answer them. Cite reasons for each.

1. If you could vote, would you?
2. How does the government affect the food that you eat?
3. Can you build a house wherever you want?
4. Who takes care of the people who cannot afford to pay for a lawyer, in case they need one?

## Organs of Government

In order to ensure smooth and systematic working of the government, it has been divided into various organs such as **executive**, **legislature** and **judiciary**. They are placed at an equal footing but work on a system of checks and balances. This is to prevent any one organ from becoming too powerful.

The legislature in India is called the **Parliament** and it makes laws for the entire country. The task of the legislature is to carry out discussions and debates to make laws. Laws are made by the **elected representatives** of the people. Their function is not only to make new laws, but also to change or amend existing laws.

▲ Parliament

After the laws are made, they need to be put into practice. The executive organ of the government helps to implement the laws. The elected representatives make laws in the Parliament and those laws are implemented by the ministries and their departments. The Ministry of Human Resource Development and the Department of Education, which comes under it are some examples. When the word 'government' is used, it usually refers to the executive because it is through this organ that the laws impact the lives of the people.

▲ The Supreme Court of India

The role of the third organ, the judiciary is to punish the law-breakers. Punishments can range from simple fines to rigorous imprisonment. There is an elaborate system of courts in our country so that justice can be ensured for all citizens. The Supreme Court is the highest court of law in our country. It is situated in New Delhi.

**Find out**

Who is the present Chief Justice of India?

## Levels of Government

India is a vast and diverse nation. One government alone cannot manage all this work so it divides its power and responsibilities among different levels. These levels are **hierarchical** in nature and are—the **union** or **central government**, the **state government** and the **local government**.

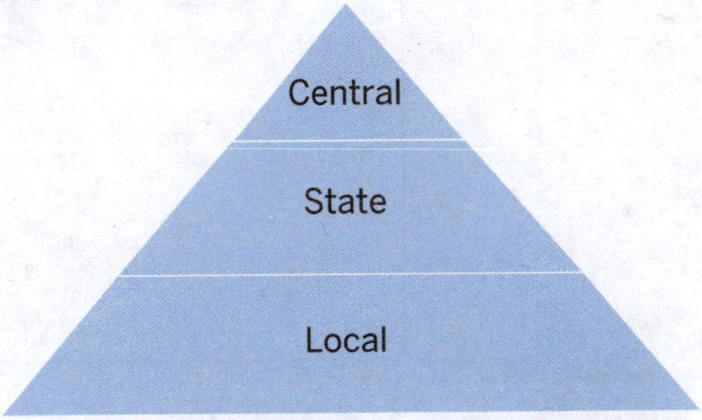


▲ Levels of government

The central government looks after the affairs of the whole nation, for example foreign affairs, external security, finance and defence. The state government looks after the affairs of the state. In this manner, specific issues related to the state are taken care of within the state. Even a state can be a large unit for only one government to manage because every street, alley, and corner of the state has to be administered. Therefore, the third level of government called the local government has been created to share the burden of administration with the state government. All levels of government are formed through the same procedure of **elections**. They carry out the same functions only their scale of work is different. The union government governs the country the state government looks into the affairs of the respective state and the local government looks into localities within a state.

### World Connect

Bhutan is a constitutional monarchy with a parliamentary form of government. The country has a monarch as well as a Prime Minister who work together and look after the affairs of the state.

Until the 1950s, Bhutan was an absolute monarchy. From 1953 the monarchs divested themselves of their power and in 2008 King Jigme Khesar Namgyal Wangchuk, completed the transfer of governmental authority to a popularly elected, multi party, bicameral legislature. While the monarch remained the titular head of state, the prime minister was the actual head. The citizens of the country have universal suffrage. The first general elections for the National Assembly were held on 24 March 2008. The national assembly called Tshogdu approves all laws.

**hierarchical:** arranged in order of rank

## Recall

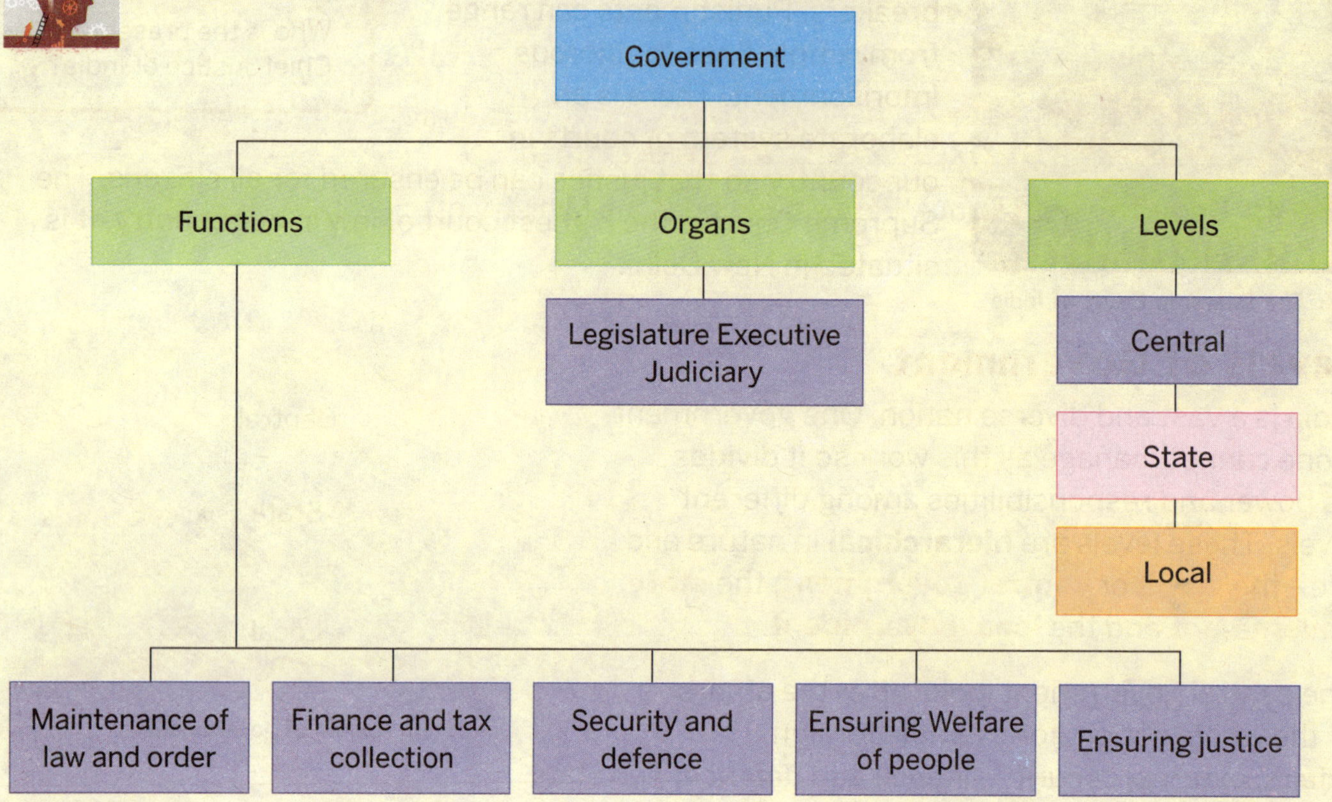


## Work out

**A. Fill in the blanks with the correct answers.**

1. The government of Delhi would look after .................................... .
   a. Uttar Pradesh　　b. neigbouring areas
   c. Delhi　　d. entire country.
2. To provide justice is the responsibility of .................................... .
   a. the legislature　　b. the executive
   c. the judiciary　　d. the government
3. To make new laws is the task of .................................... .
   a. the legislature　　b. the executive
   c. the judiciary　　d. the government
4. When people talk about the government, they are actually referring to .................................... .
   a. the Prime Minister　　b. the Home Minister
   c. the Chief minister　　d. the executive

B. Fill in the blanks.

1. A government is formed through the procedure of .................................................. .
2. The third level of the government is called the .................................................. government.
3. The level of the government which looks after the entire country is called the .................................................. / .................................................. government.
4. Department of Education comes under the Ministry of .................................................. .
5. The central government looks after the affairs of the whole .................................................. .

C. Correct the following statements.

1. There are many Supreme Courts in India.
2. Local government defends the country.
3. There are many organs of the government.
4. All levels of government are equal.
5. The legislature in our country is called the President.

D. Answer these questions in brief.

1. Name the three organs of the government.
2. How many levels of government are there?
3. What is the role of the judiciary?
4. List two facilities that are provided by the government
5. List three major functions of the Union government.
6. List two functions of the state governments.
7. List two functions of the local government..

E. Answer these questions in detail.

1. What are the functions of the government?
2. Why is a state government important?
3. Local government helps in taking care of the smallest issues of a place. Explain with example.
4. Why is it important to share the work of the government?
5. Can one organ of the government be considered more important than the other? Give reasons for your answer.

## Think

Look at the picture and answer the questions.

1. What do you think is happening in the picture?
2. Why is the person standing in the witness box?
3. What is this place called?
4. If only one level of government had been there, would the functioning of the country have been smoother? Why or why not?

## Life skills and values

A mammoth 1.26 lakh km stretch of pipelines would be laid, to quench the thirst of Telangana towns and villages, apart from providing water for the industrial needs. The government has sanctioned Rs 4,000 crore to start off the project.

Mention two important roles of the government that you can find in the above lines.

## Enjoy

The class can be divided into three groups and each group should prepare a collage on one organ of the government. The collage should only have pictures and the group members should explain their topic to the class.

## Web link

For more information, log on to:

https://www.india.gov.in/my-government/constitution-india

Last accessed on 30 September 2019

# 4 Understanding Democracy

## Take off

- The government of India is formed through the process of ..................................
- Queen .................................. rules over the United Kingdom, and she turned 90 years old in 2016.

## Warm up

What form of government does India adopt?

Every country, whether big or small, needs a government to take care of its administration. It is interesting to note that the history of a country plays an important role in the kind of government it has today. Many different monarchs ruled over India for a long time till the British came and established their rule over the country. After gaining independence from the British, leaders in India chose democracy as the best way to empower the people and develop the country. While there are many other countries that have adopted democracy, there are also countries that have adopted other forms of government. Monarchy, dictatorship and democracy are some forms of government.

## Monarchy

Before countries became politically united like they are today, most of them were divided into many kingdoms. Kings and queens used to rule over them. They were called **monarchs**. A monarch enjoyed the supreme power to make decisions on any matter regarding the country, and did not have to consult anyone. Kingship was hereditary, and the people could not elect or remove a king. In some parts of the world, monarchy exists even now. A monarch does not necessarily guarantee any

▲ The Royal Family, Buckingham Palace, United Kingdom

rights to the people and they cannot express their opinions freely. For example, in ancient India, kingship passed down from Chandragupta Maurya to Bindisar and then to Ashoka. After Iltutmish, the reign of Delhi Sultanate passed on to his daughter, Razia Sultan, one of the few woman monarch of her time.

**Fact quest**

There are 44 countries in the world till date which follow monarchical system of government. In most of them, the monarch is the titular head of the state.

## Dictatorship

**Dictatorship** is a form of government where a country is governed by one person, or political entity, that wields absolute power and is not restricted by a constitution or laws. Usually, dictatorship governments are formed when power is **usurped** from the rulers or the government forcibly. The rights and freedoms of the people are often **curbed**, and the dictator assumes absolute power over all. Protests are rare under such governments and opinions and voices often go unheard, if not punished.

**Find out**

Does dictatorship exist today? Which country is ruled by a dictator?

### Case Study

**Adolf Hitler**

Adolf Hitler was a German who served in the army and took over the Chancellorship of Germany in the year 1933. He ruled over Germany dictatorially, and established total control over the military. He established the Nazi party and dissolved the German Parliament, called the Reichstag. He took away the freedom and the rights of the people, and no one, including the media, was allowed to criticize him, or express their opinions. Hitler loved his country passionately and wanted to see it as the most powerful country in the world.

▲ Adolf Hitler

Which political theory is based on Hitler's reign and philosophy? What was his reign called in German history ?

## Democracy

**Democracy** comes from two Greek words—*demos* meaning 'people' and *kratia* meaning 'rule'. In a democracy, people have the ultimate power, and it effectively means the rule of the people. Abraham Lincoln defined democracy as a 'government by the people, of the people and for the people.' Democracy originated around fifth century in Athens, which was a city-state of Greece. It followed direct democracy in which people voted at one place and decided by a simple majority.

## Elements of Democracy

There are some elements which are present in every democratic form of government.

**usurped:** power taken illegally or by force; **curbed:** restrained

## Participation of People

A democratic government is formed after people participate in elections. Democracy works successfully only when people take interest in the working and functioning of the government.

In the olden times, when the population was comparatively smaller, people could gather at a place in the city, or under a tree in the villages, and matters would be decided by a simple majority vote. This simple form of democracy was known as **direct democracy**. Gradually, as the population increased, cities and villages became larger, elections were held. Thus, the system of electing representatives, who would govern on behalf of the people, came into being. This is known as **representative democracy**.

## Voting

In a democracy, the citizens of the country elect the government by **voting**, and they also have the power to remove someone by not voting for them in the next election. **Franchise** refers to the rights of citizenship. Today all democratic governments in the world provide **Universal Adult Franchise** wherein all adult citizens enjoy the right to vote. The elections in which the union government of the country is formed are called the **General Elections.** This makes a democratic government responsible and accountable to the people. The elected representatives know that they have to participate in an election after a fixed period of time, and if they do not fulfil their promises, the people will not vote for them the next time.

▲ Voting in India

### Case Study

**Women's Suffrage Movement**

The women's suffrage movement began in the mid-nineteenth century, in Britain. The suffragettes were treated very badly, and were also imprisoned. The campaign grew stronger with the founding of the Women's Social and Political Union 1903, by mother and daughter, Emmeline and Christabel Pankhurst. A suffragette called Emily Davison, threw herself before a horse during the Derby, and sacrificed herself for the cause. When World War I broke out in 1914, suffragettes scaled down their struggle in the larger interest of the nation, and supported their country. This won them admiration. They also managed all the work which, till then, considered a man's domain, as most of the men were away, fighting on the war front. As a result of these developments, women were granted the right to vote for the first time in Britain, in 1918. In USA, women got the right to vote in 1920, and in France, they got the right as late as 1944.

▲ Women Suffragettes, London

Find out when did countries in Africa and Middle East grant right to vote to women and plot it on a time line.

**Franchise:** the right to vote in an election, especially one in which people elect a parliament.

Democracy is based on the principle of **equality** of all citizens without any discrimination. A democratic country does not discriminate against its citizens on the basis of caste, creed, color, gender, language, or any such factors.

> **Fact quest**
>
> Many religious shrines in India did not allow women to enter and offer prayers. After a petition was filed against this in 2016, in Maharashtra, the Bombay High Court ruled that 'it is a fundamental right of women to enter places of worship and it is the government's duty to protect this right.'

## Other Forms of Participation

Sometimes, when laws and legislations are not received well by the people, they protest against them. People may protest by shouting slogans, organizing strikes or by conducting signature campaigns. In a democracy, people can express their views in many forms. They may organise strikes, harthal, dharna, rallies etc. People often organise social movements to protest or challenge policies of the government. Members of the minority community, dalits, adivasis,women and others use this as a means to participate in the democratic process.

## Resolution of conflicts

The government is responsible for helping to resolve conflicts. The duties of the government includes bringing situations of conflict under control and maintaining law and order in the society. In India, there are different groups of people practising different religions and sometimes it leads to clashes. In many instances, it has acted as a cause of tension and conflict in the society. There have been many instances when groups from different religions clash with each other, each wanting to. It is the responsibility of the government to ensure that such clashes do not occur, and all the people live in harmony with each other. Sharing of river water is always a contentious issue between states. Interstate water sharing conflicts are also resolved by the government of India by forming a tribunal and through negotiations.

> **Consider**
>
> **International Day of Democracy**
>
> 15 September
>
> 'Civil society is the oxygen of democracy. Civil society acts as a catalyst of the nation for social progress and economic growth. It plays a critical role in keeping Government accountable, and helps represent the diverse interests of the population, including its most vulnerable groups.'
>
> —*UN Secretary-General Ban Ki-moon*
>
> These words of the United Nations Secretary General, aptly sum up the importance of participation of the people in democracy. The International Day of Democracy helps foster the spirit of democracy in the world.
>
> 1. Civil society refers to the ................................ of the country.
> 2. The civil society helps in ................................ and ................................ .

## Equality and Justice

Democracy is based on the principle of equality of all citizens without any discrimination. A democratic country does not discriminate against its citizens on the basis of caste, creed, color, gender, language, or any such factors. Equality can be ensured in the society only when all religions are given equal status and are considered at par with each other. Justice for all can also be ensured if people who wish to violate these doctrines are not allowed to do so. A democratic government always guarantees equality and justice to its people. Equality and justice are upheld by the Constitution as the ideals India should strive to achieve.

▲ How can one participate in governments?

## Role of Media

Media plays a very important role in a democracy. It acts as the voice of people and provides information about work done by the government. Newspapers, magazines and TV play an important role in discussing government issues and responsibilities. **Social media** helps to garner support for protest and convey messages across the population.

Television is a popular medium which carries out debates and programs through which the voice of the people reaches the government.

### Eco feat

On 27th March 1912, the Japanese Government gifted cherry trees to the United States of America, in an effort to promote friendship and harmony among the two countries. The US government observes the day as the beginning of the National Cherry Blossom Festival to commemorate this gesture and to celebrate the onset of spring.

## Democracy in India

India became a democracy in 1950, after a long drawn struggle against the colonial rule of the British. Indian democracy allows all citizens of India to vote. The Indian Constitution guarantees Universal Adult Franchise. All citizens of India who are 18 years and above enjoy the right to vote. As the population size has grown manifold, India practices representative democracy. People elect their representatives who decide matters on behalf of people. In our country, the government stays in power for five years after which elections take place again.

### World Connect

Mustafa Kemal Ataturk was a Turkish army officer, a revolutionary and the first President of Turkey. He led the Turkish National Movement as a military officer in the Turkish War of Independence. After Turkey succeeded and gained independence, he went on to become the first president of the Republic of Turkey. During his tenure, he introduced several reforms in the fields of education, women empowerment and international relations. He played a key role in the formulation of the principles of liberty and equality, upon which modern Turkey was established.

## Recall

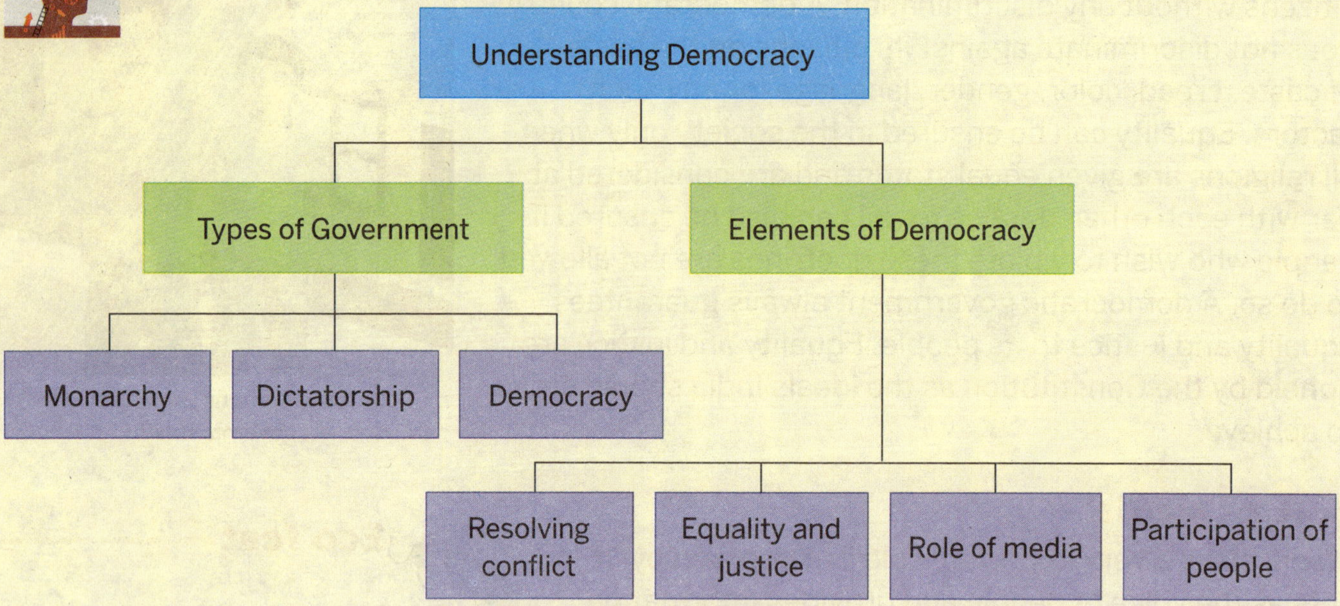


## Work out

**A. Fill in the blanks with the correct answers.**

1. Citizens have the power to remove an elected representative by .................................... .
   a. shouting slogans
   b. not voting for him/her in the next election
   c. not voting at all
   d. asking the President to remove him/her.
2. Direct democracy means .................................... .
   a. people get elected themselves
   b. everyone rules
   c. a simple majority vote is taken
   d. there is no need for the public to be asked.
3. The rule of Mauryas is an example of ....................................
   a. hereditary Kingship
   b. Direct Democratic
   c. Dictatorship
   d. Representative democracy
4. In our country, a government is formed for a period of .................................... .
   a. four years
   b. five years
   c. six years
   d. three years
5. Hereditary selection of a successor is a feature of a .................................... .
   a. dictatorship
   b. democracy
   c. monarchy
   d. all modern governments.

B. List one feature each for each of these.

1. Monarchy
2. Dictatorship
3. Democracy.

C. Write T for true and F for false.

1. Dictatorship is when power is taken illegally and forcibly. ☐
2. India has a monarchical form of government. ☐
3. Suffragettes fought for the rights of women. ☐
4. Religion does not cause conflicts between different groups. ☐
5. India was a democracy even during British rule. ☐

D. Answer these questions in brief.

1. How did Abraham Lincoln define democracy?
2. Why is direct democracy difficult to practise today?
3. Why do you think dictatorship is not a suitable form of governing the country?
4. Who were suffragettes?
5. Give one advantage and one disadvantage of public protests
6. Why are equality and justice important for a democracy?.

E. Answer these questions in detail.

1. List two differences between monarchy and democracy.
2. Why did women have to fight to get their right to vote? How did the suffrage movement shape up?
3. In a democracy, people can protest against the government. In what ways can they do this?
4. Participation of people is a key feature of democracy. How?
5. What role has India's history played in making it a democracy
6. Write a short note on elements of democracy in India.?

## Think

Look at the pictures and answer the questions.

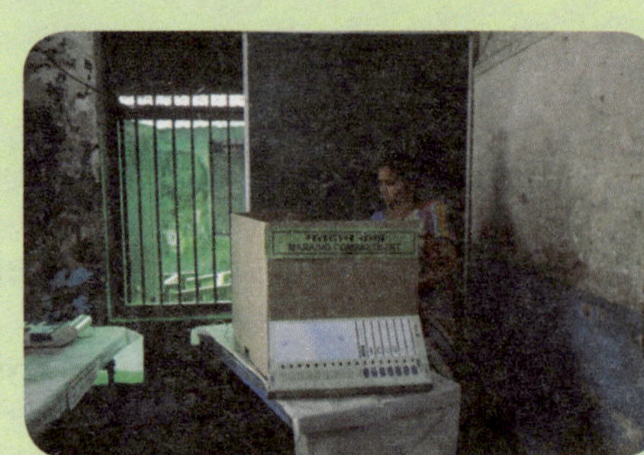

Participation of people is an important feature of democracy.

1. Which ways of participating do you see here?
2. What are the other ways of participating?

## Life skills and values

If two religious groups clash with each other while celebrating their respective festivals, who should resolve this? Most celebrations of festivals require fervent procession, which are taken out so that majority of people can participate. However, these also create disturbance for traffic and can lead to violent clashes. Write your views on the given situation.

## Enjoy

A. Conduct an election in the class to choose the Captain of the class

B. Have you read the *Little Women* novel by Louise M. Alcott? Did you know that Alcott was also a part of Women Suffrage Movement? The character of Jo was based on Alcott herself. Read about her work for uplifting women in the USA.

## Web link

For more information, log on to:

https://www.india.gov.in/my-government/constitution-india

Last accessed on 30 September 2019

# 5 Panchayati Raj

## Take off

- .................................. takes care of the needs of the people.
- It comes into power by the process of .................................. in which the people of the country vote.

## Warm up

Write two differences between a city and a village. Who do the children approach for help?

## What is a Panchayat?

The government at the local level in the villages is called the **Panchayat**. A panchayat traditionally means an assembly or a group of five (*panch*). In India, since the ancient times people in the villages have conducted elections to select leaders, usually the village elders to resolve their conflicts in a peaceful manner. As the villages expanded in size and population, this process evolved into a system of selecting five elders as heads to solve conflicts in an impartial manner.

India has both **rural** and **urban** areas and a large number of towns and cities. Their needs and requirements are very different from each other. In urban areas, proper roads, transport facilities, electricity and water supply for every area is essential. In rural areas there are a different set of problems and concerns. Local governments play a very important role in the rural areas. People living in an area best understand the issues and problems of their area if they are included in the governance of that place then their problems can be addressed in a better manner.

### Need for Panchayat

Although a similar list of facilities are required for the functioning of both urban and rural areas, with respect to basic amenities there are significant differences in their needs.

**rural:** places far away from large towns or cities, villages; **urban:** belonging to, or relating to, a town or city.

The villages are primarily agriculture-based hence wells, tube-wells and canals need to be constructed to irrigate the fields. As a majority of a population practise farming, land-related disputes and disputes over cattle are common in the villages. To solve these disputes fairly, an assembly of local people needs to be set up to arbitrate over the matters or disputes.

## Panchayati Raj System

**Fact quest**

A village in Nagaur district in the state of Rajasthan adopted the first panchayat on 2 October 1959.

Let us now understand the three levels or tiers of the Panchayati Raj system. As we already know, the village is the smallest unit of administration and it is divided into **wards**. Each ward elects its representative for the Panchayat. These representatives are known as the ward member or ***Panch***. administered by the **Gram Panchayat**. Many villages together make a group called a **block**. A block is administered by a body called the **Block Samiti** or the **Panchayat Samiti,** which is headed by an officer called the **Block Development Officer (BDO)**. Many blocks together form a district. The district is administered by the **Zila Parishad**. The **District Collector** is the highest officer in the district administration.

### Structure of Panchayati Raj

The village panchayat consists of two bodies, the **gram sabha** and the gram panchayat. If a village is small, then two or more villages are taken care of by one gram panchayat. Sometimes, a **nyaya panchayat** or local court may be formed for a group of villages. The people have the power of vote in their hands and this feature of democracy keeps the government at all levels alert and encourages them to do their best.

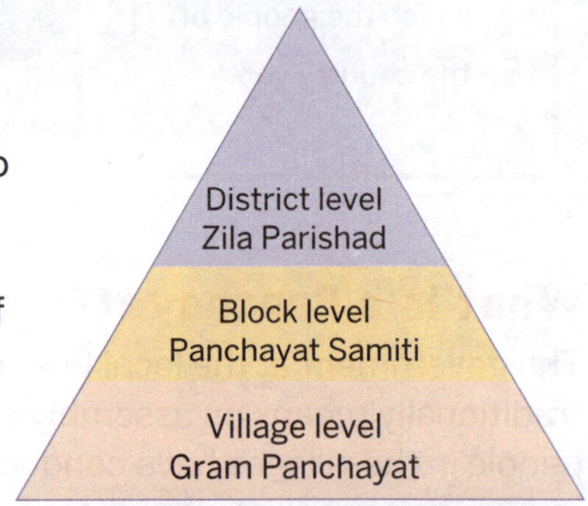


▲ **Structure of the Panchayati Raj**

### Gram Sabha

The panchayat is an elected body. In a village, all those who are 18 years and above can become the members of a village body, the gram sabha. Gram Sabha is a meeting of all citizens living in the village or villages. Every adult with a right to vote is a member of the gram sabha.

All the members of the gram sabha also elect a **sarpanch** who is the panchayat president. The ward panchs and the sarpanch form the gram panchayat.It conducts meetings at least twice a year to raise issues and concerns related to the village. The government appoints a salaried officer as the **panchayat secretary** for both the gram sabha and the gram panchayat. He performs the important functions of taking minutes of the meetings of the gram sabha and also registers the work done by the panchayat.

Some important functions of the gram sabha are:

- Members of the gram sabha elect the gram panchayat.

- It discusses and reviews the issues of economic development in the village.
- It prepares the village budget and audits the accounts of the gram panchayat.
- It looks into the issues of social justice in the village.
- It also makes the panchayat responsible and accountable to the people of the village.

## Gram Panchayat

Every village has a gram panchayat elected by the gram sabha. Sometimes, a few less populated villages are collectively looked after by a gram panchayat. All panch and the sarpanch form the gram panchayat.

## Functions of the Gram Panchayat

The gram panchayat is responsible for:

- Sanitation, conservation, drainage, and redressing public grievances
- Curative and preventive measures with respect to any epidemic
- Supply of drinking water and disinfecting the sources of supply and storage of water
- The maintenance, repair, construction and protection of public streets
- The control and administration of the Gram Panchayat Fund
- The imposition, assessment and collection of the taxes, rates or fees
- The administration of the nyaya panchayat, if required
- Regulation of market and rates of agricultural produce
- Maintain record of births and deaths in the village

On behalf of the state government, the gram panchayat has to focus on:

- Primary, social, technical, vocational, adult or non-formal education
- Rural dispensaries, health centers, maternity and child welfare centers
- Irrigation, rural electrification, and housing
- Land reforms, including bringing waste land under cultivation
- Women and child development

▲ Gram Panchayat

## Consider

At Aravi village, near Latur railway station, there was another queue at the panchayat's water tap. Raju, a grocer, said that one would lose one's place if not physically present.

People start keeping their vessels and pots in the queue just past midnight. Arvind, a Class X student, said that his family was first off the mark because it lives just across the tap on Sai Road. Sheikh Hakani, who has a rented pan shop near the tap, said he paid rupees 40 for a bottle of 18 liters. The panchayat, meanwhile, provides him 200 liters of water free.

1. Can you list at least two functions of the Panchayat from the above passage?
2. Why do people prefer to stay in the queue?

▲ Water problems

### Nyaya Panchayat

A nyaya panchayat is the local court at the village level. Usually, there is one nyaya panchayat for every three to four villages. Its main responsibility is to solve simple disputes among people. It deals with cases of petty theft, minor trespass and other such cases. One-third of the total seats are reserved for women in the nyaya panchayats. Unlike other courts it does not have powers to punish people. Nor does it have any lawyer or judge as its member. It can levy fines on the villagers, and refer cases to the district courts, in case it cannot be settled at the village level but cannot imprison people. As the name suggests, this panchayat brings justice or nyaya to the villagers.

## Funding of the Panchayats

The panchayats need money to carry out the developmental work in the villages. Some of its sources of funds are taxes collected, funds from state government, funds received from centre for its schemes and budget allocation from Finance Commission.

Ministry of Panchayati Raj (MoPR), Government of India initiated the e-Panchayat in the country. This has helped in increasing public participation as well as connecting more than approximately 2 lakh panchayats in the country.

## Eco feat

A village in Netherlands called Geithoorn. The village has no roads only canals. When people have to go from one place to another they require boats. The local authorities ensure regular cleaning of the canals and maintenance of boats in good condition.

▲ A village in The Netherlands

The Panchayti Raj system has empowered the people of the rural areas and has made them active participants in the governance of their areas. This is not only giving them a training in democracy but also making them self-confident and responsible citizens. The panchayat has also created opportunities for the women in the villages as an increasing number of women today are elected to the panchayats.

## Women in Panchayat

Today, panchayats have become a source of women empowerment. The women in villages are now taking active interest in the affairs of the village. They are no longer confined to household work. One-third of the seats in the panchayats are reserved for women so that women can get representation in the panchayats and their issues and problems can also get addressed.

### Fact quest

90-year-old Jal Devi is the oldest member of the UP panchayat. She defeated her 32-year-old rival by a record 7,213 votes at ward 28 of Jagner-II block in Agra district in the panchayat elections in 2014. Jal Devi said "I maintain a register to note down all the complaints which people bring to me."

### Case Study

**Hope for a better future**

The picture you see here is that of a sarpanch of a panchayat from a village called Soda in Rajasthan. She has worked hard to get solar power, water supply, roads, toilets and a bank for her village. She has also addressed a conference on poverty at the United Nations in New York, US. She represents a hope for a better future for the people of India as she is young, modern and an MBA degree holder, who has chosen to work for the rural areas.

1. What has been the contribution of Chhavi Rajawat?
2. What position does she hold? What do you think are her responsibilities?

▲ Chhavi Rajawat

### World Connect

Panchayati Raj system is the oldest known system of local administration in the Indian subcontinent. The word *raj* means 'rule', *panch* and *ayat* in *panchayat* mean 'assembely' and 'five' respectively, therefore meaning, 'an assembly of five'. Traditionally, panchayats were made up of wise and respected elders chosen and accepted by the local community. Apart from India, this system exists in Bangladesh, Nepal, Pakistan and Sri Lanka. Panchayats or village level administrative bodies exist in Trinidad and Tobago too.

## Recall

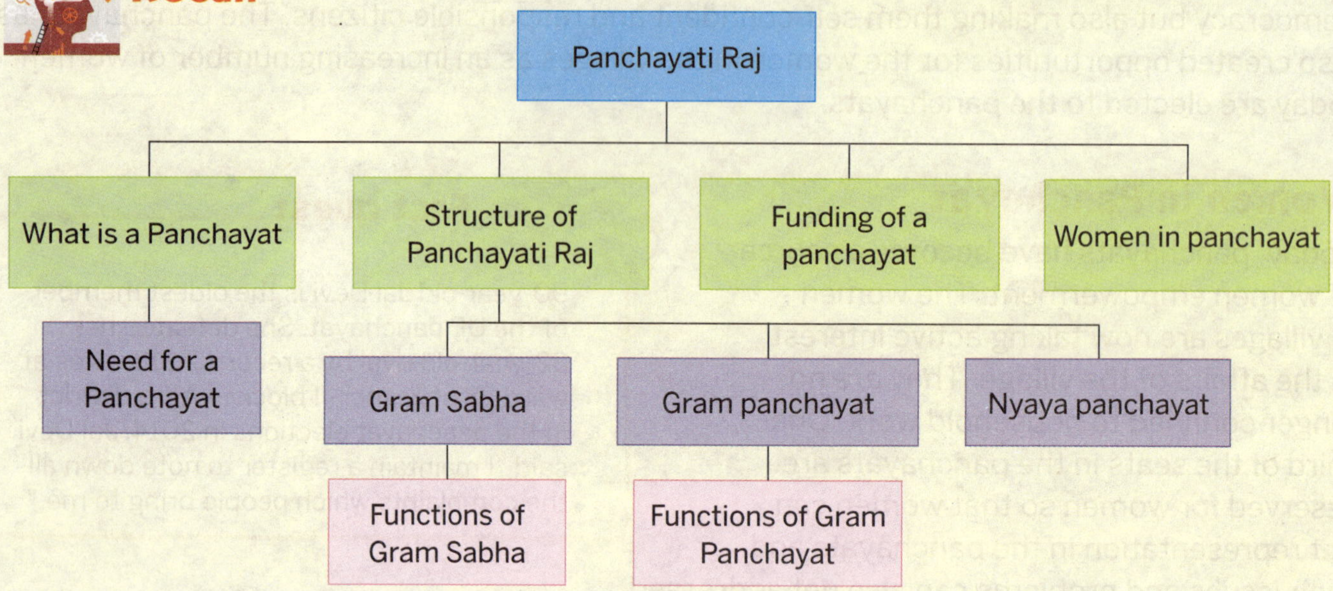


## Work out

**A. Fill in the blanks.**

1. A panchayat is headed by .................................................. .
2. .................................................. seats are reserved in the panchayats for women.
3. The three tier system was added to the Constitution by the .................................................. amendment.
4. The .................................................. takes care of the administration in a block.
5. .................................................. is the body which looks after district administration.
6. Many villages together make up a .................................................. .

**B. Fill in the blanks with the correct answers.**

1. The Panchayati Raj is a .................................................. tier system
   a. two  b. three  c. four  d. five
2. The main function of the Gram Sabha is to elect .................................................. .
   a. Zilla Parishad  b. Panchayat Samiti
   c. Gram Panchayat  d. Block Development officer
3. The smallest unit of administration is .................................................. .
   a. district  b. state  c. village  d. streets

4. The village court is called .......................................... .
   a. gram panchayat
   b. tehsil court
   c. nyaya panchayat
   d. High Court

C. Write T for true and F for false.

1. The panchayat gets money from collecting taxes. ☐
2. The women have got no role to play in the panchayats. ☐
3. The Panchayats connect approximately two lakh panchayats in the country. ☐
4. The block samiti is headed by a District Collector. ☐
5. The Central Finance Commission approves grants for the panchayats. ☐

D. Answer these questions in brief.

1. What is the Gram Sabha?
2. Why was the Panchayati Raj system included in the Constitution?
3. If you were the Panchayat Secretary, what would be your responsibilities?
4. How does a person become a member of the Gram sabha?

E. Answer these questions in detail.

1. Explain the Three Tier Panchayati Raj System.
2. Why can the Central Government not take care of the whole country on its own?
3. How can we say that the Panchayati Raj system gives the people training in Democracy?
4. Panchayats require money to carry out their responsibilities. How do they get it?
5. What is the role of the nyaya panchayat?

## Think

Look at the picture and answer the questions.

1. Ralegan Siddhi is a model village, located in the Ahmednagar District, Maharashtra. Find out more about this village.
2. Its sarpanch is Shri Anna Hazare. Write a report on the latest methods of sustainable development used in the village.

## Life skills and values

As responsible citizens, we must try to conserve the natural resources, especially water, because there is a shortage of clean drinking water in our country. Discuss with your classmates about the measures that can be adopted to save water.

## Enjoy

Divide the class into five groups. Each group can take up one region of India and find out about participation of women in the village panchayats in that region. Present the statistics in the form of a graph on a chart paper and display it in the class.

## Web link

For more information, log on to:

https://www.india.gov.in/topics/rural

Last accessed on 30 September 2019

# 6 Rural Administration

## Take off

- Rural areas are the .............................. areas.
- The needs of the rural areas are different from those of the ..............................

## Warm up

Can you think of some problems which the villages have?
Who do you think solves these problems?

India has a large number of villages. Agriculture is the main occupation of the people living in these villages. As Mahatma Gandhi once said 'If villages of India perish, India will perish too.' This tells us about the significance of the Indian villages. The villages in India have a localized form of government. so that governance becomes easy for the people living in the rural areas of India. In India, the Ministry of Rural Development spearheads the development and welfare of the rural areas.

## Administration of a District

You already know that India is divided into states. The states are divided into **districts,** which are further subdivided into **tehsils** or *talukas*. A *tehsil* is a collection of small towns and villages. The division of a district to tehsil level ensures effective governance. The highest officer in the district is known as a **District Collector.** A District Collector is an officer of the Indian Administrative Service. The main responsibility of a District Collector is to maintain law and order in the district. A District Collector is assisted by **tehsildars** and **patwaris.** Tehsildars are the land revenue officers. They try to solve the village disputes and also supervise the work of patwaris. They ensure that the land records are maintained properly and land revenue is collected. They provide the farmers a copy of their land records. Other important government offices in villages are the milk societies, *anganwadis* or day care, societies to regulate seeds and fertilizers, post offices, health care centres and fair price shops.

## Functioning of the Rural Administration

Have you seen the fields while travelling outside your city? The fields do not have any boundaries or walls yet the farmers have a well-defined land. It is the rural administration that keeps track of the land and maintains the land records. Every village has a system of recording how much land is owned by each farmer.

This job is done by the **patwari**. There are many ways of measuring the land. After measuring the land, a map is created. This map clearly shows the boundaries of each piece of land owned by the farmers. However, conflicts occur when the farmers claim that some portion of their land has been taken over by another farmer. Who resolves these fights? Do the villages also have courts to settle disputes related to land and revenue?

**Fact quest**

The Mughal emperor Akbar, was a great administrator and during his rule, each farmer's land was carefully measured not only for the area but also for its fertility. Tax was calculated on the basis of a tenyear assessment known as 'Dahsala.'

### Role of a Patwari

Detailed records of land holdings are maintained in the villages in order to reduce the number of complaints. Each farmer's land is measured by the government so that there is clarity over who owns how much land. It is the responsibility of the village patwari to ensure that records are maintained properly.

A patwari has these duties:

- Measurement of land and fixing the land revenue according to the size of the land.
- Collecting land revenue from the farmers.
- Maintaining a record of the crops being grown every season.
- Updating the land records every year or in case of any changes.
- Inspection of harvests in order to make an estimate of the yield it would get.

**Find out**

Find out who maintains records in your school. Talk to the concerned person and understand how they carry out their day-to-day work.

## The Role of Police

In case of a conflict, the villagers reach out to the respective police station of their area. In the rural areas. The police station is an important link between the people of the village and the district administration. At the police stations written complaints are lodged. Then, a **First Information Report** (FIR), is registered for the case. Land disputes are the most common complaint in the villages.

▲ Police

**patwari:** a government official who keeps records showing who owns areas of land

## Consider

**The Hindu Succession Amendment Act, 2005**

The Hindu Succession Act came into force in 1956. It was passed by the Parliament of India. There were many different laws about inheritance of property in the Hindu society before that. This Act consolidated all those laws in one Act. The Act was amended in 2005, to uphold the equality of women in inheriting a share of the family property. According to the new law, daughters and their mothers can get an equal share in the land. This Act is considered a landmark law in promoting equality because it has helped the women in the villages become more empowered.

1. How does the Hindu Succession Amendment Act promote equality?
2. Can you think of some benefits that women enjoy women due to this law?

## Case Study

**Story of the largest village in India**

The village of Gahmar is located in the Ghazipur district of Uttar Pradesh. The village has a total population of about 26,000 people. The village is known for the number of soldiers it has given to the Indian Army. Soldiers from Gahmar also fought in the First World War and there is a memorial in the village to commemorate the sacrifice of the martyrs. It is believed that each family in the village has at least one member in the Indian Army.

## Changes in Villages

Rural administration helps the people to implement technological changes such as usage of tractors, harvesters, solar panels, organic farming and others.

In European countries, many farmers are now turning to organic farming. This is a practice followed in India also. Organic farms are those where instead of chemical fertilizers, natural manures are used. Chemicals used in the fertilizers make the soil dependent on chemicals, and they lose their natural richness. The organic manures make the crop healthier, and also rich in nutrients, thereby giving a bumper harvest.

▲ Organic produce

### Eco feat

Find out why the Charanka village in Gujarat is important. Do we need many more places in India to be like that?

## World Connect

At Benta village in eastern Pahang state of Malaysia, an experiment is changing the way some poor people live. A farmer is growing rice without soil. Each rice stalk is grown in a plastic pot with a smart valve that allows the right amount of nutrients and water to the crop. 'The technology can turn anyone into a farmer. The system is pretty much automatic. You just need to aerate the plant, the water is piped in so it will grow by itself.' says Padang Rumbia, the farm manager.

The plastic pots have transformed this village which once used to be a swamp area where little could grow. Today, it is a self-sustaining farm, containing berry and mango trees, vegetable plants and a rice crop. Benta village is the first government-funded experimental farm to help those living in the countryside. The water is recycled from fish tanks to feed the plants. Even the chicken waste is used as fertiliser. Nothing goes waste here.

## Recall

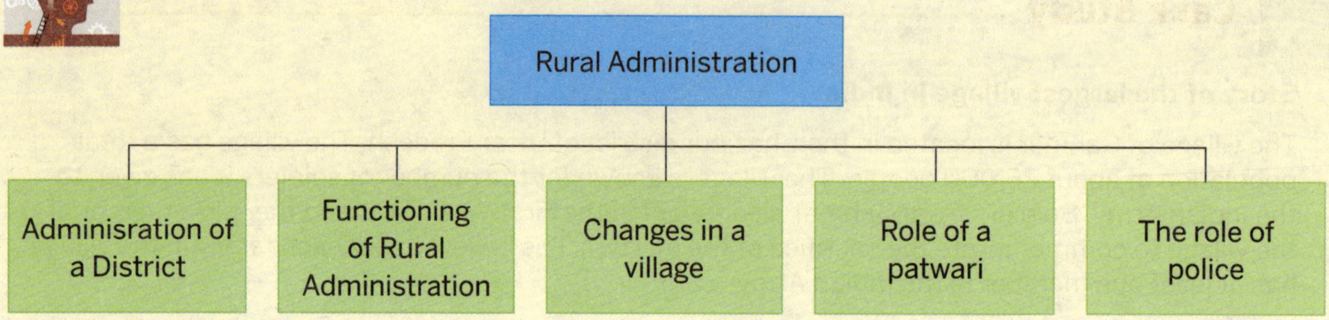


## Work out

A. Fill in the blanks with the correct answers.

1. The ministry of Rural Development has two departments—Land Resource and .................................... .
   a. Rural Development
   b. Rural Affairs
   c. Revenue collection
   d. Land Records
2. The village of Gahmar is located in the Ghazipur district of .................................... .
   a. Madhya Pradesh
   b. Haryana
   c. Uttar Pradesh
   d. Punjab
3. The police station in the village is important because it helps in .................................... .
   a. maintaining law and order
   b. registering complaints
   c. links the villages to the administration
   d. all of these

4. The patwari is .................................................. .
   a. appointed by the government
   b. elected by the people
   c. elected by the Chief Minister
   d. appointed by the Collector

B. Write T for true and F for false.

1. Local self-government helps to develop the villages. ☐
2. The patwari is an important official in the urban administration. ☐
3. The District Collector is the highest official of the state government. ☐
4. Trade is the mainstay of the rural economy. ☐
5. A district is further divided into blocks and villages. ☐

C. Given below are some important officers of administration. List two duties for each of them:

1. *patwari*
2. District Collector
3. Sub Inspector

D. Answer these questions in brief.

1. In what ways have the people of the rural areas become actively involved in governance?
2. Who is the head of the district administration?
3. Why does the Indian Army take special interest in the Gahmar village?
4. Why is it important to maintain land records in the villages?

E. Answer these questions in detail.

1. Interpret the views of Mahatma Gandhi on the villages.
2. Why are the functions performed by the patwari crucial for the rural administration?
3. Which Ministry of Rural Development is responsible for developing rural areas? How does it carry out its work
4. Write a short note on the role of a patwari in a village.
5. What is the role played by the police in a rural area??

## Think

Imagine that you live in a village and a portion of your land has been taken by a farmer whose lands are adjacent to yours. How will you get your land back? Whose help will you take to prove that it is your piece of land?

## Life skills and values

It is believed that the population of the villages is lesser as compared to the cities. Why do the villages still need a local governing body?

## Enjoy

A. Divide the class in six groups. Conduct a comparative study of life in the villages and cities. Present your work through a collage, a PowerPoint presentation or a skit.

B. A corporate employee wants to settle in a village, buy some land and start farming. What are the things he would need to know about rural administration to help him settle there?

## Web link

For more information, log on to:

https://www.india.gov.in/topics/rural

Last accessed on 30 September 2019

# 7 Urban Administration

## Take off

- Urban areas mean the ...................... and the .................................. .
- Administration means to ........................ an area and provide all the facilities required by people living there.

## Warm up

What difference has been brought out by the elderly person, between the house and the park?

The government provides certain basic **amenities** that are essential for its smooth running to all villages, towns and cities. Water and electricity are basic requirements for homes, schools and offices to function. A good network of roads and transport systems, adequate housing facilities, proper sewage tanks, schools and hospitals, recreational facilities and many more things are needed by an urban set-up.

▲ Access to water

▲ Roads

▲ Children's park

**amenities:** desirable or useful features or facilities of a building or place

**Municipal** governance was set up to create effective and responsive bodies to administer the towns and cities. Smaller towns and cities that have a population of less than 20,000 are governed by city councils, cities that have a population of more than 20,000 but less than 10 lakhs are governed by **municipal councils** and cities with a population of more than 10 lakhs are governed by **municipal corporations**.

**Fact quest**

The Chennai Municipal Corporation was the first Municipal Institution to be established in India, in 1688. The East India Company had set up a part of Madras as their Town of Fort St George, and had placed it under a Corporation.

## Municipal Corporation

The municipal corporation or **Nagar Nigam/Mahanagar Palika** is the topmost form of local government in India. Cities governed by municipal corporations are divided into municipal wards from which the members are elected. Each municipal corporation has a committee whose members are elected for a term of five years. The committee is comprised of a **mayor**, and a municipal commissioner along with councillors. The mayor is the titular head of the committee and he is elected for a period of one year. Seats are reserved for Scheduled Castes, Scheduled Tribes, backward classes and women. This institution enjoys a greater measure of autonomy than the other forms of local government.

### Functions of the Municipal Corporation

The functions of the municipal corporation include obligatory functions and optional functions.

The obligatory functions include provision of the basic requirements. These include:

- Regular supply of clean drinking water as well as construction and maintenance of waterworks
- Supply of electricity for all streets, public places and buildings of the area.
- Construction of roads and streets
- Maintaining public health and sanitation by ensuring that the streets and other public places are cleaned
- Construction and maintenance of a proper drainage system
- Maintaining public hospitals and keeping a record of births and deaths
- Setting up schools issuing licenses
- Safeguarding the public from disaster, accident or injury
- Constructing fire brigades, market places, etc

**municipal:** means associated with or belonging to a city or town that has its own local government.

The **discretionary** functions include construction and maintenance of public parks, libraries; maintenance of public transport system, providing housing for the poor and promoting welfare schemes.

In order to understand the role of these bodies, let us take one example of the functions performed by them. Along with providing facilities, a municipal corporation also organizes relief and rescue work, in case of any disaster. like earthquakes and floods, In case of tragedies like train accidents, fires etc they help the victims, and also approach the state and central governments for further aid, if required.

## Sources of Income

Funds are required by the municipal corporations to carry out their responsibilities. People living in the wards own shops, houses and other property. Various sources of income are:

- Water and electricity tax.
- Entertainment Tax
- Octroi and Toll Tax
- Tax on property
- Grants-in-aid from the state government.

**Find out**

What is the name of the Mayor of the Municipal Corporation in your city?

Thus, with this body of funds, the municipal corporation is able to provide facilities to the people. These bodies also play a significant role in addressing the grievances of the people.

**Consider**

**As Flood Water Recedes, Chennai Corporation Begins Cleaning of City on War-Footing**

CHENNAI: The rain water level may be receding in the city bringing relief to people, but it is leaving a huge trail of mess, prompting the Chennai Municipal Corporation to launch a mass cleanliness drive, for all its 200 wards today, for which some of the civic bodies from the neighboring districts have also lent a helping hand.

This newspaper report was published on 6th December 2015 by the Press Trust of India.

- What role has the Chennai Municipal Corporation played in the face of floods?
- Do you think such bodies are very important for an area? Give reasons for your answer.

## The Municipal Council

The Municipal Council or the nagar palika governs smaller cities with a population of more than 20,000. Like municipal corporations, municipal councils are also divided into wards. They are formed through elections and their tenure is five years, after which elections are held again. Seats are reserved for Scheduled Castes and Scheduled Tribes. One-third

**discretionary:** not fixed by rules but decided on by people in authority, who consider each individual case of the seats are reserved for women in the municipalities. It is headed by the municipal commissioner.

## Functions of the Municipal Council

- Maintenance of public hygiene, including disposal of garbage and provision of proper drainage system
- Maintenance of public health by organizing vaccination and health awareness camps, checking for food adulteration, ensuring regular supply of clean drinking water
- Provision of educational facilities, maintain schools, public libraries and museums
- Registration of births and deaths, and issue of certificates
- Maintenance of public places like public parks, roundabouts, roads and bridges, recreation centres, parking lots, shops, markets
- Issuing licenses for parking lots, markets, restaurants, hospitals and housing complexes
- Ensuring regular water and electricity supply, and proper street lighting
- Collecting tax and surcharge on property, water, electricity, parking and other such facilities

**Fact quest**

The Right to Information Act, 2005, enables citizens to secure access to information kept in the public offices. It ensures accountability of the public officer, and promotes transparency.

## Sources of Income

The sources of income for the municipal council are similar to that of municipal corporations. The municipal council also collects tax from water, electricity, entertainment, toll and property. It also gets grants from the state governments.

The municipal authorities sometimes hire workers on a contract basis, when there is more work to be done and less number of people to manage it. Sometimes in bigger cities the contractors **sub-contract** the job further. The contractual workers are not paid at par with the regular employee of the municipal corporation or council.

Study the newspaper report given below.

*Contractual Workers to Help Mcd Fight Staff Shortage*

HT Correspondent, Hindustan Times, New Delhi |

Updated: Apr 08, 2011 00:16 IST

To tide over the problem of staff crunch, MCD has decided to hire more people on contract basis. The Municipal Corporation of Delhi (MCD) has drafted a proposal, keeping in mind the need for more manpower. The MCD commissioner has approved the proposal, making it mandatory that contract employees should be paid emoluments or benefits in such a manner, that they can attract efficient workers.

## Case Study

### A Cleaning Drive

The City of Victoria in Canada, has an elaborate system of keeping their streets clean. The staff in the Corporation arrive early every morning and play a key role in keeping the city clean and inviting for the people. They clean the litter from the streets and sidewalks every day, and empty out the city litter bins every day. All the city parking lots are cleaned weekly. They also clean up the graffiti from the walls on the sides of the roads, and public property. Downtown Victoria is cleaned continuously, as it is a busy area, and all the shopping places are cleaned weekly. The Corporation also invites the people of the city to be part of their drive. Posters put up at places spread the message.

- Do not throw chewing gums and litter the streets.
- Dispose of waste in the bins provided.
- Recycle bottles, aluminum and paper.

The Government of India launched the Swachh Bharat Mission on 2 October 2014 to promote cleanliness in both rural and urban areas all over the nation.

How do you contribute towards cleanliness of your school and neighbourhood?

## Nagar Panchayats

With time, many rural areas change and develop into urban areas. The facilities in these areas grow, and people gradually take up activities other than farming. Such areas, which are in transition from rural to urban, are administered by a body called the **nagar panchayat**. The name of this body explains its function well. Nagar because it is looking after a city, and panchayat because a panchayat looks after rural areas. Usually, these are formed in areas which have a total population of more than 11,000 and less than 25,000. These civic bodies also perform similar functions and their source of income is also the taxes they collect from people.

### Eco feat

The New Delhi Municipal Committee carried out a Tree Census to keep a count of the number of trees in public areas.

## World Connect

The local government in South Africa consists of municipalities of various types. The largest metropolitan areas are governed by metropolitan municipalities, while the rest of the country is divided into district municipalities, each of which consists of several local municipalities. There are eight metropolitan municipalities, 44 district municipalities and 226 local municipalities in South Africa.

**nagar:** a town, a city, an area in a city, or a suburb

## Recall

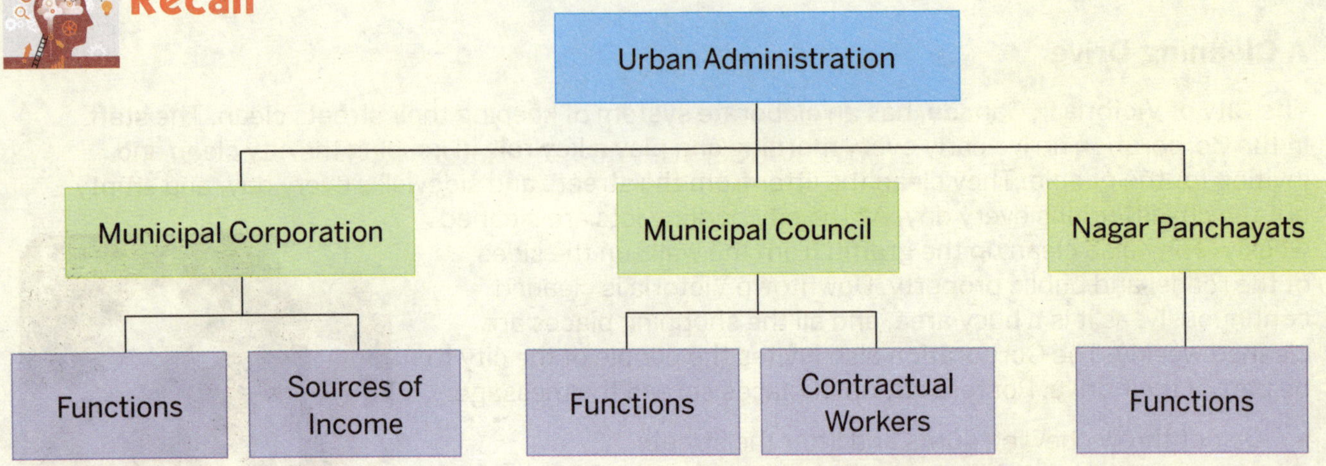


## Work out

**A. Fill in the blanks with the correct answers.**

1. The administrative body for small town is known as the .................................... .
   a. Municipal Corporation b. Municipal Council c. State Government
2. Members of the Municipality are .................................... .
   a. chosen b. nominated c. elected
3. The first Municipal body to be formed in India was in .................................... .
   a. Mumbai b. Chennai c. Kolkata
4. The tenure of a municipal council is .................................... .
   a. four years b. five years c. not fixed
5. Construction of public parks is a function of the .................................... .
   a. municipal council b. municipal corporation c. nagar panchayat

**B. Write T for True and F for False.**

1. The areas are divided into units called blocks, for the purpose of elections. ☐
2. There are municipal bodies in villages also. ☐
3. Members elected to the municipal bodies are called councillors. ☐
4. The state government provides grants to the municipal councils. ☐
5. Toll tax is collected by the municipal bodies. ☐

C. Complete these statements.

1. The urban administrative bodies are formed for a period of ........................................
2. According to the Constitution if a municipality has to be dissolved, then ........................................
3. Nagar panchayats are formed for areas with population between ........................................
4. A Mayor is the ........................................

D. Answer these questions in brief.

1. What are the responsibilities of the Municipalities?
2. Funds are needed by the municipal bodies to provide amenities. How do they get these funds?
3. Who are contractual workers?

E. Answer these questions in detail.

1. For which types of areas are nagar panchayats formed?
2. Enumerate any two features of the municipalities which show that they are democratic institutions.
3. List out the differences between a Municipal Council and Municipal Corporation.
4. What are the functions of a Municipal Corporation?

## Think

A. Look at the picture and answer the questions.

1. Which scheme of the government is being referred to?
2. How is the scheme related to Mahatma Gandhi?

B. You can write a short note or make a drawing to show how the scheme is implemented in your school and neighborhood.

## Life skills and values

Is it the responsibility of only the municipal workers to clean the neighbourhood, or do the citizens have a role to play in it?

There is dengue alert given by the municipal corporation. Elucidate the steps you would take to safeguard the health in your home and then in your neighbourhood.

## Enjoy

Interview the municipal worker who comes to clean your neighbourhood street. Find out whether he or she is a contractual worker and what difficulties he or she faces and write it in your notebook.

## Web link

For more information, log on to:

https://www.india.gov.in/my-government/constitution-india

Last accessed on 30 September 2019

# 8 Rural Livelihoods

## Take off

- The word .......................................... refers to the means of earning money to fulfill our day-to-day needs.
- In the villages, people do different types of work like .......................................... and .......................................... .

## Warm up

Why do you think most of the people in the villages engage in farming activities?

The first mention of a village brings to mind the image of green fields, cows, cottages and children playing on dusty lanes. Village life is busy, but not as fast-paced as city life. Work here is more or less clearly outlined. In India, more than half of the total land area is used for farming. While a majority of the people engage in farming activities, a small population is employed in different kinds of livelihoods like making pottery, handicrafts, weaving, spinning, fishing, etc. In this chapter, we will learn about these occupations. Broadly, these are classified into two categories—**farm work** and **non-farm work**.

▲ Farm work

## Farm Work

About half of India's workforce makes a living directly from agriculture. Since the beginning of agriculture efforts have continually been made to obtain the best yield from every piece of land. Today giant canal projects, multi-purpose projects, the green revolution and the increased use of irrigation and chemical fertilizers have made Indian agriculture more productive. There are three types of farmers in India—**large farmers**, **marginal farmers** and **landless farmers**.

## The Large Farmers

Some of the farmers in the villages own land which has been handed down to them from generation to generation. As they become more financially secure, they also buy more land and expand the existing fields. These farmers own large tracts of land and are able to use the best machinery for their agricultural practices. They plough the fields with the help of tractors, harvesters, cultivators, threshing machines, harrows, and seeders and use fertilizers, and high yielding seeds. These farmers usually don't do the work on their own, but employ other people to do the work for them. Large farms are diverse, growing different kinds of crops with a few incorporating livestock.

> Agricultural seasons
>
> *Rabi* - winter crop; crop grown - wheat
>
> *Kharif* - summer /monsoon crop, grown in the beginning of July; crop grown - paddy
>
> *Zaid* - crops grown from march to june; crops grown - muskmelons, watermelons, etc.

## Farmers with Small Landholdings

Besides the rich and wealthy farmers, there are also farmers who own and work on their own land, but their land holding is much smaller than that of the large farmers. These farms are usually less than two hectares, and the people who own the farms usually work on them themselves. They use traditional methods of farming, and cannot afford heavy machinery like the large farmers. These farmers usually produce just enough for themselves, and at times, a little more for selling in the market. The farmers who grow only as much crops as they can eat, are called **subsistence farmers**. However, since their livelihood is mostly dependent on rain-fed agriculture, these farmers usually find themselves **indebted** to traders or money lenders during times of drought, or when the crops are still not ready. Money lenders provide them with the money to buy seeds and fertilizers, but after harvesting they have to sell their crop to the trader at less than market price.

> **Fact quest**
>
> In the olden times, *bigha* was a unit of measuring land. It was not a standardized unit, and therefore, meant varying sizes of land in different areas.

## Landless Peasants

There are many people in the rural areas who are farmers but do not own lands. They do not have fields of their own to cultivate. They work on other people's farms to earn their livelihood. In this way, they become agricultural labourers. Some of them are small farmers who had land earlier but now it has been taken over by the money lender as they were unable to pay off their debt.

They take the money on interest, and this creates a **vicious cycle** from them. They are not in a position to return the principle amount, or pay up the interest, which just goes on accumulating. As a result, the money lender **confiscates** their lands in order to recover his money.

**indebted:** owing money; **vicious cycle:** a situation in which an attempt to resolve one problem creates new problems that lead back to the original situation; **confiscate:** to seize (property), esp for public use and esp by way of a penalty

## Non-Farm Work

People in the villages, especially women, also do a lot of work which is not related to the fields, but helps them earn a livelihood. This includes embroidery, art and craft work, painting, weaving shawls and other woollen items, working with jute, mirrors, glass, pottery, etc. It is noteworthy, that in a diverse country like India, arts and crafts are also equally diverse, because locally available materials are used for producing these. Since the regions are geographically diverse, the things locally available also vary from region to region.

**Eco feat**

Farmers are now turning to organic farming in order to replenish the nutrients in the soil in a natural way, and also reduce the use of chemicals in farming.

### Fishing

In the coastal areas of India and the banks of the major rivers, fishing is a popular source of earning. Fishermen set out early in the morning to catch fish, and the work involves extensive labour. Sometimes, they do not even catch much fish. The fish are sold in the local and nearby markets, so that farmers can earn money. Nowadays, fishermen from small villages can sell their catch to large corporations that sell them in big city markets. The fishermen sometimes get good returns for this. These corporations process the fish for the markets and also export fish to other countries.

▲ Fishing in India

### Cooperatives

Cooperatives are organizations or groups of people, who come together for the purpose of trade. Cooperatives play an important role here, as it buys the catch from all the fishermen in the village, puts it in large trucks, and takes it to bigger markets in far-off areas. Thus, the fishermen are able to save on the expenses, and can also sell their catch in far-off markets.

| Region/State | Small Scale/Cottage Industry |
|---|---|
| Jammu and Kashmir | Silks and papier mache. |
| North eastern states | Bamboo and cane and jute products |
| Gujarat | Mirror work, embroidery |
| Punjab | Juttis, phulkari embroidery |
| West Bengal | Jute, terracotta artefacts and jewellery |
| Kerala | Coconut fibre articles, weaving, |
| Karnataka | Sandalwood articles. |

▲ Juttis

## Cottage Industries

We have already studied about the three types of industries—large scale, small scale and cottage industries. In villages, cottage industries play a significant role. Cottage industries have played a key role in the economic development of the villages, thereby making the farmers and villagers financially independent. People make use of locally available materials and do not have to depend on raw materials from distant regions.

▲ Mirrorwork

## Case Study

**Weaving**

Rohan and Ritika return home from school, very excited about a summer holiday project that they have got. They have to interview a farmer. The family goes to the village in their car to visit their grandmother. They go to Ramdhan who is a farmer, and are greeted by him. The children ask him about what he cultivates. He tells them about how he grows rice in the big fields that he has, and that his two sons help him in this work. They own two cows, which are looked after by his wife, Sunita. Every morning she wakes up early, milks them, and takes the milk to sell in the village, which helps them to earn. After cleaning their small cottage and finishing her daily household chores of cooking, bathing etc, Sunita sits down to weave colourful mats from the different pieces of cloth that she has. Sunita never throws away old clothes and curtains, bedsheets etc. Instead, she makes strips from them and keeps them in a large box that she has carefully kept in a corner. These mats and the sacks of rice are taken by Ramdhan and his sons to the city market for sale. Sunita's mats are always in demand and sell for a good price.

▲ Mat

1. Can you distinguish between the farm work and the non-farm work in the story?
2. What are the things that keep Sunita busy?

## The Sad Truth

When we try to understand the different ways in which the people in villages earn their livelihood, we cannot remain ignorant about the difficulties they face in their day-to-day lives. Suicides committed by farmers have become a growing problem in our country.

Suicides by farmers touched a grim high in past five years. There have been thousands of farmers who have committed suicide till now. Many state governments have **waived** off farm loans for many farmers to stop this practice. This newspaper report refers to Maharashtra.

Extreme poverty, harsh weather conditions, acute shortage of funds and lack of facilities force these farmers to end their lives due to depression and hopelessness.

▲ Drought land

## Consider

Some rural areas are now emerging as busy tourist spots, especially in the scenic hills of our country. Hill stations are most sought after, not only for their picturesque landscape, but also for adventure sports. The villages around these sites give the tourists a traditional welcome, give them fresh home-cooked food, which consists of the traditional dishes of the region. The Ministry of Tourism is promoting rural tourism. The tourists can get a feel of the village homes, and also enthusiastically take part in their day-to-day activities, like chopping fodder for the animals and plucking fresh fruits. This is mutually beneficial as the urban tourists get a taste of the village life, and the villagers get to interact with different people, and also earn money alternatively.

- How is this new source of livelihood benefitting the villagers?
- What advantage do the tourists get from this?

## World Connect

In many other parts of the world, like Europe and Australia, there are many opportunities for people who love travelling, to earn on their holiday. In Australia, they can do a variety of things like grape picking in Berri, to mango picking in Darwin. Each year, thousands of backpackers find work, helping to bring in the fruit and vegetable harvests. This gives the backpackers the opportunity to combine seasonal harvest work with traveling. It is a popular trend, and is making the city people understand the intricacies of village work.

**waived:** choose not to have it or do it, also people do not have to obey in a particular situation

## Recall

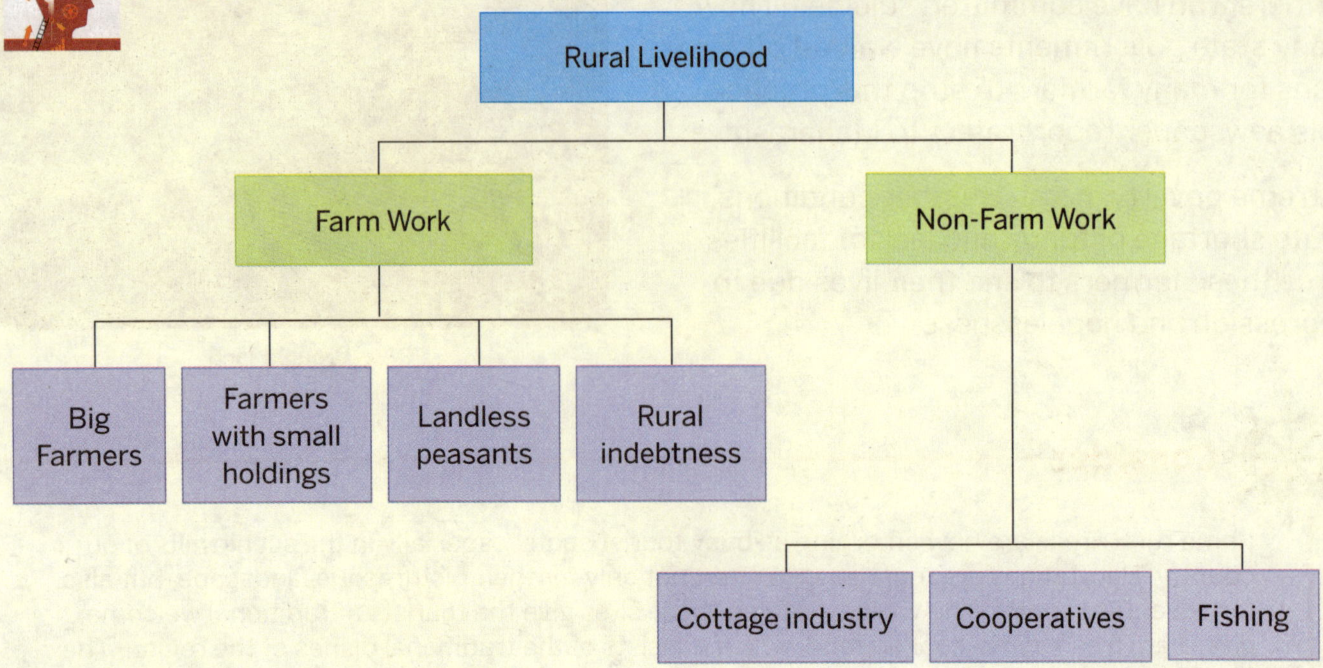


## Work out

A. Fill in the blanks with the correct answers.

1. One of the sources of livelihood for the villages is ............................................ .

   a. going to office  b. working in banks  c. farming  d. all of these.

2. When manufacturing of products is carried out at home with no big machines, it is called a ........................................ .

   a. company  b. factory  c. shop  d. cottage industry

3. In coastal areas, ............................................ is an important source of livelihood.

   a. pottery-making  b. fishing  c. bangle-making
   rope-making

4. Silk and papier-mâché products are famous cottage industries from .................................... .

   a. Punjab  b. Bengal  c. Jammu and Kashmir  d. Kerala

B. Write T for true and F for false.

1. Pottery making is farm work.
2. Harvesting the crops keeps the farmers busy.
3. New sources of livelihood are now available to the farmers.
4. Agricultural labourers own small lands of their own.
5. Women share the burden of running the household.

C. Answer these questions in brief.

1. What are the main sources of livelihoods in the villages?
2. Why do people migrate from the villages during certain times of the year?
3. What are cottage industries?
4. Who are agricultural labourers?

D. Answer these questions in detail.

1. Cooperatives help the village people in increasing their income. Explain.
2. Elucidate with examples, how people in the villages earn their living from sources other than the farms.
3. What are the advantages of cottage industries for the farmers?
4. What are the factors which lead to farmers getting into debts?

E. Solve the crossword.

**Across**

3. A region in Maharashtra, where farmer suicides are common
4. Mirror work is famous in this state
5. A group of people who follow the same profession
6. People who go from city to the villages, and vice versa, in search of work

**Down**

1. Famous embroidery from Punjab
2. Sandalwood articles from this state are famous.

## Think

Look at the picture and answer the questions.

These are the bangle makers from Firozabad in Uttar Pradesh. Firozabad is well known for its glass work. Many families here earn their living, by producing lamps, chandeliers, bangles, utensils, and other articles from glass.

1. Observe who is making the bangles.
2. Do you see a lot of machines?

## Life skills and values

If you were a farmer, list three ways other than farming, in which you would enhance your income.

## Enjoy

Divide the class into groups. Each group can take up a non-farm work and suggest ways in which it has contributed to the village economy. Make a power point presentation and share it with the class.

## Web link

For more information, log on to:

https://www.india.gov.in/topics/industries

Last accessed on 30 September 2019

# 9 Urban Livelihoods

## Take off

- There are many different ways in which people earn their .................................... in the cities.
- In my school, I see different sources of earning like .................................... and .................................... .

## Warm up

Why can't Raghav's father sell crackers in his shop? What would happen if he sold crackers in his shop without a license?

Everyone needs a source of livelihood to earn money and meet their day-to-day needs. We have already learnt about the different types of livelihood in rural areas. In urban areas too, there are many different ways in which people earn their living. Education plays an important role in shaping the lives of the people. People who are well-educated are easily able to find jobs according to their qualifications. Many companies these days select students on the basis of interviews while they are still studying. They are able to get jobs in companies, once they complete their course. People who are less educated, have to struggle to find good jobs and earn well. Thus, we see that education is a key factor in helping us choose our source of livelihood.

### Markets

Markets play a very important role in the lives of the people. Shopkeepers sell groceries, fruits, vegetables, clothes, utensils and crockeries, stationery, milk, sweets and other articles. In markets, most shops are permanent, and are owned or rented by shopkeepers. You may have noticed that shopkeepers extend their shops or set up new temporary outlets to sell things, which are needed for special occasions and festivals such as Diwali, Christmas or Holi.

▲ Market

**Shopping malls** have emerged as a major source of employment for people in the recent times. Malls have a large number of shops under one roof. A large workforce is required to clean the mall, maintain it, and manage the parking lots. The food and entertainment areas in the malls also generate employment opportunities for many people. **E-commerce** and **Online shopping** is gaining popularity in India.

### Fact quest

E-commerce means buying and selling of goods and services including digital products over digital & electronic network.

### Consider

The Foreign Direct Investment Guidelines issued by Ministry of Commerce states that:

I. A manufacturer in India is permitted to sell its products through e-commerce retail.

II. A single brand retail trading entity operating through brick and mortar stores, is permitted to undertake retail trading through e-commerce.

III. An Indian manufacturer is permitted to sell its own single brand products through e-commerce retail. Indian manufacturer would be the investee company, which is the owner of the Indian brand and which manufactures in India, in terms of value, at least 70% of its products in house, and sources, at most 30% from Indian manufacturers.

1. How does this policy protect the interest of the Indian manufactures?
2. How does permission to sell products through e-commerce help the Indian manufactures?

## Factories and Industries

Factories continue to be an important source of livelihood. They offer a wide range of jobs for both skilled and unskilled workers. Factories employ a large number of people, right from truck drivers who bring the raw materials from different parts of the country, to people who help in loading the finished products back into them. People who are involved in the manufacturing or the processing of goods in the factories, are usually **skilled workers**. Nowadays, government is promoting skill development. Skill India campaign was launched in July 2015 to train over 40 crore people in India in different skills by 2022. Due to the increasing levels of pollution in the cities, and also because big trucks add to the existing

### Find out

What kind of facilities are required by the foreign companies selling their products in India through e-commerce?

▲ Factory workers

bulk of traffic in on the roads, the government has decided to shift some of the industries to the outskirts of towns and cities.

> **Fact quest**
>
> Channapatna is a town near Bengaluru in Karnataka, which is well known for its toys. The toys are made with ivory wood and are colored with vegetable dyes. Many people are employed in making toys in the town of Channapatna.

Sometimes, a **suburban** area transforms into a bustling commercial centre because of a factory or industry located there. These are called **industrial towns**. The workers employed in the factory try to settle in close **proximity** to it, so that they do not have to spend a lot of time **commuting** to their place of work. This type of employment improves their standard of living and also benefits the area, as more facilities are developed there. It is, however, wrong to think that all factories pollute the environment. There are many small scale industries which do not cause a lot of pollution.

People sometimes run their own small businesses, by opening showrooms and shops in an independent manner. In this way, they are different from a regular market. Here, the initial investment has to be their own and they are solely responsible for the profit and loss. Neighbourhood grocery shops are usually run by independent businessmen.

## Offices

Private and government offices abound in the cities, and a sizeable population is employed in this sector. Offices generally have fixed working hours, and constitute the salaried part of the population. The office goers also impact the traffic situation, as expressions like 'peak hours' of traffic generally refer to the majority of people going to their offices around the same time, thereby adding to the bulk of vehicles on the roads. The offices and companies give various kinds of benefits to their employees, like medical allowances, insurance, leaves, pension and retirement benefits.

## Street Performers

Before computers, internet, mobiles and satellite television became the craze, street performances of different kinds used to be a popular and a common source of entertainment in the country. There were a variety of performers like acrobats, jugglers, snake charmers and puppeteers. These people earned their livelihoods by showcasing their acts in the busy parts of towns and cities. This phenomenon was common, not just in India, but in other parts of the world as well. In European countries, musicians playing instruments drew huge crowds, and it was a respectable source of earning. These musicians were recognized for their talent, and were not looked down upon. As times are changing, many of these arts

▲ Snake charmer

**suburban:** related to a suburb of a city or large town a suburb; **proximity:** nearness in space, time, or relationship; **commuting:** the activity of travelling some distance to work every day by car, bus, or train are losing their charm and importance. The younger generation is taking up more profitable jobs and vocations, instead of learning these skills.

## Hawkers and Vendors

There are many people who earn their living from the streets as they do not have the capital required to buy shops or set up business in the markets. The vendors and hawkers sell various kinds of things and go from place to place to sell their wares. It has been upheld by the Supreme Court of India, that hawking and vending is included as part of the right to livelihood.

▲ Hawker

Many a times, it is seen that people come to the bigger towns and cities from villages and other smaller towns, in search of such jobs. They migrate to the cities and add to the bulk of the population living there. When they cannot find a job some become rickshaw puller.

## Casual Workers

As so many men and women are employed in offices, they require help for their homes. Therefore, **domestic workers** are much sought after in cities and towns. This provides a source of employment to hundreds of people in the cities. These people make up the workforce, which is called casual labour. Domestic workers, as you may know, change from time to time. Their salary is also fixed by the employers, and therefore, may or may not increase with time. There is no job security in this sector.

▲ Casual worker

## Professionals

There are various professionals like doctors, teachers, engineers, journalists and bankers, who earn their living in the cities. Business Process Companies, popularly called BPO's, have emerged as a source of employment for the young, educated people. In such companies, people have to work in morning and night shifts, as they attend to the customers in their city, as well as customers around the world. Such opportunities are very important for youth **empowerment** as well.

**Eco feat**

The gardeners in homes and public parks, who keep the areas clean, green and beautiful must be acknowledged for their hard work.

**empowerment:** the process of giving power and status in a particular situation to a person or group of people

Despite so many different sources of livelihood, it is unfortunate for the cities, that the number of unemployed people is growing. Increasing population is one of the main reasons for unemployment. There are qualified people who are unable to find suitable jobs because the jobs are less and the seekers more. The government is making efforts for skilling people for different jobs.

## Case Study

**Kathputli Colony, Delhi**

The Kathputli colony is a hub of a variety of street performers. The name of the place comes from the Hindi word for puppets, *kathputli*. This colony was established almost 50 years ago, and has become home to performers from different parts of the country. These are people who had earned their living by showing their skills and acts in public. These shows would take place in street corners or busy parks. People would gather around the performers and watch them with amazement, and also cheer them on. At the end, money would be given to them. With the pace of life becoming fast, and newer and more modern means of entertainment becoming common, they are on the verge of losing their source of livelihood completely.

Find out how many types of puppets are made in India and how they are different from each other.

## World Connect

Have you wondered what could be the sources of livelihood in Greenland? The extremely cold country in the Arctic region is the least populated country in the world. The population which is permanently settled over there, have fishing as a source of livelihood. The fishing industry has emerged in a big way and cod and shrimp are the main varieties of fish caught there. People use it in their homes as well as sell it in the markets. Large quantities of fish is exported to other countries. This gives the people a source of livelihood.

## Recall

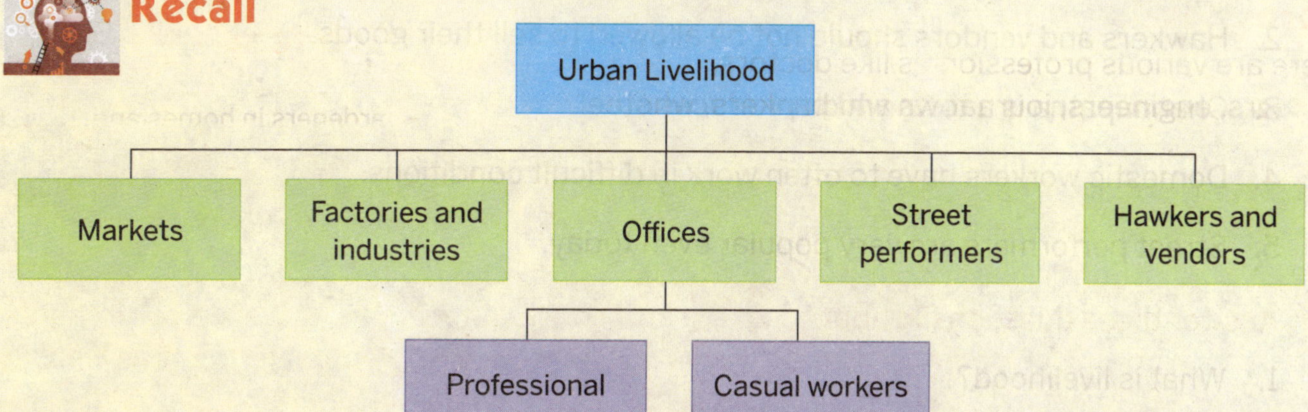

## Work out

A. Fill in the blanks with the correct answers.

1. One of the main reasons for unemployment is .................................... .
   a. lack of offices
   b. more population
   c. uneducated people
   d. less population
2. .................................... is a type of street performance.
   a. Going to office
   b. Working as a snake charmer
   c. Working as a doctor
   d. Working in a BPO
3. The town near Bengaluru where toys are made is .................................... .
   a. Mysore
   b. Channapatna
   c. Patna
   d. Agra
4. During festivals there are many shops in the market selling
   a. decorations
   b. diyas and candles
   c. flags and toys
   d. all of these

B. Complete the sentences.

1. The domestic workers comprise a work force called the .................................... .
2. The Supreme Court of India upholds hawking and vending as a .................................... .
3. The rickshaw pullers do not require a lot of .................................... .
4. The new generation is not learning to appreciate the art of street performance because .................................... .
5. The office jobs are permanent jobs, and have benefits like .................................... .

C. Write T for true and F for false.

1. In the offices, people have the freedom to work the way they want. ☐
2. Hawkers and vendors should not be allowed to sell their goods. ☐
3. Channapatna is a town which produces steel. ☐
4. Domestic workers have to often work in difficult conditions. ☐
5. Street performers are very popular even today. ☐

D. Answer these questions in brief.

1. What is livelihood?
2. The industries were moved out of the towns and cities. Why?

3. Why did people perform on the streets?
4. Why are some people unemployed in the cities?

E. Answer these questions in detail.

1. What are the advantages of working in an office?
2. What do you understand by unemployment? What do you think is the main reason for it?
3. In what ways are the domestic workers exploited?
4. Explain how shopping malls have emerged as a source of employment.

## Think

Look at the picture and answer the questions.

1. This tour group is visiting the pyramids. What do you call the person leading them, and showing them around?
2. Do you need someone like that person to show you around while you are travelling?
3. Do you know many people in this line of work?

## Life skills and values

Imagine yourself to be working in a food chain, which provides home delivery service. What problems could you face in fulfilling your task of delivering the order to its destination?

## Enjoy

Draw up a list of three family members. They could be your parents or relatives. List their sources of livelihood. Which one fascinates you the most? Collect pictures of some famous personalities from the field that you like the most.

## Web link

For more information, log on to:

https://www.india.gov.in/topics/labour-employment

Last accessed on 30 September 2019

Info Time

## Milestones in India's Polity

**1947**
India gained Independence from British rule

**1947**
Equal voting rights were granted for both men and women in India; Mahatma Gandhi was assasinated

**1949**
The Constitution of India was written

**1950**
India became a republic; the Constitution of India came into force; Caste system was abolished

**1951**
Jawaharlal Nehru becomes India's first Prime Minister

**1952**
The first Lok Sabha was constituted by the General Elections; All states became reorganized on the basis of language

**1955**
Hindu Marriage Act passed by the Parliament

**1960**
Prevention of Cruelty to Animals Act was passed

**1961**
Dowry Prohibition Act was passed

**1963**
Official Languages Act was passed

**1972**
Wildlife (Protection) Act was passed

**1986**
Environment (Protection) Act was passed

**2005**
National Rural Employment Guarantee Act (NREGA)

**2005**
Right to Information Act passed by the Parliament

**2007**
Prohibition of Child Marriage Act, 2006 was passed

**2009**
Right of Children to Free and Compulsory Education Act, 2009 was passed

**2010**
National Green Tribunal Act, 2010

**2013**
National Food Security Act, 2013

**2014**
Lokpal and Lokayuktas Act, 2013

# Suggested Assessment 1

**Max Marks: 80** **Max.Time: 3 hrs.**

## History

**Marks: 30**

A. Fill in the blanks. (½ × 6 = 3)

1. .................................... is the period in human history when humans did not leave behind written records.
2. Humans had mastered the art of farming by the .................................... Stone Age.
3. Apart from transportation, the wheel was also used to make .................................... .
4. .................................... was the first city to be discovered in the Indus Valley.
5. In the Vedic Period, society was divided into .................................... varnas.
6. Mahajanapadas could be a monarchy or a .................................... .

B. Place these in the correct sequence and explain in one sentence the importance of each period. 4

1. Chalcolithic Age
2. Mesolithic Age
3. Neolithic Age
4. Bronze Age

C. Who/What am I? (½ × 6 = 3)

1. A period of 1000 years.
2. I helped scare away wild animals and provided light in the old times.
3. First animal to be domesticated by humans.
4. The Chinese Civilization was born along my banks.
5. I am the earliest known books of the Aryans.
6. I was the most powerful of the 16 mahajanapadas.

D. Answer these questions in brief. (Attempt any 4) (3 × 4 = 12)

1. Why should we study history?
2. Name the three categories of prehistoric tools. Explain each type in one sentence each.
3. How do we know that the Neolithic people believed in life after death?
4. Give three examples to show that the Harappan people were excellent engineers.
5. Describe any three features of the Vedic religion.
6. How did urbanization emerge in the age of the janapadas?

E. Look at these pictures and answer the questions. 4

1. Name the place in Madhya Pradesh where this cave painting is found.
2. In which age was this painting made?
3. Why do you think people drew the paintings?
4. What did they draw with?

F. On a map of India, mark and name the following: 4

1. An early paleolithic site in Karnataka.
2. This neolithic site in Pakistan shows the earliest evidence of farming in South Asia.
3. This Harappan site in Gujarat was a very important trading centre.
4. This was the capital of Vajji.

## Geography

**Marks: 30**

A. Give one word answers. (½ × 8 = 4)

1. The star closest to the Earth ..............................
2. The planet often called the Red Planet ..............................
3. An imaginary line which divides the earth, horizontally, into two halves ..............................
4. This is also called the 0° meridian ..............................
5. Two days in a year when day and night are of equal duration ..............................
6. The Earth spins on its own .............................. from east to west.
7. East, west, north and south are called the .............................. points of the compass.
8. The planet with a ring around it is .............................. .

B. Define the following: (1 × 4 = 4)

1. Celestial bodies
2. Globe
3. Circle of illumination
4. Map legend

C. Answer these questions in brief. (2 × 4 = 8)

1. Why is the earth the only living plant in the solar system? Give two reasons.
2. Enumerate any two features of latitudes.
3. What are the two effects of the rotation of the Earth?
4. Why are maps prefered over globes to study the Earth?

D. Draw and label diagram of the heat zones of the Earth. 6

E. Draw a simple diagram to show the cardinal and intermediate directions. 4

F. Draw any four conventional symbols and indicate what they stand for. 4

## Social and Political Life

**Marks: 20**

A. Answer these questions in brief. (1 × 6 = 6)

1. How do India's festivals reflect unity in diversity?
2. Give one example of a stereotype.
3. What is the legislature called in India?
4. Give one difference between monarchy and democracy.
5. Explain the term panchayat.
6. What is the basic function of a government?

B. Name one woman for each of the statements who have broken the following stereotypes. (1 × 3 = 3)

1. Women don't play sports
2. Women are not politicians
3. Women cannot lead companies

C. Match the columns. 5

| | |
|---|---|
| 1. Idli, páratha, dhokla, roghan josh | a. Example of prejudice |
| 2. Looking down upon someone because they cannot speak English | b. Example of Central Government power |
| 3. Women are not allowed to drive cars in Saudi Arabia | c. Examples of food diversity in India. |
| 4. The rail budget | d. Example of panchayat authority |
| 5. Digging of a new canal to irrigate fields in the village | e. Example of discrimination |

D. Look at this picture and answer the questions. 6

1. Identify this personality.
2. Which caste did he belong to?
3. How did he contribute to society?
4. Name two things that he encouraged the people to practise.
5. Which religion did he convert to?

## Suggested Assessment 2

### History

**Marks: 30**

**A. Fill in the blanks.** (½ × 6 = 3)

1. Buddhist scriptures are called .......................................... .
2. .......................................... Mauraya established the Mauryan Empire.
3. .......................................... marked coins were the earliest metal coins.
4. .......................................... a Portuguese navigator and merchant is said to have charted a straight sea route to India.
5. .......................................... was one of the epic poem composed by Kalidasa.
6. Panini's treatise on Sanskrit grammar is called .......................................... .

**B. Match the columns.** (½ × 6 = 3)

| | |
|---|---|
| 1. Upanishads | a. Trading port town in Southern India |
| 2. Kautilya | b. Mrichhakatikam |
| 3. Arikamedu | c. Contain the essence of the vedas |
| 4. Hiuen-Tsang | d. Head of Nalanda University |
| 5. Dharampala | e. Arthashastra |
| 6. Shudraka | f. Visited India during Harshavardhan's reign |

**C. Organize in the correct sequence.** (1 × 6 = 6)

1. Samudragupta becomes king.
2. Kautilya helps Chandragupta Maurya become king of Magadha.
3. Ashoka conquered Kalinga.
4. Vedas are composed.
5. Fa Hien visits India.
6. King Harshavardhana is defeated by Pulakeshin II.

**D. Answer any four of the following questions.** (3 × 4 = 12)

1. Discuss any three of the main principles of Jainism.
2. Why do we consider Ashoka a great ruler?
3. What is understood by the term guild? Explain any two of its functions.
4. Discuss the importance of the Silk Route for Indian history.
5. How did the Gupta kings organise the administration of their empire?
6. Throw some light on the scientific developments in ancient India.

E. Read the passages and answer the questions. 4

When king De-va-nam.priya Priyadars'in had been anointed eight years, (the country of) the Kaligas was conquered by (him). One hundred and fifty thousand in number were the men who were deported thence, one hundred thousand in number were those who were slain there, and many times as many those who died. After that, now that (the country of) the Kalingas has been taken, De-va-nam.priya (is devoted) to a zealous study of morality, to the love of morality, and to the instruction (of people) in morality. This is the repentance of De-va-na-m.priya on account of his conquest of (the country of) the Kalingas. For, this is considered very painful and deplorable by De-va-na-m.priya, that, while one is conquering an unconquered (country), slaughter, death, and deportation of people (are taking place) there.

a. By which name do we know king De-va-na-m.priya Priyadars'in?
b. Which kingdom has he conquered?
c. Why is the king feeling repentant?
d. Mention any two steps that this king took after the conquest of this kingdom.

F. On a map of India, mark and name the following: 2

1. Capital of the Gupta Empire
2. The kingdom conquered by king De-va-na-m.priya Priyadars'in.

## Geography

**Marks: 30**

A. Answer in one word. (½ × 8 = 4)

1. The realm of earth consisting of rocks .................................... .
2. The ocean whose name means peaceful .................................... .
3. When all continents were joined together in one landmass, it was called ....................................
4. A mountain range in South America ....................................
5. The Greater Himalayas are also known as .................................... .
6. The coastal region of Kerala is called.................................... .
7. Tidal forest in West Bengal .................................... .
8. .................................... was the initiative taken by Indian government to protect the rhinoceros.

B. Answer these questions in brief. (2 × 4 = 8)

1. What is the importance of the lithosphere?
2. Give two points of difference between young fold mountains and old fold mountains.
3. Name any three rivers of the Peninsular Plateau.
4. Why are monsoons important to India?

C. On a map of India name and mark the following: 6

1. Any two neighbours of India
2. One major river system, with at least 2 tributaries
3. One state along the Bay of Bengal
4. One state along the Himalayas

D. Complete the following table: 4

| National Park | State |
|---|---|
| 1. Jim Corbett | a. ................................ |
| 2. ................................ | b. Assam |
| 3. Periyar | c. ................................ |
| 4. ................................ | d. Sariska |

E. On a given map of the world, mark and name the following. 5

1. An ocean that separates Americas and Africa
2. A country which is also a continent.
3. North and South Poles.
4. This continent has no countries.

F. Why is it important for us to protect our environment? 3

## Social and Political Life

**Marks: 20**

A. Who or what am I? (1 × 4 = 4)

1. It is my job to make sure that streets are kept clean in the city of Delhi.
2. I measure land in the village to calculate the owner's revenue dues.
3. I am a low investment business and can be managed from home.
4. I sell things that you need but I do not have a shop.

B. List two functions of the following: (2 × 2 = 4)

1. Urban administrative bodies
2. Rural administrative bodies

C. Answer these questions in brief. (3 × 4 = 12)

1. Briefly explain any three types of rural occupations.
2. Can you identify three types of urban occupations?
3. List any three sources of income for the municipality.
4. Who is a patwari? What are his duties?

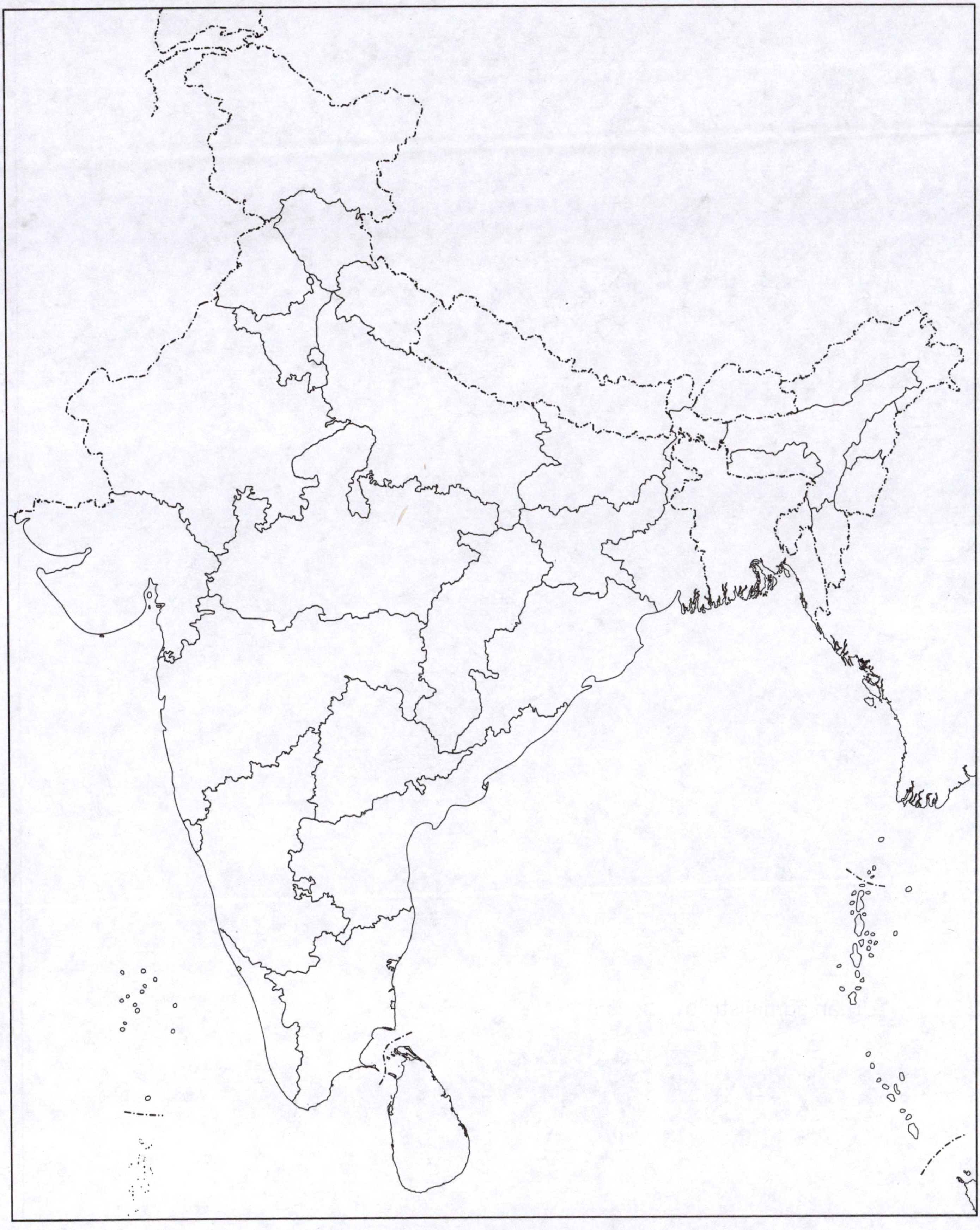

▲ Political Map of India—Outline

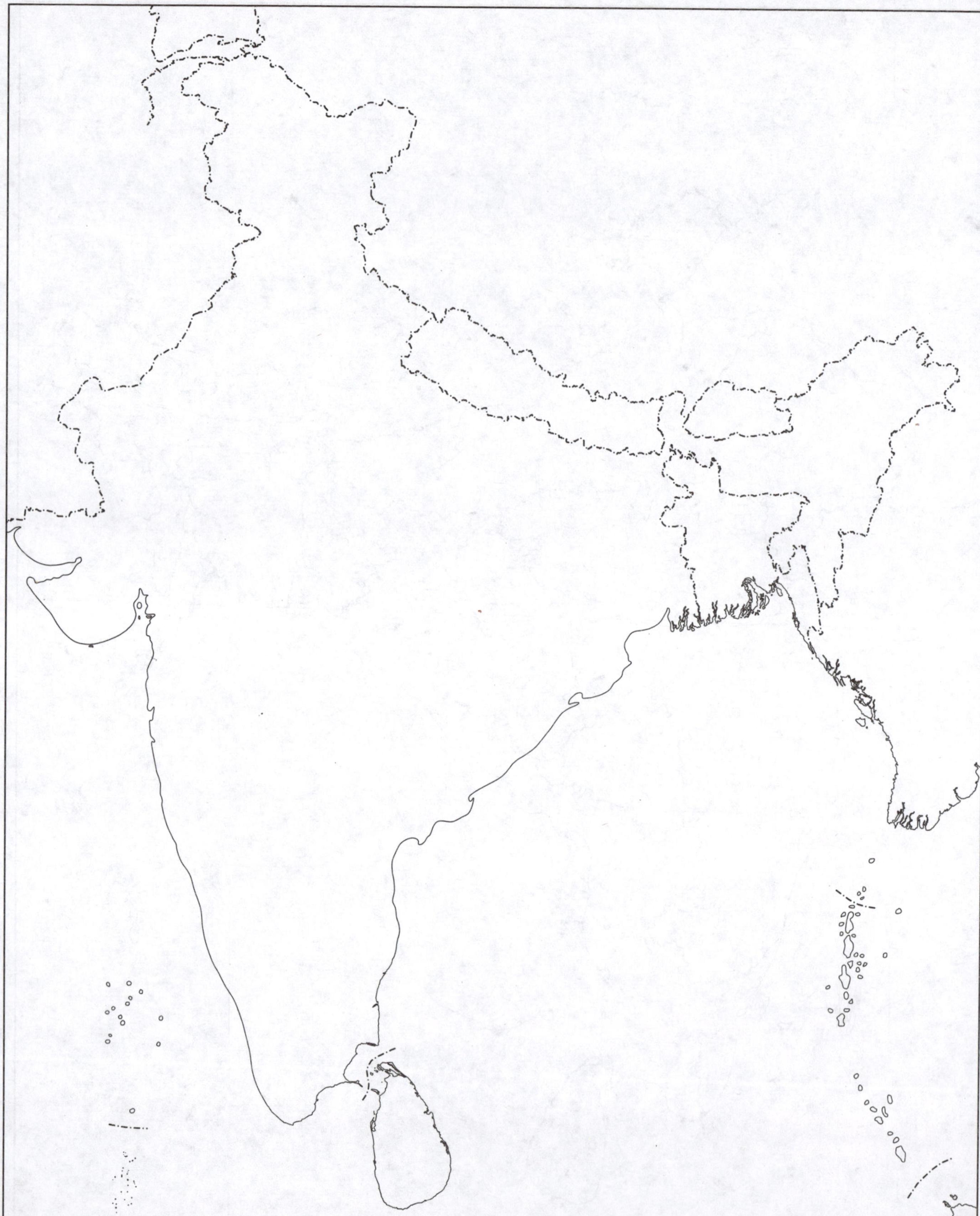

▲ Physical Map of India—Outline

▲ Political Map of World-Outline

▲ Physical Map of World-Outline